T0384353

Praise for
Run Over By the Grace Train

"Joby wrote this book with the same biblical precision, passion, and conviction with which he preaches, and you will be so blessed to read it. With Joby's signature sense of humor, you will laugh and also be moved to tears when you learn of the grace of God upon your life... This book is essential for those who want to know the truly abundant life in Christ."

—Phil Hopper, author and lead pastor of
Abundant Life Church

"In *Run Over By the Grace Train*, author Joby Martin beautifully explains how grace is at the foundation of a life of faith, and why so many of us fail to understand its rich complexity. Using rich biblical ideas, relatable analogies, and real-world application, this book demonstrates our powerlessness to save ourselves, paving the way for God's immeasurable grace to rescue us and lead us into a deep relationship with Himself. Anyone wishing to deepen their understanding of how God's unfathomable grace will transform our lives should read this book."

—Dave Ferguson, author of *B.L.E.S.S.: 5 Everyday Ways To
Love Your Neighbor and Change the World*

"In *Run Over By the Grace Train*, Joby describes why he simply cannot get over the reality and repercussions of the Gospel of Jesus Christ, and he elucidates ways for all of us to feel the same. We should never move past it. Instead, we should dwell on it. All aboard..."

—Kyle Thompson, *Undaunted Life* podcast

"Grace is a word that gets tossed around in Christian circles quite frequently, and as a result can be confusing to those of us who need it most. In this book, Pastor Joby Martin cuts through any confusion with biblical clarity regarding the power of the grace, captured in the Gospel, to liberate us from sin and sanctify us for service to King Jesus. I'm thankful for a book that is so easy to read without dumbing down the rich theology of the free gift offered to us in the grace of God."

—Clayton King, evangelist, pastor, author of
REBORN and *STRONGER*

"Joby Martin is a powerful communicator and an inspiring leader. His down-to-earth and brilliant teaching gift connects the truth of Scripture in ways that move us all to Jesus-led action. *Run Over By the Grace Train* captures his passion for the indispensable message about the undeserved, unending, and unstoppable gift of God's grace that never stops transforming our lives."

—Santiago "Jimmy" Mellado, president and
CEO of Compassion International

"With the wit and flair I have come to expect from my friend, Joby Martin weaves a beautiful tapestry of the power and reach of grace. Grace redeems. Grace restores. Grace transforms. God's grace changes everything! And if you give due attention to this book, grace will change you too."

—Léonce B. Crump Jr., founder of Renovation Church and
author of *Renovate* and *The Resilience Factor*

"I'm a big Joby Martin fan and I listen when he speaks and I read what he writes. I loved his book *Anything Is Possible* and I'm even more grateful after reading *Run Over By the Grace Train*...you will be too!"

—Doug Fields

RUN
OVER
BY THE
GRACE
TRAIN

RUN OVER BY THE GRACE TRAIN

HOW THE UNSTOPPABLE LOVE OF GOD TRANSFORMS EVERYTHING

JOBY MARTIN

WITH CHARLES MARTIN

FaithWords

New York   Nashville

FaithWords

Hachette Book Group

1290 Avenue of the Americas, New York, NY 10104

faithwords.com

twitter.com/faithwords

First Edition: September 2024

FaithWords is a division of Hachette Book Group, Inc. The FaithWords name and logo are registered trademarks of Hachette Book Group, Inc.

The publisher is not responsible for websites (or their content) that are not owned by the publisher.

The Hachette Speakers Bureau provides a wide range of authors for speaking events. To find out more, go to hachettespeakersbureau.com or email HachetteSpeakers@hbgusa.com.

FaithWords books may be purchased in bulk for business, educational, or promotional use. For information, please contact your local bookseller or the Hachette Book Group Special Markets Department at special.markets@hbgusa.com.

Library of Congress Cataloging-in-Publication Data

Names: Martin, Joby, author.

Title: Run over by the Grace train : how the unstoppable love of God transforms everything / Joby Martin with Charles Martin.

Description: First edition. | New York : Faith Words, 2024.

Identifiers: LCCN 2024008153 | ISBN 9781546008149 (hardcover) | ISBN 9781546008200 (ebook)

Subjects: LCSH: Grace (Theology) | Christian life.

Classification: LCC BT761.3 .M2859 2024 | DDC 234—dc23/eng/20240408

LC record available at https://lccn.loc.gov/2024008153

ISBNs: 9781546008149 (hardcover), 9781546008200 (ebook)

Printed in the United States of America

LSC-C

Printing 2, 2024

*To all the preachers who have come before me, on whose shoulders
I stand, who have preached the life-changing Gospel.
To all the preachers today who labor to do the same.
And lastly, to the ones to come, may they carry the torch
with faithfulness. By Grace.*

CONTENTS

FOREWORD

J. D. Greear

What does it take to impress an angel?

There's not much that angels haven't already seen, after all. They had a front-row seat to the wonder of creation. They watched as God obliterated the power of the Egyptian empire through a series of plagues. They stood spellbound as Joshua's shout brought down the walls of Jericho. They witnessed God endow a donkey with the powers of speech. They giggled as Jesus reduced a crack squad of Roman guards to a bunch of crying toddlers when he pushed back a 4,000-pound rock and waltzed out of a grave all by himself on the third day after his crucifixion. I mean, what else is left for them to be impressed with?

And yet, there's something you and I get to experience every day that angels are literally envious of, long to look more into, and just can't get enough of. One thing that still blows their minds.

Grace.

The things that have now been told you by those who have preached the gospel to you by the Holy Spirit sent from heaven. Even angels long to look into these things. (1 Peter 1:12)

Angels envy that you are getting to read this book. Well, I suppose they can *read* it, and may sneak a peek over your shoulder as you do. But they are *jealous* that you get to read this book and *experience* it for yourself.

The sixteenth-century reformer Martin Luther said that the Gospel is like a well. You don't get the best water from a well by widening its circumference, but by going deeper into it.

The grace of God in the Gospel, you see, is not the ABCs of the Christian life, the entry door into a relationship with God, the diving board off of which we jump into the pool of Christianity. Grace, as the late Tim Keller used to say, is the A–Z of the Christian life; not the diving board, but the pool itself. Or, to change the metaphor, if the Christian life were a school building, grace would not be a 101 class you'd take to begin your degree. It's not even a 401 class. It's the building in which all the other classes meet.

Joby Martin is a Martin Luther for our time. I don't say that lightly, either: Martin Luther is one of my favorite historical Christian leaders, and Joby Martin is one of my favorite contemporary church leaders. Pastor Joby speaks with boldness, earthiness, wisdom, and Holy Spirit *unction*. Spellcheck is now telling me that "unction" ain't a word. Yes, it is, Bill Gates. Unction is a word old-fashioned revivalists used to describe that special, divine power some people have when they talk about the Gospel. *When they speak, something deep and divine stirs in your soul.* You want to know God more. Your sin looks stupid. Jesus looks beautiful. You know you need to do something *now*. Joby Martin has unction. You'll feel that as you read this book.

And he's funny. Like legit, laugh-out-loud-for-several-sustained-seconds funny. I've often said that if Martin Luther, C. S. Lewis, and Jeff Foxworthy could somehow all have a kid together, that kid would be Joby Martin.

Honestly, I'm so excited you get to read this book. I've loved it. There's insight, humor, and application on nearly every page.

The Gospel of grace really is like a well. The deeper you go, the better it is. Or, to use Joby's metaphor, it's like a train barreling at you, the sheer power of which we can barely comprehend, with cabins and cars you can spend the rest of your life exploring.

No wonder the Apostle Paul said that we grow in our faith by continuing to gaze "at the glory of the Lord." The more we behold the glory of God in the Gospel, the more we are "transformed into the same image from glory to glory" (2 Corinthians 3:18).

How do we first become Christians?

By beholding the glory of God in the Gospel of Jesus and believing it was done for us.

And how do we become more and more like Jesus?

By beholding the glory of God in the Gospel of Jesus and believing it was done for us.

There really is no getting over the Gospel. If angels aren't bored with it, you won't be either. If they are still enthralled with it, there's a lot more in here for you.

If you're curious how that could be, read on. Joby will explain it better than I can. The Gospel saves the sinner and thrills the saint. It illuminates the child and confounds the philosopher. It restores the broken, heals the wounded, satisfies the hungry, illuminates the lost, and raises from the dead.

And it's for you.

Prepare yourself. Honestly, I'm not sure you're ready for what's ahead. The grace train is barreling toward you.

A NOTE ON THE TEXT

Almost all direct Scripture quotations in this book come from the English Standard Version. In some cases I've simply paraphrased instead of quoting directly from a published translation; in these cases, the Scripture is set in italics.

> In him we have redemption through his blood, the forgiveness of our trespasses, according to the riches of his grace, which he lavished upon us, in all wisdom and insight.
>
> —*Ephesians 1:7–8*

> But God, being rich in mercy, because of the great love with which he loved us, even when we were dead in our trespasses, made us alive together with Christ—by grace you have been saved—and raised us up with him and seated us with him in the heavenly places in Christ Jesus, so that in the coming ages he might show the immeasurable riches of his grace in kindness toward us in Christ Jesus. For by grace you have been saved through faith. And this is not your own doing; it is the gift of God, not a result of works, so that no one may boast.
>
> —*Ephesians 2:4–9*

> For all have sinned and fall short of the glory of God, and are justified by his grace as a gift, through the redemption that is in Christ Jesus.
>
> —*Romans 3:23–24*

RUN
OVER
BY THE
GRACE
TRAIN

PROLOGUE

So there I was…

At my house, we're Georgia Bulldog fans. Why? Because we're Believers. My Bible's written in red and black, so just take it up with the Lord.

We're pretty die-hard fans so we usually go to the opening game of the year. There are lots of reasons. One, it's Labor Day weekend, and I usually take that weekend off. Second, it's usually around my birthday, and it's a fun way to celebrate. And third, Georgia typically schedules the biggest cupcake team of the year for that game, and that's my favorite kind of game to go to. I don't need to go to a close game. I don't need stress. I have a church for that. I just want to go and watch the game. I want to sing, "Glory, glory to old Georgia," until my voice is gone. I want half the stands to be gone by the end. Hope we win by 200. That's the kind of game I like to go to.

I'm a Bulldogs fan, but I'm also a Braves fan. About five or six years ago, the Braves had just built this new stadium, and we had yet to see a game in it, so we decided to go up Saturday for the Bulldogs game and then stick around for Sunday and go to the Braves game after church.

So. Saturday. Georgia game. We won. I lost my voice. I think the score was 7,000 to nothing. We were playing the perennial powerhouse Austin Peay. I don't even know what that is, but we beat the mud out of them. Then we drove up to Atlanta and checked into this hotel right beside the Braves stadium. Pretty swanky. All the doors faced the atrium. When I was a kid, all the doors faced the parking lot. They call that a motel. This was not that.

When you walked into this one, the atrium was massive. Twelve stories. You could fly a plane in there. Shops and restaurants all around the edge. We checked in, and then my daughter, Reagan, and her friends, Wiley and Windsor, went to their room to do whatever girls do, and the boys and I went to this little bar and grill. I ordered some chicken wings and refreshments, because my throat was parched because I'd been singing "Glory, glory to old Georgia." We were just sitting there waiting on the wings when this alarm sounded. The fire alarm. "Fire, fire, please move to the exits. Fire, fire."

And I did what any good dad would do. I sat there, because it was probably nothing. Plus, I had wings coming. But my friend McCarthy said, "Well, let me check." Which he did. He walked out to the atrium, looked up, and immediately spun and ran back in, panicking. And he ain't a panicky dude. He pointed. "Bro, it's a fire."

But I was not convinced, because I had wings coming and something for my throat, so I sauntered out into the atrium and, when I looked up, it was not a little bit of smoke. It was not like, "Could that be steam?" It was not a fog machine run amok. Smoke and little fire flashes were billowing out of the ceiling.

It was legit.

Where did my thoughts immediately go? Right.

Reagan and her friends were on the tenth floor. Fire on the twelfth. And my mind went to all the places where every mama and daddy's mind goes, right? All I could think is, "Reagan is on the tenth floor, I'm down here, I have to get there." Chaos had spread through the hotel. People were running everywhere in every direction. Not to mention that the glass elevators had been shut down. So I grabbed an employee— "Where are the stairs?" He pointed. "In the corner."

I ran to the corner, opened the door, and charged into a banquet hall closet. Strike one. I grabbed a second employee. A little more directly. "Where are the stairs?"

People had filled the public space. You could smell the smoke. When you looked up, flames had overtaken the top floor. Again, my mind was in the worst place it could be. I asked again, "Where are the stairs?" and somebody pointed to the closet. What was wrong with these employees? I grabbed a third guy. More direct. "Hey, man, where are the stairs?" And he pointed, and I grabbed him by the shoulders, and I said, "Where are the—" and I used an adjective. And he tried to tell me, and so, like any good pastor, I laid my hands on him and I said, "No more pointing. Lead me."

He did. We started running. And my wife Gretchen ran up alongside, and we had this conversation about how she needed to stay down. "You can't come with me. One of us has to be down here…"

I reached the stairwell, opened the door, and was run over by a sea of people coming down. And I thought, "I got to get to Reagan. I got to go, man." And so I went huffing it up the steps and elbowing my way against the current.

About here, two things hit me with equal weight: I had not trained for this. The sound coming out of my lungs was not good. I should've upped my cardio game about eight months ago. Second, I was wearing flip-flops. My daddy used to always say, "The only thing you can do in flip-flops is get your butt kicked." Which is a fact. So, in between trying to breathe and weave my way upstairs against the flow of panicking people, I was literally thinking, "Do I kick them off so that I can run faster, or do I keep them on because, if John McClane taught us anything, it's that you might have to walk over broken glass or walk through the fire?"

That's literally what I was thinking.

About every floor and a half, I'd bump into another equally unhelpful hotel employee saying, "Sir, you can't come up here," to which I'd respond, "That's cute."

To their credit, the hotel workers had been knocking on all the doors. They had gone to our girls' door. So, about the fifth floor, who did I bump into? I turned one corner and I saw Reagan, Windsor, and Wiley, and I thought, in that moment, "Oh, thank God. My worst nightmare has not come true."

I grabbed all three. Wrapped my arms around them. Two of them aren't even mine, but they kind of grew up with me, so it was okay. Plus I didn't care. I squeezed them in and started jabbering, "It's going to be okay..." If you have been around preteen girls, you know there can be a lot of emotion on a normal day. Add a fire and no dad and, I mean, they were crying, too. There was a lot going on.

At this point, we filed in with everybody else, exited the stairwell, and got everybody reconnected with their family. We gathered outside our hotel—because it was still on fire—and we walked down the sidewalk to a wing place, because my last order got lost. We were sitting at a table, I was catching my breath, and Reagan was pretty upset. Still emotional. I was trying to calm her down. "Baby, here's what I need you to know. I don't care what's going on, I don't care what the circumstances are, I don't care where you are or what you've done, there is nothing on this planet that could keep me from coming after you. I would walk through fire for you."

This is the message of Ephesians 2: "But God, being rich in mercy, because of the great love with which He loved us, even when we were dead in our trespasses, made us alive together with Christ—by grace you have been saved—and raised us up with Him and seated us with Him in the heavenly places in Christ Jesus, so that in the coming ages He might show the immeasurable riches of His grace in kindness toward us in Christ Jesus. For by grace you have been saved through faith. And this is not your own doing; it is the gift of God, not a result of works, so that no one may boast. For we are His workmanship, created in Christ Jesus for good works, which God prepared beforehand, that we should walk in them" (Ephesians 2:4–10).

This is the message of the Gospel. God did whatever it took to rescue His children. When it says in Revelation that He has feet of burnished bronze, it's because He walked through fire, and the fire refined them. Then He prepares a lavish banquet in their honor.

The truth is this: There's nothing unique about me as a dad. Every mama, daddy, grandparent, aunt, and uncle would do whatever it took to rescue a kid that they love.

Later that night—in a new hotel—we pushed our beds together. It was like Daytona. Four wide. And Reagan said, "Daddy?"

"Yeah, baby."

"You would walk through fire for me?" she asked, with a little crack of emotion in her voice.

"Of course I would walk through fire for you."

Her realization in that moment is the same one I'm praying you have when you close this book. Let me be clear, because I want you to know this—this emotion, this thing in me that runs up the stairs, or tried to before cardiac arrest set in, did not come from me. It did not originate in me. I love Reagan because Jesus first loved me. That desire. That willingness. That first flip-flop step started with God the Father who sent His only begotten son, Jesus Christ, on a rescue mission to literally walk through the fires of hell and pay the price and die on the cross and spill His blood and to walk through the hell of whatever you've been going through, so that not only could you be forgiven of your sins, but so that you could be adopted into the family of God forever and ever and ever, and so that the name "God with us" would be your reality for all eternity.

This is the Gospel of the freight train of Grace.

When we were stuck in a burning building, smoke pouring through the cracks, and us as good as dead, Jesus ran through the flames and lifted us out. There's an old preacher story that goes around that says this little boy was trying to join the church, so he sat before the deacons. And they said to the kid, "So, tell me, how did you come to know Christ?"

And he said, "Well, I did my part and He did His part."

And they said, "Whoa. What do you mean? What do you mean you did your part and He did His part?"

And the boy said, "Yep, I did my part and He did His part."

"What are you talking about?"

He said, "I did the sinning and He did the saving."

*   *   *

For thirty years, I've been a preacher of the Bible, and one thing that was true when I started that's still true now is this: I just can't get over the Gospel.

What do I mean by that? I can't wrap my head around the fact that God would take my place. Why does this get me? Because I'm the worst sinner I know. No one has lied to me more than me. No one has let me down more than me. No one has betrayed me more than me. But when I look at me, I don't see the lying, rejecting, betraying sinner. Why? Because Jesus poured out His Grace on me. Not only did He save a wretch like me, but He adopted me into the family of God as a co-heir with Christ and even uses a nobody like me to lead thousands of people into that same saving knowledge of Jesus Christ. I mean, really…who gets to do this? Answer: I do! I'm doing it right now. This Grace is also available to you right now. There is nothing special about me.

The Grace of Jesus is the most undeniably powerful force I've ever encountered, and the only way I know how to really describe it is like being hit by a train. Given this, I like to call it "being run over by the Grace Train." And by calling the immeasurable Grace of Jesus a freight train, I'm not making light of it. I just can't find a better image. Maybe Halley's comet works better, but you can't ride that, so the comparison falls down. The word "train" actually comes from a French verb meaning to drag, which is a good image of us. We get dragged along by something that can have almost forty thousand horsepower, can be a mile and a half long, and can travel more than 350 miles per hour.

What's it like to get run over by the Grace Train? Let me give you an analogy: When a mosquito is hit by a freight train, the mosquito does not feel bigger. It doesn't take credit for the speed of the train. Or its size. The mosquito makes no claim on the train. It didn't start it and can't stop it. Can't reroute it or slow it down. It doesn't understand what powers it, how long it will last, or where it came from. The mosquito has zero control over the train. Truth is, the mosquito can't comprehend the train. All the mosquito knows is that it was buzzing along when out of nowhere, wham! The mosquito was caught up in the vortex of something so much greater than itself. A rolling hurricane, barreling toward some unknown destination.

Having been run over by the Grace Train, the mosquito quickly realizes a few things: One, it is powerless to resist. What can it do against the train? Nothing.

Two, it didn't get itself on the train, can't get itself off the train, and cannot alter the destination. The train is going where the train is going. Unstoppable and undeterred.

Third, the mosquito does not have to hold on for dear life. It can relax. The conductor has everything under control. He knows where he's going, where he came from, why, what he's carrying, where he's headed, and when he'll arrive.

Fourth, when the mosquito is hit by the train, its life changes forever. This is not a casual encounter that can be brushed off. This impact changes everything about everything.

Last, while someone obviously paid a lot of money for the train, and every seat is in a first-class cabin, the ride is free—to the mosquito. It pays nothing. When the mosquito catches its breath and realizes its inexplicable predicament, the only thing the mosquito can do is enjoy the ride—all the way to glory.

This is a loose translation of the Gospel of the Grace Train.

If you were to be hit by an actual train, wouldn't it dramatically change your life? Imagine that you showed up to church late. If I were to ask, "Why are you late? Where have you been?" and you responded, "Sorry I'm late, I was run over by a freight train!" I'd have questions. Especially if, as I observed you, nothing looked different. No bumps. No bruises. No blood. Shirt neatly tucked into your freshly pressed slacks. I would think, "Doesn't look to me like you've been hit by a train."

Now don't miss this... The Grace Train of the Gospel of Jesus Christ is infinitely more powerful than a freight train, and anyone who encounters God's Grace is changed totally and eternally.

Back in the 1900s, at Oxford, a group of professors was teaching a symposium on the universality of all religions. Basically, what they were saying is all world religions are fundamentally the same and only superficially different. And they gathered together and they began to write words to describe all religions on a chalkboard. They were words that we would all be comfortable with, like "prayer" and "meditation" and "sacred texts" and "teachers" and "devotion" and "morality" and "serving the poor" and "kindness." They wrote 150 words on this chalkboard, in essence, to say, "See? It's all basically the same. Just some of the superficial details are different."

There was a professor walking down the hallway, and they reached out to him and said, "Jack, come in here." Now Jack was his nickname. I don't know why they called him Jack. His name was Clive Staples Lewis. You may know him as C.S. Because if your name's Clive Staples, people call you C.S.

They invited C.S. into the office and said, "All right, Jack, look. We believe all religions are fundamentally the same, and only superficially different. So we came up with a list of words describing them all. How is Christianity different from all this? What sets Christianity apart from all these world religions?"

Jack read the list, then grabbed the eraser and wiped the board clean, erasing all other descriptive terms.

In their place, he wrote one word: Grace.

That's how it's fundamentally different.

And most of us don't know and/or don't believe this. A peer-researched article came out recently that said that more than 50 percent of professing Christians say their good works will play a key role in them getting into heaven. Please tell me, where is that in the Gospel of Jesus Christ?

It's not.

Every religion says we have been separated from a holy God and it's up to us to work our way back. The good news of the Gospel of Jesus Christ is that God sent His son on a rescue mission to come and get us. To bring us back to Himself. Not because we deserve it, but simply because He loves us. This is the message of the Gospel of Jesus Christ, and it is fundamentally different than every other religion and superficially similar.

If His Grace is a train, then in the first car, the engine, He justifies us. In car two, He sanctifies us. And in cars three through one hundred, He continues to sanctify us, to make us more like Him today than we were yesterday. This is a process that will take our whole life. And then the caboose is our glorification. The ride into glory. It's an unimaginable exchange, and we absolutely do not have the power to pull it off. All we did was ride the train. And we didn't even get us on the train. He did that, too.

When the Grace Train runs you over, it doesn't kill you. It saves you. "By grace you have been saved" (Ephesians 2:5). The flip side is also true. If you don't receive and accept the Grace in this life, then you get run over by the judgment of God at the end of your life. Grace or judgment: your call. One of my favorite verses is Philippians 2:10, which says that at some point in the future every knee will bow in heaven and on earth. This means, like it or not, you and I have two options. We can bow, or we can bow.

But I'm getting ahead of myself.

So, the mosquito may think, "Oh, I can step off this thing any time." Fact is, no, he can't. Jesus says, *"I've never lost the one that you gave me."* He didn't put himself on it in the first place. When people ask, "Can a Christian lose his or her salvation?" That's the wrong question. The right question is, can Jesus lose you?

Some of you are reading me right now, and behind your eyelids a slide show is playing of all your past sin, and you're thinking to yourself, "You don't know what I've done." You're right. I don't. But that doesn't matter. He does. And He's not ashamed of you. I don't care what sin you bring to the table, He's not ashamed. That slide show that's playing, that list of wrongs you carry in your pocket, He doesn't look at you through the hazy lens of all that sin. He's well aware of it; He just wants you to bring it to Him and leave it at His feet. His cross.

So here's where we're headed: In the chapters ahead we're going to look at how Grace saves us. How you can't lose it any more than Jesus can lose you. From there, we're going to dive into how Grace sanctifies both the rebel and the religious, and how Grace does not condemn but cleanses us from the inside out. Even the most outcast. And last, we're going to unpack how Grace forgives, is slow to anger, and never runs out.

For those of you who lead discipleship groups or just want to dive deeper, there's a study guide to go along with this book, to help you get even more out of this.

Grace. Say it with me: "Grrrrrace." It's a pretty cool word. Maybe the coolest ever.

So, hop on. Grab a seat on the Grace Train.

Chapter 1

GRACE SAVES

Grace is not a license to sin. It's the cause of our obedience.

When I first started dating Gretchen, I learned her dad was an engineer. Not like a rambling wreck from Georgia Tech, but the train kind. You know, conductor's hat, big horn, pocket watch, always checking the time.

The first time she brought me to her house to meet her family I was terrified. When it was time to go to bed, she set up a little bed in this front room. Call it a sitting room. There was a piano. A couch. Drapes. Lots of records and photo albums. Just across the front yard sat a CSS railroad track, which her dad used to ride almost every day. The track ran east to west, but when it reached the house, it made an S-turn, curved around the mountain, and then continued either east or west. When I fell asleep, I did not understand this little anomaly of redirection.

So I got to sleep, then about three o'clock in the morning, I was in deep REM. Blanket. Couch. Pillow. I was out. But a horn woke me up. I sat up. Lights in the distance. I rubbed my eyes. More horn. It was getting closer. Lights were getting larger. Horn again. Lights brighter. The room was bright. The windows were rattling. Horn again. This time longer. It was splitting my brain down the middle. I had no idea what was happening, but I fully believed this train had rerouted, jumped the tracks, and was coming through my couch. My first thought was, "I'm gonna die."

I vaguely remembered them talking to me about a train. Maybe I heard the train the day before, but in my defense, I was a little distracted. There was a good reason, and Gretchen is her name.

I rubbed my eyes again and tried to gather my wits. Now awake, I looked through the window, and the train was right there. This thing was about to cut me in half. No joke—I'm dead. So I opened my mouth to scream like a little girl, and nothing came out. I was too scared to even scream. I tried again. Crickets. The light was blinding. The horn was deafening. The house was shaking. My heart was pounding. I was sweating through my sheets. I tried again, but it was no use. My airway was closed off. I raised my hands, as if that was going to do any good. I was shaking. Sweating. No kidding, I thought I was dead.

Then the thing hit the end of the S-turn and routed around the house. I think somebody should've warned me. Maybe a little heads-up. "Hey, Joby, when you see the lights…" Nope. Nothing. Not a peep. Nobody said a word. I think they were all in their beds laughing while I was in there trying to figure out how to wash the sheets.

About three years later, I finally shared that story with the rest of the family, once I knew I was in. Thank God I had been too scared to scream. If her dad had heard me cry out like a baby, there is no way he would have trusted me to provide for and protect his little girl.

Here's my point—no matter what I did, I could not escape that train. No way. In my mind, it was going to squash me and, for the life of me, I couldn't understand why G's family didn't tell me. Seems like that's information I needed. The information I want you to glean from my silly story is this: We are saved by Grace alone. Period. That's it. Nothing else. Just Grace.

Sometimes, people seem to get it confused and think good deeds are what God is after. They're not.

Ephesians 2 says we're not saved by works, but we are saved for good works and we are a good work (Ephesians 2:10). We are God's workmanship, literally His poem, His masterpiece. This means we can rest in our salvation. And we don't need to question it. We didn't save us, so it's not on us to keep us saved. Or keep saving us. He did it. He will continue to do it.

This is the Gospel.

Before we dive deeper into this idea of the Gospel of the Grace Train, I first want to unpack this word "gospel." It means good news. Why is the Gospel good news? I'm glad you asked. While the Gospel is the best news the world has ever heard, it is simultaneously delivering a diagnosis that is as bad as it gets. That's what makes it so good. Stay with me. This will make sense soon.

Ephesians 2, verse 1. "And you…"

Stop right there. I guess I should warn you, I'm going to be sharing a lot of Scripture in this book, and it sometimes takes me a while to get through chapters of the Bible, because every word is important.

He says, "And you…" From the beginning, Paul is talking to you. We know this because in Ephesians, chapter 1, it says, "To the saints who are in Ephesus." If you're a Christian, you're "in Christ Jesus," you're a saint. I know it's crazy. But it's true. Paul says so. You don't have to wait to die and let some people vote on you and sell you on a necklace at a store to make you a saint. If you're a follower of Jesus Christ, then by definition, you're a saint.

"And you were dead in the trespasses and sins in which you once walked." This might shock some of you, but here's the first bit of good news—the Gospel is not about bad people getting better. There are no good people. We're all bad. Paul is about to explain this. And because we're all dead, the Gospel is about dead people coming to life. He says, "You were dead." He doesn't say, "You were bad." Sin doesn't make you bad. Sin makes you dead.

And so the good news is not God is good, you are bad, try harder. The good news is that God is life and you are death and He wants to resurrect you. He wants to revive you.

To be clear—you're not a bad person who needs to be better, and you're not a mistaker in need of a life coach. I know this is hard for some folks who grew up getting thumped over the head with this week after week. The truth of the Gospel is that you might just become a better version of you and still die and go to a Christless eternity if you are not made alive in Him.

The problem is that you and I are sinners in need of a savior. This is the diagnosis. The bad news. But hold on, don't close the book. There is a remedy.

We've got to stop here for a second. Paul wants us to know this reality. You are a sinner. Again, I know some of you will be offended by that. That's okay—that's part of my job. My job is to comfort the afflicted and afflict the comfortable.

You and I are, by nature and nurture, sinners. I know some of you reading this are asking, "Who are you to call me a sinner?" Great question. Truth is I'm the greatest sinner in the room. That's why I can recognize you so easily. Because I am one, too. We have all sinned and fallen short of the glory of God. So welcome to planet Earth. This makes you one of us.

Paul says, "And you were dead in the trespasses and sins in which you once walked, following the course of this world, following the prince of the power of the air, the spirit that is now at work in the sons of disobedience." Every one of us, if you're a Christian, was at one time on that path of the world—a path that led to a Christless eternity. The Bible says, "The wages of sin is death" (Romans 6:23). There are only two paths in this life. If you don't know Christ as your Lord and Savior, then you are—by default—on a path that leads to destruction. To hell. To a Christless eternity. If you are a Christian, if you have surrendered to the lordship of Jesus Christ, then He has rescued you from that domain of darkness and placed you on a path that leads to Him. He has brought you to Himself. These are two very different places.

Verse 3. And Paul says, "Among whom we all once lived in the passions of our flesh, carrying out the desires of the body and the mind." Part of what Paul wants us to understand, if you're a follower of Jesus, is that you can't look down your nose at any person. In order for us to arrogantly look down at other people and the way they behave, we have to take our eyes off the cross and off of Jesus to look down at those people. You can't simultaneously look up at Christ and look down on anyone else.

Paul is asking, "Who do you think you are? Don't you know that we all once lived in the passions of our flesh, carrying out the desires of the body and the mind? And we're by nature children of wrath, like the rest of mankind." I realize this is a very unpopular message. Anyone spouting the idea that we're children of wrath is not going to win a popularity contest.

The Puritan Jonathan Edwards preached that we are sinners in the hands of an angry God. And you know what? He's right. Seventeenth-century preacher John Owen wrote, "Be killing sin, or sin be killing you." (This comes from an eighty-six-page book entitled *Mortification of Sin in Believers* and the quote is referencing Romans 8:13.)Good advice.

If the message ended here, that we're sinners in the hands of an angry God, then that would not be good news, because we're all about to get smoked by lightning bolts. Bummer. But we would do well not to rush by the fact that you and I, apart from Christ, are children of wrath and that we deserve, by our own decision, by our own choices, the full wrath of God. What's more, nobody had to teach us that.

If you have children, you already know this. This is what I mean—you didn't have to teach your kids to sin. They just do it. Naturally. It's like breathing. As much as you love them, that precious little beautiful angel, that skittle, that snowflake, is—at heart—a wretched, black-hearted sinner. Like you and me. How many times did your kids walk up, snatch something out of your hand, then bite you and walk away?

Nobody taught my children to do that. But both did. It's just in there when they opened their eyes on planet Earth. This means that by nature, they are sinners. Some people hear me say this, and they respond, "No, no, no, Pastor, I'm good. Really. I'm good." Compared to who? The nightly news? Maybe. Compared to an Almighty God? Not so much.

Let's just look at basic Ethics 101. Kindergarten-level ethics. The Ten Commandments. How many have you broken? How often?

Need a refresher? The first one is to worship only one God. You ever worship another God? You ever put your trust in something other than Him? Me, too. The second one says, don't have any idols. Have you ever worshipped the created things over the Creator? Yep. Me, too. The third one says, don't use the Lord's name in vain. If you've ever driven the roads around my house at five in the afternoon, you've broken this one. I'm speaking from experience.

Right now I'm zero for three. Anybody looking at a different score-card? The fourth one commands that we honor the Sabbath and keep it holy. Let's be honest, we don't even think that one counts anymore. Whatever. I do what I wanna do. But He commanded it. When was the last time you honored it and kept it? I know—me, too.

The fifth one, obey your parents. If you've ever been a teenager, you broke this one every day from the age of thirteen.

When we get to the sixth one—thou shalt not murder—folks like to raise a hand and object, "Pastor, I've never killed someone." Well, con-gratulations. The problem we have is that Jesus comes along in the Ser-mon on the Mount and says, *"If you've ever hated someone in your heart, then you've committed murder."*

Number seven is don't commit adultery. To which many folks say, "I've never cheated on my spouse." For that I am thankful. Except Jesus says in the same sermon, "But I say to you that everyone who looks at a woman with lustful intent has already committed adultery with her in his heart" (Matthew 5:28). And every dude reading this goes, "Well, dang it." And every grown woman who's watched the movie *Twilight* or read *Fifty Shades* just got outed.

The eighth is thou shalt not steal. Have you ever taken anything that's not yours? And I don't care if you said you were "sharing" that music. Or that video. It's not sharing. It's stealing. Don't think so? Tell the FBI and let's see how they view it.

The ninth one—thou shalt not lie. I've had people tell me, "Listen, I'm not a liar. Just sometimes I tell lies." Do you hear what you're saying out loud? No, sometimes you tell lies because you're a liar. That's like saying, "I'm not a thief but sometimes I take things that don't belong to me." Which by definition is exactly what a thief is. Have you at any point this week clicked a box online that said, "I have read the terms and conditions"? Exactly. You are a liar.

Then the tenth one is thou shalt not covet. If you've ever watched HGTV, you're guilty. That's what it is. The whole network exists to feed your covetousness. How do I know? Because I'm the worst of the bunch.

All right. So you're zero for ten. And if by some chance any one of you wants to stand up and argue, then you're now guilty of the grand-daddy of them all: pride. It's what got Satan kicked out of heaven. I know, on a lot of pulpits, we don't talk a lot about wrath. And if you're thirty or under, you grew up in a world that lied to you and told you that you were a rainbow and a snowflake and puppy's breath. I hate to break it to you, but you're not. Your biggest problem is you. You are the problem. You lie to you more than anybody else. You've broken more promises to you than anybody else. You are your own worst enemy. And you are the root of your own problem.

That's the diagnosis.

Truth is, we're sinners. The problem is us. The heart of the problem is that we have a heart problem. That's what it is. That's why you've said things that you've been embarrassed of. And that's why you say things like, "Oops. That just slipped out." The only thing that can slip out is what's in there.

Jesus says, *"Out of the overflow of the heart, the mouth speaks."* That means this: You don't have a potty mouth. You have a potty heart.

And that's a problem. That's what Paul means when he says that we are sinners.

Sometimes we treat God like "the man upstairs" who doesn't really care about sin. We assume sin is not that big a deal. Not really a problem. But judging by the fact that God sent His Son to die in our place, our sin is a huge deal. One look at the cross tells us that our sin debt is insurmountable. But there's the problem—we've taken our eyes off the cross. And the only way to see us clearly is through the shed blood of Jesus. Sin is such a big deal that the Son of God had to shed His blood for it to be forgiven. God's love is so lavish that He was willing to do it for you and me.

Not far from our church, in St. Augustine, Florida, a family owns one of these big exotic cat places. Think *Tiger King* without all the weird people. There's a lion. A few tigers. Couple of cheetahs. My brother, Russ, is a police officer in St. Johns County, so sometimes when there's fresh roadkill, he'll scoop up the deer and give it to these folks, who then chuck the body in there with this lion, whose name is Mufasa. Mufasa eyes the dead deer, then saunters over and takes the head off the doe with a single bite. Eats it like a KitKat. Which surprises us. The fence gives us a false impression of who he is. We think he's a tame Disney character caged for our pleasure. Here, lick my finger. But he's not tame. He's a lion. And were it not for the fence, he'd eat us like a chocolate bar.

We treat our sin the same way as we treat that lion.

Let me poke at you a little—when you gave yourself to that guy who wasn't your husband, not only did you sin against your own body, you sinned against the Almighty God. Whenever you downloaded that picture of that girl, you didn't just sin against her and against your own body but against an Almighty God. Whenever you misused your words in a hurtful way, whenever you withheld forgiveness, when you lied, when you stole, whenever you erupted in anger, you did so against the Lion of Judah. He's powerful. He's almighty. He's uncaged. And we should stand in reverent fear.

When Isaiah, a prophet of God, encountered the Lion of Judah, he said, *"Whoa, I'm not worthy to stand in your presence. I'm a man of unclean lips and I'm of a people of unclean lips."* Why does he say this? What happened? His eyes were opened. He saw God for who He is.

Alright, back to Ephesians 2. Verse 4. "But God..." Don't skip over that part too quickly. It's the best news ever. There are some big buts in the Bible that you should pay attention to. This is a big one right here. "But God, being rich in mercy, because of the great love with which he loved us..."

Don't miss this: God is love. Even at our worst, sinning against Him and others, even when we slap the face of the Almighty Sovereign God, He is love and He is rich in mercy. He has to be stirred to anger. The reason we can even sit here today and He didn't wipe you out after your first sin is because He is love. This is His very nature. His essence. The overflow of God is love. It's why you and I are here. He was not lonely in heaven looking for some people to sing Him songs. He is love, and love begets love. And in His love for us, He didn't strike us down with a lightning bolt when He had and has every right.

"But God, being rich in mercy, because of the great love with which he loved us, even when we were dead in our trespasses, made us alive together with Christ—by grace you have been saved." "Grace" means unmerited favor. It means we do not get what we deserve. "By grace you have been saved—and raised us up with him and seated us with him in the heavenly places in Christ Jesus."

Couple of things here. One, you're the passive agent. You were dead and He made you alive. You did not make you alive. God did that. This is very different than the popular teaching across multiple denominations that doing the right stuff, like going to church enough times, saying the right prayer, or going on a mission trip, makes you okay with God. Puts you on an even playing field. Grants you access to His presence.

Look again at the verse. "When we were dead..." What can a dead man do? He can stink. Rot. Melt into the earth. But he can't make himself alive. Only God raises the dead. Which is Paul's point. You and I are the passive agent. God comes after us. He pursues us and He knows what He's getting into. And yet He pursues us anyway. This thought ought to stir you to worship and help you walk in freedom. Why? Because you didn't earn it, and if you didn't earn it, you can't lose it. It's a gift. "By grace you have been saved…"

Look at the verb tense in all the verses here. That we *were* dead, that He *made* us, He *raised* us, and He *seated* us. They're all past tense. That means it's already happened. A done deal.

One of the things you should know about me is that I record every Georgia Bulldogs football game. And if we win, I save it. If we lose, I erase it. So in my DVR, the Bulldogs have never been beaten. Greatest team of all time. Sometimes, after the season, I'll rewatch the games. And when I do, do you think I'm worried about the outcome of those games? If we fumble, if we throw an interception, if their defense blocks a punt, do you think I sweat it? Not in the least. Why? Because the game is past tense. I know the end of the story, I know what's going to happen.

The same is true with all of you who are "in Christ Jesus." Who have surrendered to the lordship of Jesus Christ. Who have said, "Not my will, but Yours be done." You are past tense. Yes, you were a wretched, blackhearted sinner. And yes, you still do struggle in your flesh and will until either you go to heaven or Jesus returns. But, by the Grace of God, if Christ is your Lord, then you have been adopted into His family as a son, as a daughter. And when God sees you, you are no longer a wretched, blackhearted sinner. You are righteous. Covered by the blood of Christ. When God looks at you, He doesn't see where Jesus ends and where you begin, because you were dead and He made you alive. You're past tense. A done deal.

Verse 7. "So that in the coming ages, he might show the immeasurable riches of his grace in kindness toward us in Christ Jesus." And verses 8 and 9. These are very famous verses: "For by grace you have been saved through faith. And this is not your own doing; it is the gift of God, not a result of works, so that no one may boast." Paul, by the power of the Holy Spirit, wants you to know that salvation is God's gift, not something you earn or produce. You've been saved by Grace through faith in Jesus. Period.

While your salvation is a free gift to you, it cost Christ everything. The message of the Gospel is not God is good and you are bad, so try harder. The message of the Gospel is that you were dead and by the power of Jesus Christ, by His death and resurrection, by the price that He paid on the cross, He brought you to new life in Christ and adopted you into the family of God.

The Bible uses two primary illustrations to describe folks like us who try to bring their good works to God as if He's going to be impressed. *Look at me, God. Look at what a good job I'm doing. You must love me more now because of all my good works.* Nothing could be further from the truth.

In Philippians chapter 3, Paul lays out a laundry list of good works that he's done. His religious résumé. Some things he earned. Others he was born into. All of which were true. Based on the list, he says, "Though I myself have reason for confidence in the flesh also." In other words, if anybody can be saved because they were good enough, Paul would say, *That's me.* "If anyone else thinks he has reason for confidence in the flesh, I have more." And then he lists his laundry list of things. And compared to other people, he's right. He says he was "circumcised on the eighth day, of the people of Israel, of the tribe of Benjamin, a Hebrew of Hebrews; as to the law, a Pharisee; as to zeal, a persecutor of the church; as to righteousness under the law, blameless. But whatever gain I had, I counted it as loss for the sake of Christ. Indeed, I count everything as loss because of the surpassing worth of knowing Christ Jesus my Lord. For his sake, I have suffered the loss of all things and count them as rubbish…" We'll come back to that word, the one translated as "rubbish." "In order that I may gain Christ and be found in him, not having a righteousness of my own that comes from the law, but that which comes through faith in Christ, the righteousness from God that depends on faith."

Paul says, *I did it all. I attended every night of the revival. I sponsored more Compassion kids than you. I went on all the mission trips, didn't even send out funding letters. I funded the whole thing myself. I pray morning, evening, night. I downloaded the podcast. I took notes. I led a disciple group, I was in a disciple group. And having done all this, when I bring it to Jesus to try to impress Him, it is rubbish.*

That word "rubbish" is *skubalon* in Greek, a slang term for animal dung. Now, if you've ever heard me speak, you can probably tell by my accent that I'm from the South. And where I'm from, when you step in some skubalon, we don't say, "Oh, no, I'm stepping in rubbish." Unless you're British. They might say that. In my part of the world, we use two words to describe that smelly pile of animal dung. The first is "bull" and the second I won't print in this book, but you can fill in the blank.

When you try to bring your good deeds to God and say, "Look at me, God. Look how I've put my whole life together. Are you not impressed?"—that would be like your child saying, "Mom, I got something for you" on Mother's Day. And then he or she brings you this beautifully wrapped present. And you open it up and you pull off the top, and there's a big steaming pile. How impressed are you? You're not. You're offended. "Are you kidding me?"

This is what it's like when we think we can earn the Grace of God. You are essentially looking at Jesus on the cross and saying, "That's not enough. Let me add to your work." You can't earn what's already been paid for. Your attempt to do so is rubbish. Skubalon. You need to get the bull-skubalon out of your life and lean into the Grace and the mercy of Jesus Christ.

The Old Testament illustration is actually worse. I really think that the Bible is trying to be graphic, and gross, and shocking. Which it is. The prophet Isaiah says this in Isaiah 64:6: "We have all become like one who is unclean, and all our righteous deeds are like a polluted garment."

Some of your translations might say "filthy rags." Literally, in Hebrew, the word used means menstrual cloths. I'm not making this up. So let me make sure you understand Isaiah's meaning. Husbands, imagine if on your anniversary, your wife said, "Baby, I love you so much. I appreciate our marriage. I appreciate you loving me like Christ loved the church, and I've got a gift for you." And she brought "polluted garments." Or used menstrual cloths. What would you think? It's graphic and it's gross, but that's exactly Isaiah's point.

Having said that—and this is important—there is no such thing as a fruitless Christian or a workless Christian. If you have been run over by the Grace Train, there should be physical evidence. Something should bubble up and out of that. Gratitude produces works not because works save us but because we *can't not* work. When we understand the Grace that saved us, works are the natural byproduct. James, the brother of Jesus, says this very thing—show me your faith without your works, and I'll show you my faith by my works. Why does this matter?

Romans 5:1–2 says this: "Therefore, since we have been justified by faith, we have peace with God through our Lord Jesus Christ. Through him we have also obtained access by faith into this grace in which we stand, and we rejoice in hope of the glory of God." Think about it. We "stand" on Grace. It's our bedrock. Our foundation. Not judgment. Not condemnation. But unmerited Grace. It seems counterintuitive because when we talk about Grace, we often do so in the context of falling. And that's absolutely right. When we fall, we fall on His Grace. But it's more encompassing than that. Every single time we fall, we fall upon the Grace that allows us to stand right before God to begin with. So, it's Grace when we fall. It's Grace when we stand. It's His Grace that picks us up, dusts us off, and grants us access to the Father—which should blow our minds.

It's His Grace that brought us there. When we fall down, it's His Grace that convicts us to repent. It's His Grace that stands us back up. And it's His Grace in which we walk. It's not like He's keeping a scorecard. "Um…Joby, this is the 1,122nd time you've fallen. My patience is at an end. You have run beyond my Grace." Nope. He won't ever say that. Why? Well, to quote my friend Charles, "There is more Grace in Jesus than sin in us." You should write that down. It's true. And it matters. A lot.

Here's the point—salvation is found by Grace alone through faith alone in Christ alone. And some of you might even say, "Hey, yeah, but I put my faith in Him. At least I get credit for the faith." Right? Wrong. The faith that you had to put into Him was a gift from God so that you can't even brag about that part. The only thing you brought to the equation was the sin that caused you to need Him in the first place.

When I was in student ministry, I would use this illustration to explain it. Now, every illustration falls down, but work with me here. I would put a kid in the back of the room on a skateboard and throw them a rope and I would say, "Come to me without touching the ground." But they couldn't. They had no way to propel themselves to me. Then I gave them a little tug and they came scooting on over, having done none of the work to get to me.

I would tell them, "Grace got you here. You didn't initiate it. Faith is what kept you on the board. Grace is what got you here." I'm not saying faith doesn't matter. It does. Without faith, it's impossible to please God. Faith is everything. But faith is a gift from God, while Grace is this unmerited favor that brought you to Him. Faith is the vehicle. Grace is the power. We need both. But it's important to understand those two things are not the same.

This takes us off the hook. We don't have to muster up enough faith to be saved. He gives us all we need. The fact that we even have faith is the gift of Grace that God gives us.

In other words, Jesus plus nothing equals salvation. It's just Jesus. It's not Jesus plus good works. It's not Jesus plus baptism. It's not Jesus plus raise your hand or Jesus plus say a prayer. It's not Jesus plus the sacraments. It's none of those things. It's Jesus plus nothing equals salvation.

Because Jesus plus anything screws up everything because it means that you don't understand the Gospel. Again, the good news is not about bad people being better. It's about dead people coming to life. It's about God paying a debt you could not pay. And when you begin to understand this, you get to verse 10, which says, "For we are his workmanship, created in Christ Jesus for good works, which God prepared beforehand that we should walk in them."

If you think, "Well, sweet, I can just pray the sinner's prayer, and become a Christian and do whatever I want," then He's not your Lord; He's a get-out-of-jail-free card, which you use to get out of the bad place you got yourself into—which makes you Lord of your life and not Him. And that has nothing to do with the Gospel of Jesus Christ. I'm trying to help you see that you were an enemy of God. But the story doesn't end there. But God, being rich in mercy, reached down, redeemed you, softened your heart, regenerated your heart, drew you unto Himself, paid for your sin, and then adopted you into His family. You were dead and He made you alive.

Gretchen and I used to have two dogs. Boxers. Sadie and Sampson. I wanted English bulldogs, like Uga from Athens, but they're like $1,500 each and I was on a youth pastor budget, so I got boxers because they were a couple hundred. But they kinda look the same. We started with Sampson, and he was awesome. He was regal, well-behaved, and smart. When it was just him, we could leave him alone in our house and he would be fine. Obedient. Didn't get into stuff. No problem. Then we got Sadie, and everything went downhill fast.

One day, we came home, opened our apartment door, and it looked like it had snowed in there. They had chewed the couch cushions into a bazillion little white, fluffy pieces. And Sadie was so dumb that when we walked in the room, she didn't even know she was in trouble. She just got all wiggly and turned in a circle. Sampson, on the the other hand, had a pretty good idea they had messed up.

But we were young and we didn't care. We loved them. Too much, but whatever. We bought them birthday and Christmas presents and let them sleep in our bed. We treated them like our kids. Some of you wise people would tell us, "When you have kids, your kids will be your kids and your dogs will just be your dogs." And Gretchen and I would look knowingly at each other and shake our heads. "No, not us. We'll always love our dogs." And then we had kids.

So Sadie and Sampson were living in our fenced-in backyard. And they hated the fence. They wanted to be inside with us, so they saw the fence as a punishment. But what they didn't understand is that the fence was set in place, in their lives, for their provision and protection, because our house backed up to a main road. Without the fence, they're roadkill.

One day, I was at work. It was about lunchtime. Maria, one of our worship leaders, who used to watch our kids, gave me a call and she said, "Hey, uh, I'm looking out in the backyard and I haven't seen Sadie and Sampson all morning. I think you might need to come home."

I hustled home, walked around the back, and saw that apparently I'd left the gate open that morning. I'm sure what happened is that Sadie saw the open gate and then said to Sampson, "Hey, Sampson, it's open. We should go for this." Sampson was probably thinking, "No, we really shouldn't. The fence and the gate are for our provision and protection. The master loves us so that's why he has put the boundaries around us." But she nuzzled her way through, opened the gate, and like most mates would do, he followed her out into the road. Once free of their boundaries, you know they stood in the front yard and thought, "Sweet, no more fence. No more rules. The man can't hold me down. We can go left, we can go right, we can pee in the neighbor's flowers. We can chase cats. We can do anything we want, baby. Freedom!"

But Sadie and Sampson would soon learn that while rebellion feels like fun and freedom, it is not. It only leads to bondage and death. Those are your only options.

So I started looking, driving around my neighborhood holding a piece of cheese out the window. Why? Because they like cheese. So, like a goober, I'm driving around the hood with a piece of cheese hanging out the window shouting, "Saaaadiiieeee, Saaaaampsoooon."

That's about when my neighbors flagged me down and ask, "Have you lost your dogs?'

Frustrated, I answered, "Nah, Nanna and Grandpa got out today. But they love cheese!"

Of course I lost my dogs.

Nieghbors can be so dumb. This is probably why Jesus commanded us to love them.

When I got to our little guard gate, the lady said, "I saw 'em about nine-thirty this morning." It was after lunch by then. She said, "I saw two dogs, two boxers. They went right onto Hodges then took a left on Atlantic." When I first heard they were gone, I was thinking, "If I find these dogs, they're going to feel my wrath." But staring at a four-lane road with a fifty-mile-an-hour speed limit, I only had one thought— "Oh, Lord, please just help me find them."

An hour in and Gretchen called. "I found them! I found them!"

"Sweet. Where are they?"

"They're on the internet."

"What? Huh?"

"They have their own Facebook page."

"What do you mean?"

Somebody found the dogs and took them to the pound. Downtown. And someone at the pound took their pictures and put them on their website so people like me could identify them. I thought, "Great."

And so I called them up. "Hey, I think you've got my dogs. We saw them online."

And they said, "Alright, well, you're going to have to come on down here."

I drove downtown, found the dog pound, walked in, and told the lady, "Hey, I'm here to pick up my dogs."

My first problem, she informed me, was that we'd failed to put tags or collars on them. It was clear she was not a fan of someone like me. Let me just say her people skills were not that great, which may explain why she was working with dogs.

She said, "Do you realize you failed to properly tag your dog? And that the law, as an owner, requires you to do so?"

"Yes, but—"

"So, what you're saying is that you have no way to identify them."

"Yes, but—"

"And therefore you have no way of proving they are yours."

This was my first clue that this would not go smoothly. "Lady, can I just get my dogs?"

We walked into the back, where the kennel area was. The little doggy jails. Sadie and Sampson were incarcerated in the seventh kennel back. As I was walking by all these other little captive dogs, they were all running to the front like, "Pick me, pick me." Then we got to kennel number seven and found our two little sinners. Sadie, the dumb one, saw me, and she lit up, like, "Hey, where have you been? We've been looking for you everywhere." Sampson didn't even look at me. He walked to the back of the kennel, tucked his tail, and sat down. He was like, "My bad, dog."

Rebellion, though it feels like freedom, always and only leads to death or bondage.

Having found my dogs, I followed the lady back to the front desk to fill out the paperwork. "Okay, what do I need to do?"

Without pause, she said, "Two hundred ninety dollars. For each one."

And I blurted out, "What?"

My hands were pretty well tied. What was I going to do? Walk back to the kennels and explain to Sadie and Sampson, "Hey, I can get you out, but here's the thing—you owe me two hundred ninety dollars. Each. This means you have to get jobs. A paper route. Greyhound racing. Something. But you both owe me two hundred ninety dollars."

Now look at it from the dogs' perspective. What are they going to do? They have incurred a debt that they cannot pay. Ever. They are unable to repay the debt that they, by their own sin, have incurred. Even if they were to come to me and say, "Okay, Master, tell you what, here's the deal. You get us out of here, and from now on, we'll be perfect. Best dogs ever. We'll fetch your slippers. Bring you the paper. Teach the kids to walk and talk and add and subtract. We'll even clean up our own mess."

Well, while that would be great, they would still have one insurmountable problem: the debt. And their good behavior will do nothing to pay down that debt. So I said to the nice and understanding lady, "Ma'am, that's almost six hundred bucks."

She nodded knowingly.

"What happens if I don't pay?"

"Well, then fill out some paperwork and put them up for adoption."

"What?"

"You'll turn over ownership, legally, to Duval County."

"Well, what do y'all do with them? I mean, do you euthanize them or what?"

And she shakes her head. "No, no. We bathe them, shampoo 'em, clip their toenails." Then she paused. "We'd need to fix the male 'cause he isn't fixed yet, and then we'd put them up for adoption on the website."

I look over my left shoulder and a big poster is hanging on the wall. SPECIAL TODAY, ADOPT A DOG FOR $30.

So I looked at the girl and said, "Alright, I wanna relinquish ownership of my dogs."

She looked at me like I was the devil incarnate. And so I filled out some paperwork. And she notarized it and handed it back to me and I took my piece of paper, took about three steps toward the door, then turned around and came right back to her face and said, "Hi, ma'am, I would like to adopt some dogs, please."

And she smugly shook her head. "You can't adopt your own dogs."

I hold up the paper she'd just signed. "Ma'am, I have a notarized piece of paper from Duval County saying that I don't own any dogs. You own dogs, but I don't own any dogs. I wanna adopt two, a male, a female. Preferrably boxers. You got anything like that? I'm going to call them Sadie and Sampson."

She was angry, so she scooped up her papers and walked into the back to have a conversation with her manager. Then he came back out with a clipboard. Truth was, I had found the loophole. He slammed down the board, required me to fill out this paperwork proving that I was a capable dog owner, and then I gave them thirty dollars for each and legally adopted my two errant, rebellious, sinning dogs back into my family. I redeemed my dogs.

Having paid, I said, "Okay, can I pick 'em up now?"

This is even better. He said, "No, you have to wait three days."

"Why three days?"

"We have to bathe and shampoo them, and then clip their toenails."

Three days later, we picked them up. Clean and better than when we gave them up.

This is the Gospel of Jesus Christ.

Rebellion always feels like freedom but ends in bondage and a debt you can't pay. Not in ten thousand lifetimes. Even if you were to be perfect from this day forward, your perfection would do nothing to pay for the sin you've already committed. And yet God, rich in mercy and full of Grace, because He loves you, pays your debt and forgives your sin. When Jesus died on the cross and shed His blood for you, your and my sinfulness was imputed onto Him. As a result, He received the full wrath of God. And because He did, His righteousness was imputed unto us. And we were justified before God. This justification brought us back into right relationship before God. But that's not the end of the story. Having been justified, we were then adopted into His family, making us sons and daughters of the Most High God.

That's the Gospel. By Grace we have been saved, through faith, and not by works, so that none of us can boast.

Some of you reading this today might believe that there's a God, but you've never surrendered your life to the lordship of Christ. That invitation is open today. Maybe today, for the very first time, you've heard the Gospel, and God's softened your heart. Maybe you're ready to surrender your life to Him and receive Christ as your Lord and Savior. "God shows his love for us in that while we were still sinners, Christ died for us" (Romans 5:8). And yet, it doesn't end there. Right this moment, you could be adopted into the family of God as a full heir.

What's required? What do you need to do? Accept His Grace. Just tell Him that you're a sinner, and admit you have incurred a debt you can't pay, and that you believe Christ is the Son of God and the only way to God, and that, right this moment, you want to put your faith and trust in Him. There are no magical words. Just pour out your heart to Him and, in this moment, you are being saved.

If you've already surrendered to His Lordship, I praise God for you. I pray you are strengthened in your faith. Will you please pray with me and for all the folks who might read this and surrender for the first time?

Pray with Me

Our good and gracious Heavenly Father, that is who You are. You are good and You are so gracious. We thank You for Your Grace. Because You are love, You have placed Your love on Your children. God, we thank You for Your Grace. Your unmerited favor. You don't love us because we deserve it but simply because it is just who You are. It is Your Grace that chases us down when we have rebelled against You. It is by Your Grace that our sin debt has been paid. It is by Your Grace that we can be called children of God. Lord, we repent of our arrogance that would lead us to think that we, by our effort, could add anything to the perfect Grace poured out for us on the cross. I pray that through

the power of the Holy Spirit, our lives would be forever changed by that
same Grace that saved us.

Father, if there be someone reading this book right now who has
never surrendered to Your Grace, I pray that they would do that right
now. (If that is you, would you receive the free gift of God's Grace
right now? Would you admit that you are a sinner in need of a
savior? Would you put your full trust in Christ's finished work for
you on the cross and believe that God raised Him from the dead?
Would you confess Christ as your Lord and Savior?)

God, may we never get over the good news of the Gospel of Grace.
We pray this in the undefeated and matchless name of Jesus Christ.
Amen.

- If you prayed this prayer for the first time, I don't want you to
  live as a secret Christian or live in isolation. I pastor a really
  great church made up of a bunch of really great and broken
  sinners like you and me, and we'd love to hear from you—not
  to count you as a number but to help disciple you and help you
  deepen the relationship you've just discovered with Jesus.
- Please email me at Joby.Martin@coe22.com. We'd love to hear
  your story and know how we can be praying for you.

Chapter 2

GRACE CAN'T BE LOST. AND NEITHER CAN YOU.

Grace is not anti-effort. Grace is anti-earning.

I love walking around Walmart. I've led two strangers in Walmart to Christ by just paying attention to what's going on around me. One time, I was standing in line, and the lady in front of me was trying to check out, but her card wouldn't work. Her bill was around a hundred and fifty bucks, and it was all groceries. When her card wouldn't work, she started getting frantic. So she tried again. And again. But it wouldn't work, wouldn't work, and wouldn't work. And she just broke down in tears. So I just paid for it.

And she said, "Thank you, thank you, thank you."

So I pressed into the pain I was seeing on her face. "Are you okay?"

To which she said, "Uh, I am fine. I just needed—"

So I interrupted her.

"No, hold on, hold on." I made sure she was looking at me. "Are you okay?"

Something must have broken through, because she shook her head and said, "I'm not." She told me her story, which was terrible, and a few minutes later, I was praying with her to receive Christ in Walmart, in Jacksonville.

Another time, I was standing in the ten-items-or-less line at Walmart, and there was a lady in front of me with a full cart and a kid who was driving her crazy. Which brings me to another point—I'm convinced that the people at Walmart hate you and your children. Why else do you think they put all of the sugary snacks right there at toddler level? The kid was throwing Reese's and Skittles into the basket hand over fist and the mother was throwing them out. Then, just before she lost her ever-loving mind, she looked at the kid and screamed at the top of her lungs—which is totally normal in Walmart, by the way—"Relax!"

I remember thinking, "He's never going to understand what that word means, ever." After I checked out, she was still there trying to wrangle the kid. "Uh, excuse me. Ma'am, are you okay?"

She looked at me with both suspicion and offense. "What do you mean okay?"

I said, "No, no." I tapped my heart. "I mean like in here. Are you okay?" She shook her head. "No. I'm not. My husband just left." Boom. Waterworks. Ten minutes later, she's RSVPing to the marriage supper of the Lamb. Saved in Walmart.

I tell you these stories because before you finish this chapter, my guess is that you might look back on this chapter and think it sounds a lot like the first chapter and ask yourself, "Why'd he do that twice?" Or, "I thought he already did that. Why'd he say the same thing a second time?" My answer is simple. Because we're sheep. And sheep are dumb. Totally lost without their shepherd. And because God knows this, He says things two, three, and umpteen times. God, through His inspired Word, goes to great lengths to make sure we understand both our need for Him and His desire to return us to Himself, along with what it cost Him. What we term "unmerited Grace." And maybe no place in Scripture does that as well as Romans 3, which might be my favorite passage in the Bible.

Actually, I have several favorites. Ephesians 2. Philippians 2. I have about four favorites. Whatever. You understand what I'm saying.

But before we can dive into chapter 3 of Romans, we need the context of chapter 1. Let's pick it up at Romans 1, verse 5, where Paul says, "Through whom we have received grace and apostleship to bring about the obedience of faith for the sake of his name among all the nations." See that phrase "the obedience of faith"? Notice what it doesn't say. It doesn't say "the obedience *for* faith." While subtle, that distinction matters a ton. "The obedience for faith" would be an obedience motivated by a belief that I can work my way to God. Such as, "If I obey, then I'm okay with God. I can get in His good graces."

But that's not what Paul says. Paul says, "the obedience *of* faith." Obedience that grows out of faith. I grew up on the NIV, which says, "from faith." I like both. "The obedience of faith" means God brought me into His good graces through the life, death, and resurrection of Jesus. So my obedience is birthed out of a grateful response to what God has done for me.

Then when you get to chapter 1, verses 16 and 17, Paul says, "For I am not ashamed of the gospel, for it is the power of God for salvation to everyone who believes, to the Jew first and also to the Greek. For in it, the righteousness of God is revealed." You might want to underline that in your Bible, "The righteousness of God is revealed from faith for faith, as it is written, 'The righteous shall live by faith.'" Paul then explains how the righteousness of God is revealed in the Gospel. When you get past 1:16 and 17, you will probably ask the question, "So, Paul, who needs the Gospel?" And Paul goes, *Well, it's funny you ask. There are two groups of people. Religious people and nonreligious people. People who think they're good and people who're pretty sure they're bad. Which means, all people need the Gospel.*

In chapter 1 verses 18 and following, he says, *Okay, we'll start with the evil pagans. You know who they are.* Then he lists the sins. Sexual immorality. Idolaters. Inventors of evil. Paul then lists some stuff going on and says: *That's so shady we don't even have a sin word for that. You just made up a new sin, okay?* Then he throws in "disobedient to parents." I think he does that just to make us aware that they are us.

In chapter 2, he shifts gears and points a finger at the religious who think they're good. "Therefore you have no excuse, O man, every one of you who judges. For in passing judgment on another you condemn yourself, because you, the judge, practice the very same things." In short, you're just as bad even though you think your good works make you better, which they don't. They make you self-righteous, which is sin. Paul explains how all of us need the Gospel and nothing we can do earns us righteousness before God.

The natural question that follows is, "Paul, if what you're saying is true, then are we all too far gone?"

Everything he's written leads to this point. And his answer is, *No way*. Or, "by no means" is the way he would say it. *By no means. Righteousness has been made available even for you.* To which we would respond, "Okay, Paul. This is contrary to everything I know about the law of Moses. How can I, a sinner, be made righteous? How can I stand rightly before God?"

Well, Paul responds, *funny you ask*. And here we go. Some of the greatest words ever written in any language. Chapter 3, verses 9 through 26, answers this question. How can a sinful man stand rightly before God? Martin Luther would later say that this passage is a really big deal. He called this the chief point of the whole Bible. Remember the line in *The Sixth Sense*, where the kid says, "I see dead people"? This is that moment. This is the reveal. This is what it's all about.

We'll pick it up in 3:9: "What then? Are we Jews any better off?" In our context, this would be, "Are we religious people any better off?" And he answers, "No. Not at all." And you say, "Well, how come? I'm trying really hard."

The reason is that we all start at the same place. Whether you grew up really bad or you grew up really good. Or you grew up really good at being really bad—which was me—we all start at the same place. Paul says, "For we have already charged that all, both Jews and Greeks, are under sin." Underline those words "under sin." This is the singular diagnosis for all mankind. This means every single one of us is born under sin. Making us, by both nature and nurture, sinners.

We are no different than the seagulls in *Finding Nemo*. We are born saying, "Mine, mine, mine, mine, mine." This phrase, under sin, is like a title. Like if you had a spiritual passport. You can only have citizenship in one of two places. There is no dual citizenship here. You can only be marked as a citizen under sin or under Grace. That's it. And every single one of us is born in the country of sin. We're born in the city, in the nation, under the dominion of sin in the kingdom of darkness.

Sin is not just breaking random rules in a book that you don't read that much. Paul personifies sin as an enemy. He states we are under the power, the dominion of that domain. We are slaves to sin. We are slaves needing freedom, not just guilty people needing forgiveness. He also says we are all sinners equally, every single one of us. Wretched, blackhearted sinners.

No matter how good you think you are. In fact, if you think you're really good, that thinking in itself is your sin. Let that explode your brain for a second.

And then there's a whole crowd of you, probably the crowd that I would be most likely to hang out with, who don't even have to be convinced. When I say, "You're a sinner," you're like, "Yep, it's worse than you think, Pastor."

Now, though there are degrees—from a horizontal perspective—of our sin, all sin leads to death, and there are no varying degrees of death. There's just death. When you're dead, you're dead. Whether you've been dead for a minute or dead for a long time, you're just dead. There's not dead, deader, and deadest. There's just dead. And all sin leads to this dead place.

Look at it this way: If we all tried to swim to Europe from Jacksonville, Florida—my hometown—some of you that don't swim very well wouldn't make it past the breakers. Right? You just wouldn't. You'd be dead in the breakers. Some of you freakish athlete kind of people, you would swim day and night, putting ten or twenty miles between yourself and the shoreline. You'd lose sight of the shoreline due to the curvature of the Earth and you'd think, "I'm going to make it. I got a chance."

No, you ain't. And you don't. You're dead, too.

Now, who's more dead? The dude in the breakers or the CrossFit freak at mile twenty? Nobody. The breaker-dead people and the past-the-horizon swimmers are both dead. And they're all the same dead. That's the result of our sin. This is what Paul means—we are all under sin. I know there's a segment of our population that hears me say this and thinks, "Well, I'm offended. How can you call me a sinner?" Actually, it's pretty easy, snowflake, but let me explain.

I call you a sinner because the Bible does. Let me just warn you, be really, really careful of the people that only say things to flatter you. They're not for you. They want something from you—usually a vote—but be careful, alright? And I'm not trying to label you. I'm trying to help you see your own diagnosis, so you understand the truth of you *and* that you need a cure that you are powerless to provide yourself.

That's what this is.

Paul then says, "As it is written," and quotes from the Old Testament. He quotes Psalm 1, Psalm 14, Psalm 53, Psalm 5, Psalm 140, Psalm 10, Isaiah 59, and Psalm 36. He rattles them off like they're written on notecards in his pocket. What's amazing is that he probably does that from memory. So he's grabbing all these Old Testament verses. And the way it's indented in your Bible means this is a song, basically. A song about how evil, and corrupt, and depraved we are. He finishes with this. "None is righteous, no, not one."

"Righteous" means right standing with God. There is no person who in and of themselves has a right standing with God. Think of the best person you can think of, like your grandma. According to the Bible, she's a sinner. A wretched, depraved, crooked, evil, grandma sinner. Think about that for a minute. Apart from Christ, "none is righteous, no, not one." This means that everybody rejects God. Some of us reject God in our rebellion, and that's who we typically think of when we think "sinner." "I do what I want with who I want, when I want." You know, sex, drugs, rock and roll. The flip side is that if you don't reject God with your rebellion, then you do reject God with your religion: "God, I don't need You. I got this."

I explained in the last chapter how Isaiah declares that even our righteous deeds are filthy before the Lord, like used menstrual cloths. "None is righteous, no, not one; no one understands; no one seeks for God. All have turned aside; together they have become worthless." Hang in here, I know it's painful. "No one does good, not even one. Their throat is an open grave; they use their tongues to deceive. The venom of asps"—you've really got to enunciate that one—"The venom of asps is under their lips. Their mouth is full of curses and bitterness. Their feet are swift to shed blood; in their paths are ruin and misery, and the way of peace they have not known. There is no fear of God before their eyes."

So you think, "That's pretty rough." Truth is, that is you and me. Typically, we compare ourselves to one another. And when we do, if you've got a brain in your skull, then you always win, because you get to pick your opponent in the comparison game of morality, right? Compared to the nightly news, most of us are doing pretty well, but compared to a holy God, we've got no chance. In the last chapter, I ran quickly through the Ten Commandments, just to see how we stack up. And we all received the same score. Zero. 0-10.

Then I talked about the granddaddy of them all. Pride. Of which we are all guilty. Starting with me. Lastly, I talked about our laws. We don't call them laws. We call them "promises to ourself." Same thing. "I will never text him again." "Won't drink that anymore." "Won't date her again." And yet despite the fact that we don't want to and we promise not to, we do them all. It's as if there is something inside us that is at war with us. We know it's not good for us. We know it's not right. We don't even agree with it, and yet we almost feel like there's this other thing, this dominion, this power, this thing in us that drives us to want to do things. You look in the mirror and ask, "What is that?"

Good question. Paul asks the same and gives this answer: *You see, you are under sin.* "Under sin" is our fundamental condition. Square one. Step one. It's there when we open our eyes at birth. The problem is not that you or I tell lies. It's that we're liars. The heart of the problem is that we have a heart problem. And the impact of sin on our life, the legal status of being under sin, affects our minds, our motives, our wills, our tongues, our relationships, and primarily our relationship with God. It is all-pervasive. We are all snakebitten, and the venom runs in our veins.

In verse 19, Paul turns a corner. It gets better. Thank the Lord. "Now we know that whatever the law says it speaks to those who are under the law, so that every mouth may be stopped, and the whole world may be held accountable." In the Old Testament, God says, "Be holy, because I am holy." Which means be set apart. *Be perfect because I'm perfect.* To which you respond, "Can you please explain what that means, God? My track record with perfect is not all that great."

Part of the reason God gives us the law, like the Ten Commandments, is because while it is a map, it is also a mirror. The map to show us what being holy looks like, what being set apart looks like, what a righteous life looks like. But equally important, it is a mirror for each of us to hold up and stare into. When we do, it only takes a nanosecond to realize, "Uh-oh. If that's what it means to be holy, and perfect, and righteous, then there are some serious problems going on here."

When you get a speeding ticket, it's because you exceeded the speed limit. The speed limit is the law. And have you ever noticed that your opinion of the law has very little effect on that law? God gives us the law as a guardian. A keeper. So that we don't have to guess what God's standards are. He makes this abundantly clear in His Word.

While I'm writing this, it's tax season, and Gretchen and I are working on our taxes. Render unto Caesar. Can you imagine if we all got a letter from the IRS that said, "Everyone…just pay your fair share." Well, I'm sure we'd all pray, make adjustments, then we'd write a check or ask for a refund based upon our feelings. I also tend to think that the federal government's tax income would drop dramatically, but that's another thing. Now imagine, later that year, the same IRS came back to you with another letter and they said, "You are in violation of the federal tax code. You are going to federal prison for tax evasion. And here are all the federal tax laws you broke." Immediately, every one of us would raise our hand. "That doesn't feel fair."

Here's the thing: What you feel like the law says and what it says are not the same things. Part of the reason we have laws is so that we know what it's like to live within those laws. Paul is telling us that the law is here to remind us, it never passes away, and what's more, we are accountable to it. Every jot and tittle. Jesus didn't come to abolish the law, and God hasn't changed His mind. The law still stands. So, if that's true, and it is, the question for you and me is, "How do we obey the law?"

Enter the inconceivable Grace of Jesus. We now obey the law, completely, when we *pisteuo* in Jesus ("believe in," "trust in," "place all my faith in") and the fact that His sacrifice on the cross counted for me. He took my place. He obeyed the law that I could not and when He said *tetelestai* ("It is finished"), He credits His righteousness to me. Let me make this clear, when God the Father looks at the sin debt ledger of my life, which is more than I could account for in ten thousand lifetimes, and which is deserving of all the wrath of God, if I have *pisteuo*'d in His Son, He flips the thousands of pages in my multivolume book of sin and they've all been wiped clear. Every page. And they haven't just been covered or scratched through, they've been taken away. Hence John the Baptist, "Behold, the Lamb of God, who takes away the sin of the world!" Instead, my sin ledger is reduced to one single page and on it is written, "It is finished."

Then we get to verse 20. "For by works of the law no human being will be justified in His sight, since through the law comes knowledge of sin." We can never be good enough on our own. There's not a human being alive who can obey the law. Only one man did. His name was

Jesus. And we killed Him. Paul is saying, *No matter how good you are or think you can be, no one will ever be good enough to be justified through the law in God's sight.*

Reminder—every single religion outside of the Gospel fundamentally teaches that if you do X, Y, and Z, you can be reconciled with God based on your behavior. Your deeds. When you boil down every other religion outside of the Gospel, they all boil down to this. Right behavior + right behavior + right behavior = reconciled to God.

This is not the Gospel of Jesus Christ. The uniqueness of the Gospel is that through belief in Jesus—that He is who He says He is and did what Scripture says He did—we can be brought back into right relationship with God. In a sense, we are justified through good works. They're just not ours. They're His. We are not made right with God through our scars, but Jesus's nail-pierced body. The law is fundamentally like an MRI. It can expose a problem, but it's powerless to fix it.

I have raised a couple of athletes. You've heard about my daughter, Reagan Capri, a rising ninth grader. She's on a competitive back-to-back state champion cheerleading team. My son, JP, is eighteen years old and is a three-year starter at free safety for the Providence Stallions. In case you don't understand football, the free safety is the last line of defense. Get past the free safety and it's six points. He's lean, fast, tough. Thank the Lord he takes after his mother. This year at his team's awards night, he received the Grit Award, which is given to the pound-for-pound toughest kid on the team.

We were playing our crosstown rival this fall, and the opposing team called a toss sweep to their star running back. This kid signed to go play for an SEC school, so you know he's a giant and he's fast. Kind of like a locomotive. This kid catches the ball and turns north. JP comes downhill, runs the alley, drops his shoulder, head up, textbook tackle, and absolutely torpedoes this kid. Right on the hip. Blowing him up for a one-yard gain.

I'm a coach for the team, so I was on the sideline. I don't really coach anything. I just share my faith with the kids on the team and help out where I can. JP got up and I could see him wincing in pain. But remember, he got the Grit Award so he didn't come out of the game. He shook it off. Rubbed dirt on it. Continued to play. Back to the huddle.

Not that it matters, but we won, 17–14. After the game, he came over to me. "My shoulder's hurting me pretty good." But hyped up on Powerade and adrenaline, he played through. The next day, his shoulder was completely immobile. Couldn't move it. So we went to see the orthopedist. The doc examined him but said, "There's really only one way to know what's going on in there." So JP went in for an MRI. An MRI is a detailed look at what is actually going on inside the human body. When he returned, the doc said, "Rotator cuff damage."

The good news is, he didn't need surgery. Bad news is he definitely had a problem. Our hearts sunk, because it was his senior year, and the only thing that would help it was time and rest.

Here's the truth about the MRI—it's helpful because it lets us know what is going on inside. However, what I hate about the MRI is that it's powerless to fix the shoulder. We could have taken two hundred MRIs, printed the images, and then wrapped them around his shoulder and said, "There. All better." But that's silly. It does nothing. What he needed was healing from the inside.

The law is like the MRI. It not only diagnoses the problem but shows it to us. "Here's the problem. You have broken the law and are a sinner before a righteous God." The problem with the law is that it is powerless to change us from the inside out. We need an alien righteousness to do that. A righteousness that does not come from us.

The law is the X-ray on our hearts. We are, in our heart of hearts, a rebel. A rebel who continually rejects God. We say, "God, either I got this or I don't need you." And the law is the X-ray that confirms that eternal condition in us. We are all traitors and have committed treason against the Most High King.

Romans 3, verse 21, "But now…" Hold it. Hold it. Hold it. These are glorious words, man. I've told you before, I like big buts in the Bible, and this is a big one. (If that reference escapes you, then you probably didn't grow up listening to rap music in the nineties. God bless your ministry.) You should circle this. You should put an underline under it. Do whatever you need, because it is the beginning of what He has done. "But now the righteousness of God has been manifested apart from the law." Now, I know that's a weird way to say it, but we should be getting really excited right here. I was talking with a couple folks on my staff about this, and I was getting really excited about this verse. "Do you realize how exciting this is…?" I get excited about stuff like this, so they often get little sermonettes in the hall. My staff was not as excited as I was.

"Do you know what it says?" I continued as they struggled to not back away. "It says, but now, a righteousness of God has been made manifest, apart from the law. Do you know what that is?"

And the poor woman closest to me said, "Jesus?"

I said, "Yeah. I think you just said Jesus 'cause it's a church question and no matter what the question is, you go, 'I think it's Jesus.' But you're right."

If you go back to chapter 1, verse 17, the one I told you to underline, when he says, *For in the Gospel, in it, the righteousness of God is revealed from faith, for faith.* Now here he explains it: *Now, the righteousness of God, a right standing with God, has been manifested apart from the law. Although…*

Pause right here. Christian, don't throw your Old Testament away. It's super important. The whole Bible is about one thing. It is about Jesus. From "In the beginning" to "Amen." And all of it matters. Every jot and tittle. Paul says, "But now the righteousness of God has been manifested apart from the law, although the Law and the Prophets bear witness to it" (Romans 3:21). In other words, a right standing with God comes apart from being good enough. This means you can't and never will, by your own bootstrap works, measure up. You can't work your way back to Him. Because of this, Jesus came to do for us what we could never do for ourselves. Because no matter how good you are from this day forward, you can do nothing about past sin.

To which Paul responds, *I've got good news. Righteousness, a right standing with God, has been made manifest apart from the law.* And then he says, *This is what the whole Bible's been talking about.* For instance, when God first says to Adam, Eve, and the serpent, way back in the Garden in Genesis 3:15, *I will put enmity between your offspring and the serpent's offspring. And one day, somebody from your line, Eve, will show up on the scene and the enemy will bruise his heel. But this, this singular Jewish male from your line will crush his head.* This is what we call the "Proto-evangelium." The first Gospel. It's the first time the Gospel, the remedy, the One who will reconcile, is mentioned. Then God, before He kicks them out of the Garden of Eden in His justice, makes a covering to show His love and Grace. It's a picture of the Gospel. The entire Old Testament is pointing to the Gospel.

And none bigger than the feast of Passover, which remembers and celebrates God freeing His people out of slavery in Egypt. In short, He told them to sacrifice a lamb and paint the doorposts of their homes with the blood, and if they did, the angel of death would pass over, giving life to everyone inside. Paul is wanting us to understand that when Jesus shows up on the scene and John the Baptist says, "Behold, the Lamb of God, who takes away the sin of the world," then all of the people who grew up reading the Old Testament would think, "Oh, you mean like the Passover lamb?"

Then when you get to Leviticus, chapter 16, which talks about the Day of Atonement, God sets up this sacrificial system where they build a tabernacle. And inside the tabernacle is a room. And inside the room is a little room, called the Holy of Holies, where the very presence of God exists. And in that room is this little box called the Ark of the Covenant. And once a year, the high priest would shed the blood of a lamb, walk into the Holy of Holies, and paint the mercy seat, thereby covering over the broken law of God. This is called the Day of Atonement because "atonement" means payment—payment that satisfied the wrath of God for a year. Through the shed blood of a lamb, the confessed sins of the Jewish people would be covered over for one year.

Paul is saying, *All of that was pointing to the one day when Jesus would be the Lamb of God, who came to take away the sins of the whole world.* And then God sent prophet after prophet after prophet to remind the people. Prophets like Isaiah, who spoke hundreds of years before Jesus shows up.

And Isaiah says, "But he was pierced for our transgressions. He was crushed for our iniquities. Upon Him was the chastisement that brought us peace and with His wounds we are healed." Isaiah was saying, *Get ready. One day, God's going to send His Son and by and through something that happens to Him, we will be the beneficiaries.*

David says it this way in Psalm 22: "My God, my God, why have you forsaken me?" And then he goes on to give a play-by-play of the Crucifixion; five hundred years before crucifixion was ever even invented by the Persians as a form of torture and death, and nine hundred years before Jesus quotes Psalm 22 on the cross, David foretells it through the inspiration of the Holy Spirit. All of which is declaring what is to come.

Paul is speaking to those around him, and us, saying, *I'm not sure how you missed it because the whole thing, all of the law and all of the prophets, is about this righteousness from God that has been manifested apart from the law.*

And so he keeps going, verse 22—which is a power-packed verse. He says, "The righteousness of God through faith in Jesus Christ for all who believe. For there is no distinction." There are four segments to this verse. The first is this: "The righteousness of God."

This means the right standing before God. All of us know at the soul level there is a disconnect between me and God. And I both want and need this thing that reconnects me. I've heard of this relationship with God and I know I'm carrying around guilt, and shame, and unforgiveness, and condemnation. And somehow, I know He is a holy God and I am not a holy person. I don't really know how I know this, I just do. It's like it's written on my heart. So how do we reconcile these things? How do these two things come together?

Segment two, he says this: "The righteousness of God through faith in Jesus." Not faith in me and what I'm doing, but faith in Him and what He did. Big difference. The way you stand righteous before God is not through faith in what you can do. What you can do got you into this place to begin with. The Gospel is not "God is good. You're bad. Try harder. See you next week." This is what I heard in church as a kid. But it's not the Gospel.

Segment three is "for all who believe." The way we are connected to an almighty, perfect, holy, just God is through faith in Jesus for all who believe. This is the Gospel. This is the Good News. So if you fall into the "all" category, I've got good news. Believe in Jesus and you too can be reconciled to God.

Lastly, segment four, he says, "For there is no distinction." I talked about this in *If the Tomb Is Empty*, but it's worth repeating. That word "believe" is the Greek word *pisteuo*. It's unfortunate the translators just put "believe." It does mean believe, but it means believe *in*, not believe *that*.

Pisteuo is like commitment. It means all in. Not a little bit. It's a full surrender. Like being on the diving board. When I was a kid, all of us had this experience. Way before we were ready, Dad would make us go up there while he treaded water in the deep end. I stood on the end of the board, staring down at the water, knowing full well I couldn't swim, and yet he said, "Come on, buddy. Trust me. Jump in." I stood up there, and while I knew I could not swim, I also knew that man was my dad. I believed *that* the man with the Marlboro dangling from his lip and the Thomas Magnum mustache was, in fact, my dad. That was easy to believe. But that's not faith. That's not trust. That's not this word *pisteuo*. To *pisteuo*, to believe, to trust is not just acknowledging that, "Yeah, he helped make me. There he is. I live at his house and sometimes he gives me stuff." Everybody with a brain would get that. *Pisteuo* is to trust *in* him. Even though it doesn't make sense, even though I was filled with fear. Even though the people behind me were not very encouraging at all. And even though I knew that if he did not catch me, I would drown. To *pisteuo* is to just say, "Okay, I believe 'in' you. I place my trust fully 'in' you. You are who you say you are and you will keep your promise that if I jump off this thing, you will catch me."

This is what it means to trust in, have faith in, and believe in Jesus.

Here's why this matters—when we believe in Jesus, place our faith in Jesus, surrendering to His lordship, God wraps us in His righteousness. Like a blanket. He imputes the righteousness of His Son, Jesus, to us.

Paul says it this way: "The righteousness of God through faith in Jesus Christ for all who believe. For there is no distinction." No matter who you are, what you've done, what your struggles are, what your doubts are, there is no distinction.

Now, in verse 23 to the end, Paul gives a summary statement of the Gospel. Verse 23—and if you grew up Baptist, you definitely memorized this one—"For all have sinned and fall short of the glory of God."

I love this. That phrase there, "fall short," has two meanings. In Greek, it means "miss the mark." To miss the mark of the glory of the perfection of God. It's actually an ancient archery term. The analogy is this: If you were in an archery contest and you had to go 3 for 3 to move on to the next round but you miss the first one, you have missed the mark. Therefore, you do not move on. You are forever disqualified, and it does not matter if you hit bull's-eyes a thousand times in a row from that first miss. It doesn't matter because you missed the mark. You sinned.

The glory of God is perfection. So even if from this moment forward we were perfect, we cleaned our act up, even if that was possible, it doesn't matter because cleaning up our act does nothing to alleviate or deal with the penalty of the sin we've already committed.

Verse 24: "And are justified by His grace as a gift, through the redemption that is in Christ Jesus." Folks, we should be jumping up and down and shouting at the top of our lungs. "Justified" is a legal term. It means that you walk into the courtroom, guilty as the day is long. Our rap sheet is well documented, and the evidence of our guilt is overwhelming. And yet, due to a love we can't fathom, the judge takes one look at us and declares us innocent. An inconceivable verdict. How does he do this? Because while you and I are guilty, someone has already paid our penalty. Paul told the Corinthians, *One died for all, therefore all died* (2 Corinthians 5:14). Christ's death on the cross counted for all mankind who believe. The sinless One for all the sinners. That death satisfied the wrath of God and, in return, justified you and me.

Said another way, when God looks at us, He sees us just as if we'd never sinned. It's a mind-blowing thought. To which you might respond, "But I've sinned. A lot." This is what makes His Grace and mercy so overwhelming. Remember Ephesians 2? When we were dead in tresspasses and sins, Christ died for us. We are justified, not because we've done anything to earn it, and not because we deserve it, but by His Grace as a gift.

Here Paul is being redundant trying to make his point. Grace is a gift. It's like he's saying, "We are justified as a gift of the gift." How, Paul? "Through the redemption that is in Christ Jesus." Let me explain it this way: You ever clip coupons? Ever use coupons? Did you know that every time you've used a coupon it is a picture of the Gospel? It is a picture of redemption. What do you call it when you trade in a coupon? You redeem it, right? You redeem this coupon for whatever the coupon's for. And it is a picture of the Gospel. You go to your mailbox. You open it up and you're pumped: "Oh, look. Somehow I have been chosen to get the free ham at Publix." And then you take your coupon and place the ham in your cart. And you stand in line and then the checkout person says, "That'll be twenty-three dollars." To which you laugh. "Maybe for your average pagan, but not me."

So what do you do? You hand them the coupon, and in exchange, they hand you the ham. Boom! Redeemed. Now, here's my question:

What did you pay for the ham? Nothing. You received a free gift at the redemption of the coupon. What did the manufacturer pay? Full price. While the pig paid it all.

This is a picture of the Gospel. Some of you will be standing in line at the checkout counter, this image will return, and someone will get saved in Publix. "Oh my gosh. This is it." You're going to get saved at Publix, alright? You are. And when you do, please let me know.

Paul explains, *We're justified. We're declared innocent by His Grace as a gift through the redemption that is in Christ Jesus.* The free gift is offered to us but God paid it all through the blood of His Son, "whom God put forward as a propitiation by His blood, to be received by faith." Some of your translations will say "expiation." That means to wipe away sin. Some will call it an atoning sacrifice, because Jesus is the sacrifice that paid for our sin. Whatever the case, the Greek word is *hilastérion*. Think back to the Old Testament, the sacrificial system and the Ark of the Covenant. Once a year, the high priest would enter the Holy of Holies and sprinkle the blood on top of the box. We call it "the mercy seat," but it's not really a seat. It's more of a place of meeting. The word used is *hilastérion*. It was called the place of propitiation. The place where payment was made. The covering over the broken law.

The way we define "propitiation" is that Jesus is the propitiation for our sin; 1 John 4:10 says, "In this is love, not that we have loved God but that He loved us and sent His Son to be the propitiation for our sins." This means that Jesus is the payment that satisfies. Satisfies what? The wrath of God. Jesus, through His death, fully satisfies the justice, and the law, and the wrath of God. Now, here's why this is important. Because God is holy and just, it would be unholy and unjust for Him to overlook sin. And so when Jesus goes to the cross and He says, "It is finished," He is the payment that fully satisfies the wrath, the judgment, the justice, the holiness of God.

Now, here's something very, very important for you and me. Right now. If Jesus is the payment that satisfies and you are in Christ, that means God cannot be dissatisfied in you—no matter what you've done. You should let that sink in. He doesn't regret and never has regretted saving you. You may feel that way, but that does not change the character and nature of God. You didn't surrender to Jesus—"Okay, I love You, Jesus. I surrender my life. I'm all in"—to which God said, "Okay. I save you," only for you to screw up two days later and lose it. He doesn't look at you and say, "Never mind. Give it back." He's not looking at your sin. He's looking at His Son's righteousness, which He imputed to you, wrapped you in, when you surrendered. Remember, it's not our good deeds that save us. And if it's not our good deeds that save us, then our bad deeds don't un-save us. You can't lose your salvation. People often ask me, "Can I lose my salvation?" The answer is "No, you can't." But that's the wrong question. The right question is, "Can Jesus lose me?" And He gave His answer in John 17. Spoiler alert—He lost no one.

We are justified by His Grace as a gift through the redemption that is in Christ Jesus, whom God put forward as a propitiation, a payment that satisfies, by His blood to be received by faith. The key is that it has to be received. Now, this next little part is so stinking important because I've had people ask, "So why did Jesus have to die for us to be saved?" These next few lines explain. Now, Paul's not going to write it very simply, alright? Remember he's wicked smart, but what he is talking about here is the character and nature of God being put on full display at the cross of Jesus Christ. So how could God be totally holy and be love and simultaneously full of truth and Grace? How could He be full of both judgment and mercy? Here Paul both describes and explains it: "This was to show God's righteousness." Putting Jesus forward as the penalty and payment for our sin was to display God's righteousness.

In other words, because God is holy, our sin must be paid for. We've talked about this before. If there was a judge in our community who looked at a rapist who had killed a child or molested a child and said, "You know what? Don't worry about it. I mean, everybody messes up," every single one of us would say, "That is an unjust judge. You are unfit for service. Get off the bench."

So God pours His wrath out on His Son. "This was to show God's righteousness because in His divine forbearance, He had passed over former sins" (Romans 3:25). Here's what this means. Because God is just, He requires payment. But because He is merciful, He delayed the payment. By the way, this is also how the saints of the Old Testament are saved by the blood of Jesus. You see, every time they participated in the propitiation, they participated in the sacrificial system. Then they were putting their faith in what God would do when the Lamb of God would show up. And when we put our faith in Jesus, we are putting our faith in what God has done through His Son, Jesus Christ. To quote a Shane & Shane song, "What they knew by faith, we know by name." And you think, "Well, how did that happen?" Because in His divine forbearance, God passed over former sins.

That wasn't just for the saints of the Old Testament. That's for us, too. So because God is holy, sin must be paid for. Because God is merciful, He delayed the payment. And then, this is the best part. Verse 26: "It was to show His righteousness at the present time, so that He might be just and the justifier."

And because of His Grace, He made the payment.

You see, because God is holy, sin must be paid for. Because God is merciful, He delayed the payment. But because God is full of Grace, He is the just and the justifier. And He makes payment on our behalf. Perfection is required because He's a perfect God, and the perfect sacrifice was made through Jesus Christ. Every time you see a cross, I want you to see the two unique beams of a cross. Think of that vertical beam as God's wrath poured out on His Son. At the cross, the law of God, the justice of God was fully satisfied. And yet Jesus's arms were wide open on that cross. And that horizontal beam represents the perfect love of God that was displayed at the cross. Poured out on us. *That God demonstrated His love for us in this, that while we were yet sinners, Christ had died for us.* That's Romans 5:8. At the cross of Jesus Christ, the character and nature of God were put on full display for His glory. And because He is love, we are the beneficiaries of that—anybody who says, "Okay, when that happened, somehow, that counted for me." Why?

Because God is righteous, sin must be paid for.

Because He is merciful, He delayed payment.

And because He is full of Grace, He made the payment for us.

This is what he's saying. This is the good news of the Gospel.

Then he says, in verse 26, "It was to show his righteousness at the present time, so that he might be just and the justifier of the one who has faith in Jesus." "Faith in Jesus" means to believe that when Jesus died on the cross, somehow that death counted for me, and He died in my place.

Some of you may hear this and think, "Okay, that makes sense theologically, or I understand it when you explain it like that, but what's the application to my life? How does that apply to me?"

Let me take you quickly to Luke chapter 23, and I'll end this chapter with this: I believe God put this in the Bible so that people like you and me could see a real-life picture of what it looks like to discover a relationship with Jesus Christ by Grace, through faith, not by good works.

Jesus has been tried, convicted, and is headed to the cross. We'll pick it up in verse 32. It says, "Two others, who were criminals, were led away to be put to death with him. And when they came to that place that is called The Skull, there they crucified him, and the criminals, one on his right and one on his left. And Jesus said, 'Father, forgive them, for they know not what they do.' And they cast lots to divide his garments, and the people stood by watching, but the rulers scoffed at him, saying, 'He saved others. Let him save himself if he is the Christ of God, his chosen one.' The soldiers also mocked him, coming up and offering him sour wine and saying, 'If you are the King of the Jews, save yourself.' There was also an inscription over him, 'This is the King of the Jews.'"

Verse 39. "One of the criminals who were hanged railed at him, saying, 'Are you not the Christ? Save yourself and us.'" In other words, if you are who you say you are, then how could this be happening to me? If you are who you say you are, then fix me. Fix my problems. Verse 40: "But the other rebuked him, saying, 'Do you not fear God, since you are under the same sentence of condemnation? And we indeed justly, for we are receiving the due reward of our deeds.'" In other words, the other criminal looks around, surveys what will be the end of his life, and admits, "Yep, this is fair. I've spent a life in crime and what I am receiving is fair." In this moment, he admits he is a sinner. But he sees something different about Jesus.

He says, "But this man has done nothing wrong." Verse 42: "And he said, 'Jesus, remember me when you come into your kingdom.'" In other words, in this moment, he surrenders his life to the lordship of Christ. But look at what he does not ask for. He does not ask Jesus to fix his current situation. Why? Because I think the thief on the cross realizes that a relationship with Jesus is greater than any kind of temporary prayer request that he might have, that an eternity with Jesus is so much more valuable than any temporary thing of value he may have in his own life. And in this moment, he surrenders his life to Christ.

Both thieves have the exact same information. They were in the exact same circumstances. And yet one of them, by God's sovereign Grace, discovers the treasure while the other guy just doesn't see it.

In verse 43, Jesus says to him, "Truly, I say to you, today you will be with me in paradise." So, if anybody in the whole Bible makes it to heaven, we are assured that this brother goes to heaven. Jesus assures him, *"Today, when you breathe your last here on Earth, the next breath you take is going to be in paradise with Me and My Father."*

And this is how we know we are saved by Grace, through faith, and not by works. Because what could the guy on the cross promise to do? I mean, he can't make a deal. Can't barter. Can't negotiate. He's not hanging on the cross saying, "All right, Jesus, from now on, for the rest of my life, I'll go to church." Brother, you ain't going nowhere. The rest of your life comes down to the next three hours. Those soldiers are about to break your legs with that big iron bar and church ain't again until Sunday, so you're stuck right here. This is literally the end of your road.

He can't get baptized. Can't take communion. Can't serve anybody. Can't confess his sins to a priest. Can't do anything. Literally nothing. Except the only thing that matters: He believes Jesus is who He says He is and confesses it with his mouth. He is saved by Grace through faith.

If you know anything about me at all, you know I am driven by a deep desire to tell everyone about the Someone who died to save us all. But I don't want to assume that just because you're reading my book, you've surrendered to Jesus. If you have not, my question to you is this: Do you want to? Would you like to, right now, discover a relationship with Jesus? Maybe you've been trying to impress Jesus with how good you are. He's not impressed. Remember the filthy rags? Truth is you need a Savior, not a life coach. Or maybe you think you are too far gone. Maybe you think your sin has disqualified you from His Grace. Nothing could be further from the truth. No one is too far gone. That means that nothing can separate or disqualify you from His love. Not the sum total of all your sin, not angels, not demons, not any other power. Nothing. See Romans 8. There's more mercy in Jesus than sin in you. Some of you need to hear that. There's more Grace and mercy in Jesus than sin in you and me.

Maybe today, by Grace, you would see the treasure in the field— which is a relationship with Jesus—and you would be willing to lay down everything else in your life and surrender your life to the lordship of Jesus Christ. And for every single person that does this, no matter how good you are, or how bad you are, for every single person, you'll be adopted into the family of God. You go from being a son or a daughter of disobedience, a child of wrath, to being a son or a daughter of the Most High King. Adopted into His family. Sins washed away. You and I get to spend forever and ever and ever in paradise with our Father and Creator. For any who would believe, who would receive Him, He gives us the right to be called a child of God.

Are you ready to admit you're a sinner? To believe that when Christ died on the cross, it counted for you? In this moment, do you want to confess Him as Lord? If that's you, pray with me.

I promise you by the power of the Holy Spirit, the authority of the Word of God, the love of the Heavenly Father, and the shed blood of Jesus, that like the thief on the cross, you will one day breathe your last here, and then breathe your next breath in paradise with Him.

Pray with Me

Our good and gracious Heavenly Father, Your Grace is so good. Lord, we thank You that we can't earn Your Grace, that we can't lose Your Grace, that we can't outrun Your Grace. I pray that right now Your Grace would overwhelm the person that has yet to experience the life-transforming love of God. God, would You please allow us to never get over the Gospel? May we always be awed by the freight train of Grace that has radically and forever changed us. May the same Gospel of Grace that saved us be the power that sustains us and sanctifies us. Lord, I thank You that Your love toward us is an outpouring, an overflow, of who You are as one God in Three Persons. Lord, I thank You that nothing can separate us from Your love. Nothing in heaven or on earth or under the earth. Nothing in our past or in our future. Nothing in our hearts or in our minds. That nothing—no, nothing—can separate us from the love of God. Lord, I thank You that to see Your love for us we do not need to look at the circumstances surrounding us. To see Your love fully and finally demonstrated for Your people, we can look to the cross. God, I thank You that You demonstrated Your love for us in this, that while we were yet still sinners, You sent Jesus to die in our place. It is by His blood and in the name of Jesus that we pray. Amen.

Chapter 3

GRACE SANCTIFIES BOTH THE REBEL AND RELIGIOUS

There is more Grace in Jesus than sin in all of mankind for all time.

I spent the first two chapters attempting to show how the Grace of God is an unmerited gift and that it is His Grace alone that saves. Based on that, I now want us to look at what Grace does. First, Grace celebrates. Or, said another way, Grace throws a lavish party.

This is what I mean...

When I was younger, several things about the church made little sense to me. For one, the Holy Trinity. One of my Sunday school teachers told me the Trinity was like a peanut butter and jelly sandwich. Which, as an analogy, only made me hungry and didn't really help much. Then I was told the Trinity was a triangle: God the Father, God the Son, God the Holy Spirit. That was even less help. Sometime later, I was taught that the Trinity was like an egg: shell, yolk, and whatever the other stuff is. Yes, it paints a picture, but how helpful is that?

The problem with each of these is it suggests that each part of the Trinity is one third of God, rather than each being fully God. In fact, any and every analogy that I've ever heard to describe it is woefully inadequate at best and outright heresy at worst. As I grew older, I came to understand that we worship one God in three persons—which is how someone arrived at the word "Trinity."

So how do we explain this? The Father—the Creator of all things—sent His Son to live a life we could never live and die in our place; then, through the Holy Spirit, He raises the Son to life. All three are equally God. Equally distinct. And equally at work in us, for us, and through us. Still confused? Yeah, me, too.

People have been trying to figure this out for the last two thousand years of church history. But in the next few pages, we're going to clear it all up.

Now, the word "Trinity" is not necessarily found in the Scriptures. But the idea of one God in three persons exists from the very beginning to the very end. And it is key to understanding the Gospel and is key to understanding who you are. In fact, the Bible starts out with this idea that there's one God in three persons.

In Genesis chapter 1, the Bible starts this way: "In the beginning, God created the heavens and the earth. The earth was without form and void, and darkness was over the face of the deep. And the Spirit of God…"

So you've got God creating, and you've got the Spirit of God hovering over the face of the water. And God said, "Let there be light" and there was light. In John chapter 1, we see that the second person of the Trinity, God the Son, is the Word, and the Word was God, and the Word was with God. So right here, at the very beginning of the Bible, we get this idea of one God in three persons.

Look at the baptism of Jesus in Matthew chapter 3. The Bible says: "And when Jesus was baptized, immediately he went up from the water, and behold, the heavens were opened to him, and he saw the Spirit of God descending like a dove and coming to rest on him; and behold, a voice from heaven said, 'This is my beloved Son, with whom I am well pleased.'" So God the Father, God the Son, and God the Holy Spirit are all present, three in one, at the baptism of Jesus.

You may be asking, "What does this have to do with me?" It has a lot to do with you. In Genesis chapter 1, when God created us, this is what the Bible says: "Then God said, 'Let us make man in our image.'" Who is God talking to if there's only one God? God is not confused. He doesn't have voices in His head. The Trinity, one God in three persons, is having a conversation with Himself. "Let us make man in our image, after our likeness. And let them have dominion over the fish of the sea and over the birds of the heavens and over the livestock." This is why you fish and hunt, praise God. It's right here in the Bible. "And over all the earth and over every creeping thing that creeps on the earth." Verse 27: "So God created man in his own image, in the image of God he created him; male and female he created them." So part of what it means to be an image bearer of God is that male alone does not rightly image God, and female alone is not enough to image God. And when male and female get married, the Bible says, "The two shall become one." So they are distinct, and yet in the covenant of marriage, they are one.

Notice also—the first time you get a "not good" in the Bible is when God says, "It's not good for man to be alone." Because as an image bearer of God, aloneness doesn't image God. When God said, "It's not good for man to be alone," it didn't just mean he needed a date, or he needed a wife to tell him no or how not to burn down the garden. It means that you and I were wired for relationship. Stick with me. God exists in a perfectly submissive love relationship with Himself. We think that sounds weird, but it's because we bring our own baggage, and we don't understand it. Look at it this way: God in Himself is love. Both the object of God's love and the subject of God's love is God. This is why the Bible says that God is love. So out of God's love for God's self, His love spills out into creation, and now here we are with the ability to give and receive love.

So there are three persons of the Trinity: the Father, the Son, the Holy Spirit—and yet one God. Now, anytime anyone has ever tried to explain the Trinity to you using almost any illustration, as I stated earlier, it's usually heresy. That's just how it goes. So maybe you have heard things like the Trinity could be understood like water. Water can be, you know, a liquid form that you drink, it can be a gas form like steam, or it can be a solid form like ice, so it's three different forms, but it's all H_2O. And you're like, "Oh, that kind of makes sense."

Except, that heresy is called modalism. Modalism says that God reveals Himself in three separate modes and not three distinct persons. I've also heard some people say, "Well, God is like the sun." So, He's a star, but there's also heat, and there's also light, and this heresy is called Arianism, which means that the Holy Spirit and Jesus are products of the Father and not coequal with the Father.

I've heard people describe God like a three-leaf clover. That is the heresy called partialism, in which the Father and the Son and the Holy Spirit are three parts that make up the whole. Kind of like the cartoon *Voltron*. That kind of thing.

Really, the best way to talk about the Trinity is the way it's been talked about through church history. In short, the Trinity is a mystery, a mystery that cannot be comprehended by human reason, but is only understood by faith, and is best confessed in the words of the Athanasian creed, which states: "We worship one God in Trinity and the Trinity in unity, neither confusing the persons nor dividing the substance...we are compelled by the Christian truth to confess that each distinct person is God and Lord, and that the deity of the Father, the Son, and the Holy Spirit is one, equal in glory, coequal in majesty." Got it?

Now. You're probably saying, "What in the world does that have to do with me?" And what does it have to do with being run over by the Grace Train? Well, let me tell you. A. W. Tozer says, "The most important thing about you is what you think about when you think about God." It defines everything. The most important thing about you is what you think about when you think about God. And if you don't understand Father, Son, and Holy Spirit, then we'll never be able to understand who we are and how we even relate to God.

If we don't understand the Trinity, we won't understand how to pray, because when we pray, we pray to the Father by the power of the Spirit in the name of Jesus. This very idea of God informs how we pray. And if we don't understand the Trinity, we won't understand our own salvation, because our salvation means that we are reconciled to the Father by the atonement of the Son, and the Spirit of God dwells within us as a deposit until we reach heaven.

You see, you can't rightly love God without right thoughts about Him. And not only that, in the Gospels of Matthew, Mark, Luke, and John, Jesus primarily refers to God as Father. In fact, 189 times in the Gospels, Jesus calls God not Sovereign King—which He is—not Creator and Judge—which again He is—but He calls him "Father." "Abba." Now, He doesn't call God Father as an illustration so that we can understand Him better. He's not like, "You know, God's like a dad. 'Cause dads do this kind of thing." That's not what He's saying. He's saying that God *is* Father.

I know for a lot of folks, the moment you say that God is Father, it messes you up. We have a lot of messed-up fathers. The statistics on fatherlessness right now are not good.

According to the US Census Bureau, 19.7 million children in the United States—that's one in four—live without a father. And if you grew up without a dad, you have a four times greater risk of living in poverty. Daughters are seven times more likely to become pregnant teenagers. Children are more likely to have behavioral problems. They're more likely to face abuse and neglect. The babies of those children are twice as likely to die very early. Children are more likely to commit crimes and go to prison. Children without a dad are more likely to abuse drugs and alcohol. Children that grow up without a dad in their home are two times more likely to drop out of high school.

In 1960, only 6 percent of children grew up without fathers. In 1998, the number grew to 24 percent. Now, when you hear that, the obvious response is, "Don't throw away the father." This is why we need to disciple those men to stand up, act like men, and raise young boys and girls underneath a loving, caring father like God intended. And so when we say that God is our Father, it doesn't mean that He is a reflection of your earthly father. But He is the perfection of what it means to be a perfect father. Some of us had great dads. My dad is awesome. I love him. Not the most affectionate man I've ever seen in my life, but even the greatest dad on the planet is still evil compared to the perfect Heavenly Father. Jesus says that when we pray, we should say, "Our Father." That's how we should know Him. Paul says that when we surrender our lives to Christ, the Father gives us the Spirit of His Son, and inside of us, we cry out, "Abba, Father."

If you don't know God the Father, then you don't know God. And so I think of one of the most famous parables ever. Even if you're brandnew to Bible study, you've kind of heard of this one before. It's in Luke, chapter 15. I want to look at the parable known as the parable of the prodigal son.

Now, problem number one—I think it's misnamed. We'll talk about that in a second. But what I really want to look at here is the character and nature of God that Jesus rolls out in this parable through the prodigal's father. And what we are going to see is the lavish Grace of God that the Father shows toward His children.

To understand this parable in Luke 15, you've got to read it in context. Luke 15 actually includes three parables: the parables of the lost sheep, the lost coin, and the lost son. In verses 1 and 2, the Bible says this: "Now the tax collectors and sinners were all drawing near to hear him." If you grew up in church, that doesn't land on you as heavy as it ought to. When it says "tax collectors," it doesn't mean you just work for the IRS and nobody likes you. It means you are a sell-out, and you extorted your own people to fund the terrorism of Rome against Israel. This is much worse than you could think. When it says "sinners," it's describing a category of people committing mostly sexual sin, like prostitutes. People that the religious people would look down upon. In turn, these people that everybody looked down on really looked up to Jesus. What's crazy is people that were most not like Jesus at all really liked Jesus the most.

If you go to church a lot, you might want to check yourself on that one. Because if we were like Jesus, people who are not like Jesus at all should probably like us. They did Him. They loved to gather round and hear Him talk. Mostly because He loved them. Now Jesus does warn us that this world will hate us because it hated Him. But there He is talking about power brokers. The systems and structures that use and devalue people for their own ideology and agenda. But there is something in the soul of the image bearer of God that is drawn to the love of God through the people of God.

So you've got sinners mixed in with Pharisees and scribes. But they're not listening. They're grumbling, saying, "This man receives sinners and eats with them." And so in response to this, in Luke, chapter 15, they ask the same question. *"Jesus, why do you hang out with such awful people?"* And He answers, *"Can't you see? I'm like a doctor. The doctor doesn't come and hang out with the healthy people, the doctor comes and spends time with the sick people."*

Which should be a picture of the church. Can you imagine walking into the ER and asking, "What are all you sick people doing in here?" Of course they should be in there. It's the reason for the ER. Same with church. The church is a hospital for the sick. Not a museum of the perfect.

To help them understand, Jesus shares three parables—back to back to back. In the parable of the lost sheep, the shepherd leaves the ninety-nine to find the one. In the parable of the lost coin, a lady loses one of her ten coins. To find it, she turns her house inside out, does whatever it takes to find the lost coin. And in the last parable, He tells of the lost son. We call it the prodigal son, but that's a bad name because there are two lost sons. One is lost in his rebellion, and one in his religion. Really, the parable is about two lost sons and one lavish father.

We pick it up in verse 11. And Jesus said, "There was a man who had two sons. And the younger of them said to his father, 'Father, give me the share of property that is coming to me.' And he divided his property between them." Not just him, but them. This is important. Both sons received their inheritance.

Essentially, the younger son is saying, "I want my inheritance now." To make this request in this day and age would be like saying, "Dad, you're dead to me. I want what's mine." I don't know how you grew up, but in my house, if I went to my daddy and said, "Daddy, you're dead to me. Give me what's coming to me," he would have nodded and started unbuckling his belt. "I'm about to show you what's coming."

That is not what happens here. The dad honored his request. He divided his property, which meant he sold off a part of his estate or land and gave it to the boy. How much did he get? One-third. The older son would have received two-thirds. That's just how it went back then. But I need you to see that both of the sons have what once belonged to the father. And in this moment, the younger son chooses entitlement over gratitude. He could have been very grateful to live on this estate with his dad and have room and board and food and a relationship with the dad. But instead of gratitude, he chooses entitlement. Which is a great picture of us. Every single one of us lives on a continuum between entitlement and gratitude.

The younger son packs his bag, says, *"Dad, I reject you. You're dead to me,"* and, motivated by his own rebellion and selfish desires, goes after self-indulgence. Now, here's what's crazy—the father knows it. And he allows it. He even funds it. Why? Why in the world would this dad, knowing what this boy is going to do, fund this adventure? Because he knows the son will never fully understand, appreciate, and know the father's love without freedom. Command and control never work well in relationships.

And yet, the father, while he gives him what he's asking for, doesn't keep him from the consequences of his rebellion. Verse 13: "Not many days later, the younger son gathered all that he had and took a journey into a far country, and there he squandered his property in reckless living." That reckless living in the New King James Version is called "prodigal living." "Prodigal" literally means "without restraint." This is where we get the phrase "prodigal son."

On the front end, rebellion always feels like fun and freedom, but it only leads to bondage. I remember being at a Southern Baptist church growing up, and they would tell me, "Rebellion is not fun."

To which I'd respond, "Then you're not doing it right."

Rebellion may start out with a single act, but in truth it's a journey. Anyone who struggles with alcoholism started with one drink. Then a few at a party. Anyone who's been unfaithful in their marriage started with a look, or a thought, before it was an act. Anyone who's upside down in debt started with one bad decision that led to several compounded decisions. And in each of these three cases, the root problem below the action was this thought: "I got this." Three of the most dangerous words that you can ever utter. Truth is, they didn't. And we never do. This boy thinks, *"Forget you, Dad. I got this. I am going to discover myself by indulging myself."*

"And when he had spent everything, a severe famine arose in that country, and he began to be in need. So he went and hired himself out to one of the citizens of that country, who sent him into his fields to feed pigs." Jesus is talking to a Jewish audience. According to the law of Moses, Jews didn't touch pigs, didn't eat pigs, didn't get around pigs. As soon as Jesus says this, everyone within earshot knows this is the lowest of the low. The boy has hit rock bottom. "And he was longing to be fed with the pods that the pigs ate, and no one gave him anything."

The reality is this: The lure of sin always has a hook. There's always a gotcha. And for this boy, gotcha is a brand-new low. Total isolation. Broke. Feeding slop to pigs. None of his family would touch him or be around him. He couldn't go to temple anymore. He's completely unclean.

Notice what does not happen. No one gives him anything. Including the father. Why? Because he will not enable bad behavior or reckless living. The father cares, a lot, as we will see, but he's not a helicopter dad. In fact, the dad lets him fall flat on his back. Why? Because only then can the son look up and see the dad. The Bible says that it's the kindness of God that leads us to repentance. That's what's happening here.

Honestly, the most gracious thing God could do in some of your lives is let you get caught so that you would come to your senses. Which is exactly what happens in verse 17: "But when he came to himself." The NIV says, "When he came to his senses." He says, "How many of my father's hired servants have more than enough bread, but I perish here with hunger!" Notice the transition in his thinking that happens here, which did not happen anyplace else. When he hit rock bottom, he didn't then look to himself and say, "What am I doing?" He looks to his father and he says, "I think my father can help me." So in verse 18, he says, "I will arise and go to my father."

This is repentance. A beautiful picture of repentance. The son decides, *"I'm going to quit heading in this direction that led me to this place, and I'm going to turn back to my father"*: "I will arise and go to my father, and I will say to him, 'Father, I have sinned against heaven and before you. I am no longer worthy to be called your son. Treat me as one of your hired servants.'"

How many of you, back in the day, when you knew you were going to get busted, started rehearsing your apology before you got home? Am I the only one? This brother, in his conversation with himself, even throws in a little Jesus: *"When I get home, and I'm standing in front of my dad, I'll start talking about how I've sinned against him. Yeah, that's a good word. He'll like that. Maybe he'll have some mercy on me."* But his words are evidence that he doesn't understand the Gospel. Which is true of most Christians. I quoted a research article in the prologue that said more than 50 percent of professing Christians say their good works will play a key role in them getting into heaven. Despite the fact that this is not how it works, it is exactly how this boy is thinking: *"I'll go home and make a deal with my dad. 'Sorry I screwed up, that's on me. Now, how about hiring me out as one of your servants so that I can pay you back, and I will prove to you that I'm good enough at least to be able to eat food around here?"* That is not how it works, and it is the opposite of the Gospel. The truth is, yes, you are saved by works. Just not yours. You're saved by the finished work of Christ on the cross. Ephesians 2:8 says, "For by grace you have been saved through faith. And this is not your own doing; it is the gift of God, not a result of works, so that no one may boast."

Romans chapter 3 says, "For by works of the law, no human being will be justified in His sight, since through the law comes knowledge of sin. But now the righteousness of God has been manifested apart from the law, although the Law and the Prophets bear witness to it—the righteousness of God through faith in Jesus Christ for all who believe."

The Gospel of Jesus Christ is not about you cleaning yourself up. Quit cussing so much. Quit drinking so much during the week. The Gospel of the cross is that every single one of us is invited into a relationship with Jesus because of what He did for us at the cross. When we try to work for God, in a vain attempt to earn His blessing and approval, it only reveals that we don't know Him. Here's the truth of you and me—we are not primarily servants to the master. We are primarily sons to a Father.

These are fundamentally different.

For sure sons work for the Father, but a son has a different motivation than a servant. The son is not trying to prove himself. He doesn't have to. He knows whose he is. He belongs to the Father. Because of this, he knows who he is. Ownership births identity. The son is working because he knows the Father loves him and he loves the Father. He's happy to be about the Father's business. A servant clocks in and out. He works out of compulsory obligation. The son does not. These are very, very different things.

Luke 15, verse 20. "And he arose and came to his father. But while he was still a long way off, his father saw him and felt compassion, and ran and embraced him and kissed him." The father does five things. And please hear this. The father in the parable represents the character and nature of God the Father. Jesus is telling you and me that this is how the Father feels about us. Why does this matter? You've heard me say this before, but theology matters. You can't rightly love God without right thoughts about God. If I were to write a long, eloquent love poem to my wife, Gretchen, with all the affection and romance a man could muster under his own power, except that I talk about her beautiful, bright blue eyes and how we met on the coast of California, and I then read this to my wife, the reality is she wouldn't like it at all. Matter of fact, she'd probably be angry and suspicious. Why? Because her eyes aren't blue, and we met in Virginia, not in California. She would look at me and think, "I don't think you're talking about me. You're talking about another girl."

Jesus is trying to teach us about God the Father. When the son returns home, the father sees him—from a long way off. Listen to me. God the Father sees you. Yes, you. I know you feel alone, and I know you feel like maybe you screwed up too bad, but you haven't. There is no place on planet Earth where the blood of Jesus won't snatch you back. It does and will travel to the far ends of the Earth to rescue you.

When he sees the son, the Bible says he "felt compassion." The Greek word there is *splagchnizomai*. It literally means "to have the bowels yearn." Which means "from the gut." Or "to feel extreme sympathy." It means when God sees you, something stirs on the inside of Him, and He is not disgusted by you. He feels deep compassion.

He saw him from a long way off, and he felt compassion, and he ran. First-century Jewish men, especially of this stature, didn't run. It was beneath them. Plus, they wore big old robes to show how rich they were. But apparently running to us is not beneath God the Father. Notice, too, he's been out there looking, standing on the porch, scanning the horizon. Day after day after day. And when he sees him, he doesn't calculate what people think about him. He doesn't care. His son—who was lost—has come home. The prodigal has returned. The father launches himself off the porch, hikes up that big old robe, and shows his man thighs. That was not okay in the first century. In the first century, if you were the boss, people came to you. You sat in your authority, and people addressed you. Further, according to Deuteronomy and Leviticus, this boy should be stoned. By law. It was called an honor killing.

In the first century, this story was well known. A son rejects his father, leaves with his inheritance, and wastes his life. Broke and ashamed, he returns and grovels, but it does no good. He gets what he deserves. They stone the boy to death. That's the way the original first-century story was told and understood. And everyone listening agreed that's what should have happened to the boy. But not Jesus. Jesus turns that on its head. The honor is not in the killing, but in the living. In the repentance and forgiveness. In the love of the Father.

Jesus says, "Not in my kingdom." When the father sees his son from a long way off, he humiliates himself, hikes up his robe, and runs—after the son. And then the Bible says that he hugs him, and he kisses him. Why is he hugging him and kissing him? Part of the reason is to prevent the servants from stoning the boy like the law requires. He knows if he can get to him first, and wrap his arms around him, he will take the beating instead of the boy.

What would you do if this were your boy? My boy is eighteen years old, and I still kiss him. He doesn't like it, but I don't care. I want him to know what it's like. I want him to miss it when he's left home. I want him to remember me hugging him and kissing him. I want that memory to be the thing that finds him when he's far from home.

Dads, kiss your boys. Show them affection. Wrap your arms around them. This is God's heart toward you and me. We are all just rebellious sons.

Verse 21. "And the son said to him..." Remember, he's been practicing this thing the whole ride home. "'Father, I have sinned against heaven and before you. I am no longer worthy to be called your son.' But the father said to his servants..."

Look at that. He's not finished with the apology. He's about to do the part where he takes ownership: "Hey, my bad. And here's what I'm bringing to the table." Even though the boy feels like a failure, which he is, he still thinks he brings some merit. "I can at least qualify as a hired servant."

But the father won't hear it. His boy—who was lost—has come home. That's enough. The son's theology's all jacked, but the dad doesn't care. He doesn't need right theology to get in his presence. Some of you need to hear that. You don't have to get cleaned up to take a bath. You can come home even when you're dirty.

The dad's not having it. He just cuts him off. "But the father said to his servants..."

Notice what happens. And here is why I think this parable is wrongly named "The Prodigal Son." "Prodigal" means without restraint, which does describe the boy, but it better describes the father. We should call this thing "The Prodigal Father," because the father lavishes the son with Grace and love. He takes all he has and spends it without restraint. But not on himself—he spends it on loving his children.

"Quick, bring the best robe." The best robe would have been his robe. Notice too that nowhere in the text does it say that after he came to his senses the son went by a Holiday Inn Express, got all cleaned up, and came home feeling like a million bucks. He's covered in pig manure.

Notice what the dad does not do. He does not tell him, "Well, we may plan a party, but you need to go take a shower. You stink. You smell like pigs." That's not what he did. He says, *"Bring the best robe."* And he says, *"Put it on him."*

This is a picture of imputed righteousness. When you put your faith in Jesus Christ, not only are your sins forgiven, but His perfect, sinless, spotless life is credited to you. His righteousness, His right standing before God has been imputed, not imparted. "Imparted" means if I do something, then I earn that. That's an if-then sort of thing. That's not what it is. "Imputed" means you didn't do anything but receive it. The only thing you brought to the equation was the sin that caused you to need the Son's righteousness in the first place. When we return to the Father, He wraps us in the perfect record of His Son, Jesus Christ. So when everybody sees the boy, when they see us, they don't see the pig slop. They see the love of the Father imputed to the Son.

Colossians chapter 1 says that we used to be alienated and enemies against God, but because of Christ's death on the cross and His resurrection, we are presented to God as holy and blameless. From now on, when people ask how you're doing, you should say, "Holy and blameless." They might think you're being arrogant, but you're not. You're just agreeing with the Bible. When we surrender to the lordship of Jesus, He wraps us in His robe. It's not our robe to begin with. It's His. He gave it to us. Paul says it this way to the Corinthians: *God made him who was without sin to be sin for us that we would be made the righteousness of Christ.* This is what happened when he wrapped that robe around him.

And the father says, "Bring quickly the best robe, and put it on him, and put a ring on his hand." In this moment, the father is reclaiming his son. Giving him his name. Making sure he and everybody else knows that the boy is his. That's what's happening at this moment. The son sold his first ring to pay for his prodigal living. It's gone. Now the father gives him a new one. A signet ring. In giving it to the son he is saying, "You have the ability to write checks from our ranch now." It's an extravagant gift. The father gives the son access to the bank accounts.

And then it says, "And shoes on his feet." It's a symbol of adoption because servants didn't get shoes. They had to run around barefoot. Only sons got shoes. So in this moment, Jesus wants us to know that at the cross of Jesus Christ, for anybody that would come home, the Father imputes us with the righteousness of the Son, He changes our name to His name, and He adopts us into His family.

Verse 23. "And bring the fattened calf." This is my favorite part. "And kill it, and let us eat and celebrate."

Now, I'm going to tell you, post-resurrection, we can celebrate better than they could pre-resurrection. Let me tell you why. Because if I'm throwing a party, I'm going bacon-wrapped filet, medium rare. None of those are okay under the Old Covenant. You can't have the blood. Or the bacon. But when Jesus says, "It is finished," we get the bacon-wrapped filet. That's Gospel meat. Remember that the next time you eat a perfectly cooked medium-rare steak wrapped in bacon.

Now look closely at the father's why: "'For this my son was dead, and is alive again. He was lost, and is found.' And they began to celebrate." This is why we celebrate salvations in our church. Because dead people coming to life is worth celebrating. Now, don't forget who's listening to this story. Remember the crowd? The rebellious and religious are thinking, "No way. That's not fair." And all the sinners are thinking, "Wow, that's not how I got treated when I came home. But you mean there's hope for me? I can come home?"

That's exactly what Jesus means. I've been in the church a long time, and I've noticed something about myself and others like me. The longer I'm in a church, the more likely I am to be the older brother. Look at what happens. Verse 25. "Now his older son was in the field"—again, this is the Pharisee, the scribe—"and as he came and drew near to the house, he heard music and dancing." This is a good party. Not some little TikTok wiggle. These people are getting after it. I mean, it's one thing to hear the music. But these guests are dancing in a way that you can hear it from out in the field. "And he called one of the servants and asked what these things meant."

Now, pay attention here. The more religious you are, the more you want to talk not to the Father, but the people that work for Him. And religion will set it up that way. Like, "Whoa. Not now. He's kind of busy. You can't talk to him. I will take the message for you." But that is not how it works. When Jesus says, "It is finished," the curtain in the Holy of Holies that separated the presence of God from the people of God tore from the top to the bottom. This means that if you're an adopted son or daughter, you get to walk right into the throne room and hop up on your dad's lap, who just happens to be the King of the universe. Who gets to walk into the king's chambers in the middle of the night to ask for a cup of water? I'll tell you who—only the son or daughter of the king.

What's more—you don't need me to get there. You have the same invitation and same access that I do. The older brother, because he's religious, hears music and dancing and calls one of the servants, and asks what these things mean. Verse 27. "And he said to him, 'Your brother has come, and your father has killed the fattened calf, because he has received him back safe and sound.'" This is good news. But religious people always get ruffled when Grace transforms lives.

"But he was angry and refused to go in." Now, look what happens. His father came out and entreated him. His selfishness and self-righteousness cause him to reject the party. It's evidence that he doesn't really know his dad. But the father "entreats" him. That word means "begs." To plead. He humiliated himself when he ran after his rebellious son; now he humiliates himself again in front of the whole party, when he runs after his religious son. "Please. What are you doing? Won't you come, please? Won't you come? It's awesome in there. We got a band. We got dancing. We got food. We got filet. Won't you come in here? We are not leaving you out. Won't you please?"

Think about this. The sovereign King of the universe, who foreknows and predestines and calls and sacrifices, and gives law. Who inspires Scripture. Comes out of heaven, embarrasses Himself in front of you who have been going to church your whole life, and says, "Don't miss the party. Please. I beg you. Don't miss the party."

This is the love of the Heavenly Father.

If you are a churchgoer, please don't be satisfied with a little bit of church attendance and some morality and miss a relationship with the Father. I think sometimes it's hardest for church people to get saved. It's easier to get saved when you're jacked up, because when you're in the pit, you look around and think, "This ain't good at all. I need help. How about Jesus? I'll take it." But some of you are just sitting in your own self-righteousness, and you don't even know you're dead. You think your church attendance counts for something. It doesn't. This is the older brother. It's obvious by the way the older brother talks to his dad that he doesn't know his dad. He answered his father, *"Look, many years I've served you. I never disobeyed your command. Yet, you never gave me a young goat, that I would celebrate with my friends."*

This is not a covenant rooted in relationship. This is a contract of services. I did my part, you owe me. The son is lost in his goodness. This is, by definition, self-righteousness. Because he just declared, *"I kept the rules, and you never threw me a party."*

This is the comparison trap. I'm guilty. We all are. We compare ourselves to others and our own self-declared righteousness. "God, You know what I do for You? I've loved You, I've served You. I raised my kids in the church, and You let them run off? God, I love, I pray, I give, and You let me get sick?"

Religion puffs up. Here's a little test to let you know which son you are. When you were confronted with someone else's sin, what do you feel? Disgust or compassion? If you thought, "How could they…" then you're in the big-brother category.

But look what happens next. Verse 30. "But when this son of yours." Not "brother of mine." Not only does religion puff up, but it divides men. Because at its root, religion brings comparison and arrogance and condemnation. "But when this son of yours came, who has devoured your property with prostitutes, you killed the fattened calf."

Nowhere in the beginning of the story did it specifically mention prostitutes, but religious people love to accuse the sinner. Meanwhile, they can't even see the Father because of their own pride. But the Father doesn't give up. He continues to entreat. Notice this is a different kind of father. I wish I were like this. He keeps pleading. It's unbelievable mercy. The Grace of God is mind-blowing. And he said to him, "Son." It's translated "son" but the Greek word is actually not the same Greek word used when it says "son" before. It means little boy. But I don't think he's saying it in a condescending way. He's not saying, "Little boy." That's not how he's saying it at all.

I think he's saying, "My child, my boy. Man, I raised you. Mom and I brought you home from the hospital. You were our firstborn son. We held you in our arms, and all we wanted is to have a relationship with you. My son, my little boy. I remember going to your baseball games. I remember you opening your Christmas presents. I can remember a day when I would walk in the house, and you would run to grab onto my neck. And now here you are, and you're a million miles away from me. Son, you were always with me. And then secondly, all that is mine is yours."

This is God's response to us. God is relationship first. Stuff and blessing is secondary. All of it is just a byproduct. Essentially, both of these sons treated their father the same way. "I'm going to reject a relationship with you, so that I can serve myself." One was self-indulgence, and one was self-righteousness. But they were both just using God to get what they wanted.

The father goes on to say, "It was fitting to celebrate and be glad, for this your brother was dead, and is alive; he was lost, and is found." He's saying, *I did for him what I have done for him, and I have always been here for you. Not because of you, but I have done this because of who I am. I am Father.*

I started this chapter talking about the Trinity. One God in three persons. God the Father, God the Son, and God the Holy Spirit. I did that to help us understand that God is the good Father who lavishes His love upon His children. And yet, while that is who He is, every single one of us, by nature and nurture, reject God. All of us. Some of us rejected Him with our badness. Some reject Him with our goodness. Some by rebelling. "I do what I want with who I want, when I want." And some by religion. "I don't need You. I got this. I'll obey all the commandments."

In the Garden of Eden, Adam and Eve lived in a right and perfect relationship with God. But then sin entered, and they rebelled by eating forbidden fruit. Rebellion. In their sin and shame, they continued to reject Him with religion by sewing fig leaves together to cover up their sin and shame.

And yet, while they were a long way off, God came down. He walked through the garden and called to them by name. God is not an indifferent commander or an insensitive and unjust lawgiver. He's our Father. He's not looking for a bunch of servants. He doesn't need service. He doesn't need our help.

Despite what the enemy would like us to think, you and I are not condemned to hell due to our bad behavior. Now, it's true, we're all prodigals. Every one of us is a wretched, crooked, blackhearted sinner. But thank God that's not the whole story. We have an enemy who whispers lies and piles on the misinformation campaign.

Several weeks ago, I had to see my doctor at the Mayo Clinic. Man, I praise God for Mayo. And just to be clear about this, God is the Great Physician. Sometimes He heals through miracles and sometimes through medicine and sometimes through prayer. I'm in for all three. Whatever it takes. However He wants to do it. I'm going to give Him all the glory because He's the One who heals.

I had this nasty cough that made it difficult to do my job. My doctor examined me and agreed, "Yep, you're sick."

Here's my question: What kind of doctor would he be if he stopped right there? If that's all he did? If he only diagnosed but didn't treat? Further, what if he piled on? "What are you doing? This is your fault. Who do you think you are? You know, if you don't sleep enough, this is going to happen. And why are you being around people? Don't you know people are nothing but germ bags trying to kill everybody? Do you not watch the news lately?" What kind of doctor would he be? Not a good one. And not my doctor.

My doctor is the opposite of that. He actually prays over me. I don't know Mayo protocol, but he writes out these prayers and prays over me. Then he gives me medicine. The enemy stops with the diagnosis and plays it on repeat. He wants you to know your sin. He wants you to feel the stain of your sin. He wants you to look at yourself and say, "What a wretched man am I!" Exclamation point. This is one of the primary lies the enemy uses, to shackle Christians to sin and shame, so they cannot walk into the freedom that Christ has purchased for them. It's called condemnation. And it's in the enemy's playbook.

Most of us think we're about 90 percent saved, but in our heart of hearts, we think there are some things God can't forgive. Or won't. Or doesn't. The dictionary has three definitions of "condemn." The first one is this: "To express complete disapproval, typically in public." Does that describe you? Is that the whisper you get when you get to the place in your life where you say, "What a wretched man am I"? And then you hear the voices in your head in public go, "Yeah, that's right. That's exactly who you are. You are a bad mom, you are a bad dad. That divorce was your fault. That abortion. That prison stint. How in the world could you consider yourself a Christian if you continue to struggle with these same thoughts? What is wrong with you?"

The second definition is "to sentence someone to a particular punishment, especially death." And this is the world that the enemy lives in. The only thing he wants to do is steal and kill and destroy. And he begins to whisper the lie of condemnation. "You're not alive in Christ." And so you live with the debilitating lies of sin and shame defining you. And you roll into church, but you've got a crick in your back because you've been carrying around the lies of the enemy in your heart and in your mind for years now. And then maybe your church looked at you and said that sin that you struggle with is one sin that is too far. You don't belong here. And maybe some person with my position joined the accuser and told you that you were condemned. Let me pause and say this to anyone who's ever been condemned by the church: There is no excuse. The church is not in the condemnation business. But the church is full of broken people. Sometimes we get it wrong. Please don't equate the abuse of the church, or the offense of church people, with the love of the Father. He loves you like crazy even when His people don't.

The last definition for "condemned" is a building term. It means unfit for use. I know this from personal experience. When I was a junior in college, we were standing outside throwing the football on campus when a fire truck came screaming by. I remember thinking, "I wonder where they're going." Well, it didn't take long to figure it out, because they stopped at my fraternity house. It had caught on fire. And after they put it out, they put a big sticker on the front door. CONDEMNED. UNFIT FOR USE. And they kicked us to the curb.

This is what the enemy does to you. He wants you to think you're defined by your past. By your scars. "That abortion. That sexual immorality. That divorce. That addiction. That mental health issue." It's a dirty war campaign by the liar, the accuser, the evil Satan, who does not want you to walk into the freedom that Christ has for you. And so what he says is, "Because of your past, you are unfit for use."

But the Good News of the Gospel is, "Nope." Paul starts with the right statement and ends with the right question in Romans 7. "Wretched man that I am…" This is a good place to start. Matter of fact, it's the only starting place. Jesus will say it this way: "Blessed are the poor in spirit." Someone who realizes they are poor in spirit knows they are spiritually bankrupt. We need someone else to do for us what we cannot do for ourselves. But Paul doesn't stop there. Notice his next question. His next question is not "What do I do?" That's the American way. That's fueled by the idea that "I got me in this mess and I can get me out." No, you can't. If you could have, you would have. You don't need self-help, you need a Savior. Paul's question is not "What do I do?" His question is "Who will deliver me from this body of death?" And the who is the Savior who came on a rescue mission.

Paul gives the answer in verse 25: "Thanks be to God through Jesus Christ our Lord! So then, I myself serve the law of God with my mind, but with my flesh I serve the law of sin." And then he makes a turn to the greatest chapter in all the Bible, Romans chapter 8, verse 1. Paul is struggling with condemnation in Romans 7, which leads him to ask the question *Who will save a wretch like me?* And his answer is *Praise God for His Son, Jesus Christ, that came on the rescue mission.* Verse 1 says this: "There is therefore now no condemnation for those who are in Christ Jesus."

You should let that sink in. Write it on your bathroom mirror. Post it on the fridge. The truth of you is this: You are not condemned if you are in Christ. And what's more, the enemy doesn't get to hound you with those lies. He's a liar. Tell him to shut up. The enemy tries to slap CONDEMNED on you like you're going to wear this around for the rest of your life, because he wants you to be defined by your scars. Well, Jesus came and died on a cross, and He's got his own scars, and He wants you to be defined by His. The enemy may look at you and say, "Hey, man, because of the things that you've done, because of the labels this world has given you, you are unfit for use." I need you to know that Jesus Christ, because of His life, death, resurrection, and return, looks at that same vessel, you, and He says: "Nope. You're not condemned. You're not unfit for use. You're actually going to be the temple of the Spirit."

Here's how Paul says it in 1 Corinthians 6:19–20: "Or do you not know that your body is a temple of the Holy Spirit within you, whom you have from God? You are not your own, for you were bought with a price. So glorify God in your body." Jesus came to set us free from condemnation, that we would be filled with the Spirit of God, that we would be able to walk into freedom that He purchased for us. And that's not some future freedom. It's not just when you get to heaven. Not next week. Not when you get your act together. Not when you get control over this sin in your life. It's right-now freedom. Because of what Christ has done on our behalf. "There is therefore now no condemnation for those who are in Christ Jesus."

And then I need you to hear this. This is not just a bunch of Bible verses. They matter. A lot. So stick with me. Paul is going to give commentary on how you are set free to walk in freedom and not under the heavy burden of condemnation. He says, *For the law of the Spirit of Life has set you free, past tense, in Christ Jesus, from the law of sin and death. For God has done what the law could not do; by sending His own Son in the likeness of sinful flesh and as an offering for sin, He condemned sin in the flesh. In order that the righteous requirement of the law might be fulfilled in us, who walk not according to the flesh, but according to the Spirit. For those who live according to the flesh set their minds on the things of the flesh, but those who live according to the Spirit set their minds on the things of the Spirit, for to set the mind on the flesh is death.*

Christ came to set us free, and this includes from the enemy's dirty war campaign of the mind. "For the mind that is set on the flesh is hostile to God, for it does not submit to God's law; indeed, it cannot. Those who are in the flesh cannot please God. You, however, are not in the flesh but in the Spirit, if in fact the Spirit of God dwells in you. Anyone who does not have the Spirit of Christ does not belong to him. But if Christ is in you, although the body is dead because of sin, the Spirit is life because of righteousness. If the Spirit of him who raised Jesus from the dead dwells in you, he who raised Christ Jesus from the dead will also give life to your mortal bodies through his Spirit who dwells in you."

The way I like to say it is this: "If the tomb is empty, anything is possible." That's what he's saying. And that means even you, no matter what you struggle with in here, no matter what you've done, no matter what your current challenges are, you can be set free in Christ.

So, here's my question: Do you want to walk in freedom? Do you want to shake off the shackles of condemnation, sin, and shame? I know some of you want to, but there's a dirty war campaign against my question in your mind. The enemy is whispering, "You know what, man? I did that last time. And it didn't work. I tried Jesus and He let me down." To that I would say this: How often does Jesus say that we're to take up our cross and follow Him? Every day. Every single day. Martin Luther, in the first of his ninety-five theses, writes that the life of the Christian should be that of daily repentance. None of us graduates from this moment. None of us graduates from daily repentance. So don't let your experience of yesterday keep you from the freedom of today. That's like saying, "I ate one bad meal, so I quit eating forever."

In my life as a pastor, I struggle with this as much as anything in my life. The whispers of the lies of condemnation of the enemy. And not because it's going badly, but because it's going really well. Let me tell you what's true about the enemy: He only knows your past. Not your future. His goal is to wreck your life by keeping you looking in your rearview mirror, chaining you to the regret and shame of your past.

James, the brother of Jesus, says this: "Is anyone among you suffering?" Some of you reading this are suffering under the weight and heaviness of condemnation, and to you Jesus says, *"Come to me all you who are weary and heavy burdened and I'll give you rest for your soul."* James then tells us how to do it. He says, *Anybody suffering? Alright, let him pray.* So that's what we're going to do. If you need the chains of sin and shame and condemnation to be broken and fall off of you, then come and repent for the sin that brought the prison to your soul. Bring it before the Lord and cast all your cares upon Him, because He cares for you. You can't tell Him anything He doesn't already know. And nothing you say will surprise Him or disqualify you. Repentance leads to freedom. Period.

The bottom line is this: There is more Grace in Jesus than sin in you. You can't out-sin His Grace. It's not like there's some tipping point, some point of no return. That's the point of the cross. Jesus went to the point of no return and brought us back. He bought us with His very own blood. James says, "Is anyone among you sick? Let him call for the elders of the church, and let them pray over him, anointing him with oil in the name of the Lord. And the prayer of faith will save the one who is sick, and the Lord will raise him up. And if he has committed sins, he will be forgiven. Therefore, confess your sins to one another and pray for one another, that you may be healed." Then he says, "The prayer of a righteous person has great power as it is working."

So let's pray.

Pray with Me

Our good and gracious Heavenly Father, Your Grace toward us is so good. God, I pray for the rebel. For the person who is rejecting You and Your Word right now to chase after the temporary pleasures of this world. Lord, I pray that very quickly and maybe even through the pages of this book, they would come to their senses. Lord, I pray that they would come to the supernatural understanding in this moment that turning away from the things of this world, the lies of the enemy, the temporary pleasures of self and returning to You, their loving Heavenly Father, is the only thing that makes sense. God, I pray that You would help us realize that it is Your kindness that leads us to repentance. Lord, I ask that You would help us believe the entire Gospel message. That not only does Your Grace save us from our sin, but it also sanctifies us to be more like You and even imputes us with the perfect righteousness of Your Son, Jesus Christ. I also lift up to You the older brother, the religious person who thinks their good works bring merit. I pray that You would humble them. I pray that they could see themselves for who they really are: another sinner in need of a savior. God, what kind of king begs his children to come home? Lord, You do, and because of that I am overwhelmed with gratitude. The only word to describe that kind of God is... Grace. Thank you for Your Grace. We pray this in the name of Jesus. Amen.

Chapter 4

GRACE DOES NOT CONDEMN

When we fall, we fall on Grace.

arly in my life, my church experience was not entirely positive. Matter of fact, parts were pretty horrible. Add to that the fact that I grew up in Dillon, South Carolina, where we missed some of the memos on church etiquette. I didn't know when to stand or sit, didn't greet the ushers with "Hey, brother," or "I'm just blessed and highly favored," and I didn't wear pleated Dockers, which meant I stuck out. My memory of that time was this: Church people did not make me feel at home. They did not welcome me. I felt like in order to fit in, I needed to become some better version of myself before I walked through the doors. Or I needed to get cleaned up before I took a bath. It left a bitter taste. After college, I became a youth pastor and if you read *If the Tomb Is Empty*, you know of my story inviting Sunshine, an exotic dancer, and her daughter to church. That was a painful experience. But what made it painful was not Sunshine and her daughter, but the "good, Christian folk" who were supposed to be like Jesus but, in truth, weren't at all. What I've learned both in my life as a sinner and as a pastor is that the Grace of God does not condemn. It is not bitter. This is what I mean...

After our services, I usually stand down front and just pray with whoever walks up. A few years ago, a woman named Chauntel walked up and stared at me. She had really short hair, like a buzz cut around the side, a button-down shirt, a vest, and very masculine shoes. She was beautiful. Problem was, she was crying. So, I said, "What's wrong?"

She pointed to herself and she said, "What do you mean what's wrong?"

So I sat her down in the chair. Let me interject—one of my biggest fears is that somebody in our church would judge someone like her at the front door based on her appearance, and she would not be greeted with the Grace of Jesus. I pray all the time that the lost would always be greeted with Grace.

To her credit, she had been listening. The Word had pierced her heart, and she was crying. She could hardly talk because what was happening was the Grace of God getting on her, and she didn't know how to deal with it. So I just knelt down in front of her and said, "You're my guest. You're my friend. I want you to know that we love you and you are always welcome here and"—I pointed to the seat next to Gretchen and me—"Imma save you a seat right here with me. Every Sunday."

For the next six or eight weeks, Chauntel sat right next to me in the front row. Not much changed in her appearance. A few months later, she came walking down with her girlfriend. She was like, "Hey. This is my girlfriend, and we have a house together and we have a dog together and I would like you to do our wedding." She said all of this in the thickest Boston accent. She was half a breath from "How do ya like dem apples?"

So I said, "Well, why don't we sit down and talk about this?" And we did. Her, her girlfriend, me, and my Bible. And we just talked about what it means to claim Jesus as your Lord. I was not thumping them over the head. I was just telling them what the Bible says. And I told them that according to the Bible, you can choose each other or you can choose Jesus, but not both. That may offend you, but I'm just the mailman. Fundamentally, when we submit to the lordship of Jesus Christ, we do what He tells us to do, not what I think I should do. I give up my rights to His.

Long story short, she put her faith in Jesus, surrendered her life to the lordship of Jesus Christ, and broke it off with her girlfriend. They sold the house that they owned together and had to figure out who kept the dog. Then she faithfully began following Jesus. When this happened, the LGBTQ community came after us really hard. They said that we were using brainwashing techniques. And I was saying, "Nope. That's not what we're doing, man. We love you enough to tell you what you don't want to hear. Which is if you continue in unrepented sin, hell is your destination. We don't want that. We want you in heaven with Jesus." It's not a very popular message right now. But here's the truth of the Gospel: God says we were created in His image and that we are to flee sexual immorality, and that sex is for married people, and marriage is between a man and a woman for life. So we just walked with her through it.

One day she said to me, "What if I'm born this way and I just have these desires?"

Great question. And I said, "Well, we all have desires, but our desires are not our lord." The world will tell us that our desires are our lord. But according to the Bible, they're not. He is. Period.

When I married Gretchen, though I love her and I'm committed to her, my desires did not just all of a sudden scale down to one beautiful woman. I still have all kinds of desires, but my desires are not my lord. Jesus is my Lord, so I do what He tells me to do. Which is to remain faithful to my wife.

I'm not saying it's easy. And according to the book of Romans, these desires are outside of the created order. More evidence that we live in a broken world. Broken by sin. But Jesus came to make all things new. So I told her, "Listen, quite honestly, Jesus says take up your cross and follow Him. Your cross is different than mine. What's your cross? It's where your will and His will cross. It's the place where you die. Where you lay down your will and take up His. So, yeah, it might cost you more than it feels like it costs me to follow Jesus. The things that you have to walk away from in the flesh may just be more difficult to walk away from. But here's where Grace comes in. He will meet you wherever you are."

So she did. She took up her cross, spent a few years as a missionary in Africa, then came home and now runs a coffee truck in Asheville. She's fully embraced her femininity: that God created her, with loving intention, purpose, and His perfection—to be a woman. To my knowledge, there hasn't been a change in regard to who she's attracted to, but every single day, by the power of the Spirit of God, and stumbling along with His Grace—as we all do—Jesus is her Lord, not her desires.

Every day, she brews coffee in Asheville and shares the Gospel with whoever will listen. And here's the thing: She's my friend. I love that girl and I'm really, really proud of her. The fruit of her life is beautiful. By the way, there is no such thing as a fruitless Christian. Chauntel is different today. She looks different. Walks different. Her countenance is different. Why? We didn't strong-arm her. Didn't condemn her. Didn't judge her. She got run over by the Grace Train. I'd like to think we played a part in that, but in truth, we're just trying to be obedient to follow Him. Which brings me to my question—if you say you've been run over by Grace, then what's different about you? Does the fruit of your life back you up?

Go with me to John chapter 8. Actually, if you back up a little to 7:53, it says, "They went each to his own house." Now look right above that. You see those little brackets that say, "The earliest manuscripts do not include 7:53–8:11"? Let me just cover this real quick. First of all, the Bible is not only true, it's trustworthy. Biblical scholarship is letting us know that the earliest Greek manuscripts of the Gospel of John did not have this section in it. They were in the earliest Latin manuscripts, but not the earliest Greek manuscripts, so what do you do with it?

First and foremost, there's two things I want you to know: 2 Timothy 3:16 says this: "All Scripture is breathed out by God and profitable for teaching, for reproof, for correction, and for training in righteousness." Second, 2 Peter 1:20 and 21 says this: "Knowing this first of all, that no prophecy of Scripture comes from someone's own interpretation.

For no prophecy was ever produced by the will of man, but men spoke from God as they were carried along by the Holy Spirit." So we can trust that the Bible is correct, and the scholars are taking great pains to point out that there is even a little bit of confusion about this bit.

Basically, there are two schools of thought as to why this section was not in the earliest manuscripts. Augustine, an early church father, thought that the story was in the original manuscripts but the early church pulled it out because—spoiler alert—this lady is caught in the act of adultery and doesn't get punished for it, so the early writers took it out because they thought it would encourage adultery in the church. So the church fathers thought, "Well, let's don't tell them they can do that." So they cut it. This is what Augustine thought.

Jerome, another church father, believed that it was not in John's manuscript, but it was an actual event—a true story and everybody knew it. In fact, it was so well known and they talked about it so much that John's disciples added it in a later manuscript. Whatever the case, Bible translators are dedicated to the truth of the Scripture, and so because there is some concern as to whether this was in the original manuscript, translators bracketed that part that warns us the earliest manuscripts do not include this.

Can you imagine if cable news did this? Can you imagine? "We have an eyewitness. Not sure if he can be trusted, but we just wanted to show it anyway."

Here's what we know. Everything in this account lines up with who we know Jesus to be in all of the rest of the Bible. It's consistent with His nature. So I believe it actually happened just as it says.

Here we go. Chapter 8, verse 1. "But Jesus went to the Mount of Olives." He went there often to pray. Jesus finishes teaching at the temple, He's probably tired and needs somewhere to sleep, so He goes to the Mount of Olives. He could also be going to Bethany, which is just over the edge of the Mount of Olives. He has some friends who live there, but we don't really meet them until we get to John chapter 11. Verse 2:

"Early in the morning he came again to the temple. All the people came to him, and he sat down and taught them."

He's been teaching in the temple during the Feast of the Booths, the sixth of God's seven annual commanded festivals. This one is a harvest-time festival in which the Israelites construct tabernacles, or what we might call small huts, out of tree branches and other natural materials to remind them of God's provision for them during their exodus and sojourn in the desert. Incidentally, special psalms were sung as the Israelites approached Jerusalem. Specifically, Psalms 113–118 and 120–134, known as the Psalms of Ascent.

Given the festival, big crowds are showing up to listen to Him because He teaches with such authority. And as a result, people are believing in Him. The fact that there is a large, believing crowd listening intently to Jesus matters a lot because of what we see in the next verse.

Verse 3: "The scribes and the Pharisees brought a woman who had been caught in adultery, and placing her in the midst they said to him, 'Teacher, this woman has been caught in the act of adultery. Now in the Law, Moses commanded us to stone such women. So what do you say?'" And then John gives commentary as to the thoughts behind what they're saying. "This they said to test him, that they might have some charge to bring against him."

This is a setup. A total setup. These religious men couldn't care less about the holiness and righteousness of God. And they couldn't care less about the purity or sin of this woman. Jesus is a threat to their power, so they hate Him. Plain and simple. They're trying to trap Him and use her as a pawn. They think they've got Him in a lose-lose situation.

I imagine some of them have heard some of the teachings of Jesus. It's possible some of them have heard of His interaction with the Samaritan woman and how He said whoever drinks of the water He gives will never thirst again. Or, just a few verses earlier in John 7, Jesus stood and cried out on the last day of the feast and said that if anyone is thirsty, let them come to Him and drink. Or maybe they've heard snippets of the Sermon on the Mount and they know about His Grace and for-giveness. We don't really know what they knew, but we do know that in their minds, the message of Jesus was scandalous and radical and, hence, a threat to their power and position. And to knock Him down a few notches, they give Him a theological test. It's as if they dragged this poor woman into the temple and said, "Alright, Jesus, you want thirsty people? Here's one who's thirsty, but she's looking to be filled in an unrighteous way. And since you claim to be such a good rabbi, what are you going to do with her? Will you extend law or Grace?" They think they've got Him, because no matter what He says, He loses.

It's also a political trap, because by the time we get to the first century, the Roman Empire occupies Jerusalem, and the Roman Empire passed a law that basically says, "You little silly Hebrews with your theological laws, you are not allowed to exact capital punishment on anybody. You need our permission." This is why, by the way, when we get to the end of the Gospel of John, the chief priests can't crucify Jesus on their own. They have to ask Pilate's permission.

This test is meant to put Jesus in a political pickle. Which one's it going to be, Jesus? Are you going to obey the law of Rome or are you going to obey the law of the Hebrews? Either way, you lose. In the Old Testament, the Bible says multiple witnesses are required to execute someone by capital punishment. Hearsay doesn't count. Someone has to actually see it. And, in this case, the men saw it. They said, *"We caught her in the act of adultery."*

Which begs the question, how do you catch somebody in the act of adultery? These dudes were walking around hunting for someone to step over the law, the line. Some people speculate it was a setup. "Hey, man, why don't you go get her, we'll watch, then we'll let you off the hook." I don't know what happened—the Bible doesn't tell us—but at a minimum, they were spying on her. Also, look around. Who's missing from this equation? Where's the man? Adultery takes two. So where is he? This is total spiritual abuse. Spiritual abuse always goes after the weakest. The ones who can't stand up for themselves. They're simply using her as a pawn for their own means, and because they're cowards, they're hiding behind the law.

Any time any leader uses any person and does not value that person as an image-bearer of God but uses them for their own means or gain, then they are abusing that person for the sake of themselves. This is what they're doing to this girl. The problem is that when they do bring her forward and say, *"We witnessed it. The law says that we should stone her,"* they're right. They should. Exodus 20:14, the seventh commandment. "You shall not commit adultery." And then in Deuteronomy 22:22 and Leviticus 20:10 the Bible gives us this law: "If a man commits adultery with the wife of his neighbor, both the adulterer and the adulteress shall surely be put to death."

What's crazy is before you get to Leviticus 20, if you go all the way back to Leviticus 16, we get a whole chapter on what's called the Day of Atonement, when every year the nation of Israel would gather together. They would confess their sins out loud. And then the high priest would receive the confession of the sins of the nation of Israel and then transfer the sins of the people to the head of this goat, which was called the scapegoat. They'd then take that goat to the edge of town and release it into the desert. This visibly showed the people that their sins were removed from them as far as the east is from the west. Then the high priest would consecrate himself and shed the blood of a second lamb, a perfect, spotless lamb, and he'd then carry the blood of the lamb into the Holy of Holies and sprinkle the blood of the lamb over the mercy seat of God on the Ark of the Covenant. And inside the Ark of the Covenant were the laws of God, the Ten Commandments, the idea being that when God looks down on His people in the Holy of Holies, He did not see His broken law but He saw the shed blood of the lamb that would cover over the sins of the Jewish people for one year. And they did this year after year after year.

Here's what's crazy about it. The Day of Atonement, Leviticus 16, comes before all of the laws and the consequences of breaking those laws. In other words, the verdict comes before the performance. Please don't miss this—the offering of forgiveness for sin, or in their case the one-year covering for sin because it's before the cross of Jesus, comes before the sin occurs. Do you see the Grace of God in this? Only after the Day of Atonement do you get into Leviticus 20:10, which says this: "If a man commits adultery with the wife of his neighbor, both the adulterer and the adulteress shall surely be put to death." In God's kingdom, the consequence of sin is death. Period. No ifs, ands, or buts. Don't like that? Take it up with Him. I'm just the mailman. I don't write it. I only deliver it. The point is this—in His Grace, God offers forgiveness before the offense.

In our twenty-first-century mind, we think this seems crazy. Why in the world would God say that adultery is punishable by death? You have to understand that when He gave this law, God had just saved His people out of Egypt. They had been slaves, but now that they were not, they had to learn how to live together and work together and how to treat one another. So basically the law, the Old Covenant—starting in the book of Exodus, but also in Leviticus and Numbers and Deuteronomy—is saying, *"This is how we're going to treat one another. Treat our neighbors. Treat our enemies. This is how we're going to buy and sell. We're not going to lie, cheat, or steal. We're not going to do those things we did back there when we were slaves, because if we do, before the nation ever gets started, we will tear ourselves apart."*

I think the reason the sentence is so severe for adultery is because adultery kills. It kills relationships. It kills families. It kills children. It kills hopes, and it kills dreams. And sometimes if there is adultery and nothing is done about it, then the person who is offended comes in and literally kills somebody, and then that family responds in kind and kills a bunch of people. And so before any of that happens, God says, *"We're going to wipe it all out before we ever get started there."* To God, adultery is a really, really big deal. He takes marriage very seriously.

Back to this woman. She's busted. Guilty. Probably barely dressed. The Bible does not give us specific words on her clothing, if she was clothed at all. They wanted to shame her, so I doubt they let her get all dressed up. However she's dressed, they drag her in and drop her in front of Jesus. She knows she's about to die. The law demands it. I don't know if she has kids, maybe she does, but she knows, "I'm never going to see them again." I imagine she's just cowering, expecting the rocks at any moment. And the religious leaders say, *"Okay, here she is, man. We're right. We've got Bible verses on our side. What say you, Jesus?"*

I love this. Instead of answering right away, Jesus bent down and wrote with His finger on the ground. The New King James Version says, "As though He did not hear." You know how frustrating this must have been for the chief priests and the scribes? Jesus is doodling. Now here's what I love. No one has any idea what He's writing. No one. That part is not recorded. So whatever you guess, as long as it's not bad words, it could be right.

What's He doing? I think a part of what He's doing is getting right down on her level instead of standing in judgment. This is what Philippians 2 tells us that Jesus does for every single one of us. That Jesus, being in very nature God, did not consider equality with God something to be grasped, but He stepped out of heaven and He dressed Himself as a human, even more than that, a servant, and even more than that, He was obedient even unto death on the cross. That Jesus Christ, no matter what you've done, who you've done it with, no matter what condemnation you have heard from anybody else, Jesus, through His life and death, puts Himself down on our level. God made Him who was without sin to be sin. And He's down on her level. He's doodling on the ground.

What's He writing? I don't know. Maybe He wrote, "Thou shall not commit adultery." Maybe. Just total speculation. Some people think maybe He wrote the names of the men holding the stones. I don't know. But, for sure, He is taking the attention off of her because, while they want to use her as a pawn, He treats her like the daughter that she is. He is going to distinguish her as an image-bearer, even though she's guilty.

When He's finished writing, He stands up and says, "Let him who is without sin among you be the first to throw a stone." And then once more He bent down and He wrote on the ground. So, total speculation. This is my opinion, but can you imagine if Jesus says, "Oh, y'all want to play the judgment game? We can do that. We can play the judgment game. I'm good at this." In fact, later in the Gospel of John, the Bible is going to say that God has given over the authority for Jesus to judge everyone. "You want to start now? Let's start now." And maybe He just begins to list the names of every single person there and all of their sins, known and unknown, next to them. "So, alright, boys, let's go. Everybody brought their rocks? Cool. Let's go. Who wants to go first? 'Cause here's what we're going to do. If you judge this woman, by the same measure that you judge, that's what I'm going to judge, too." And He leans back down and continues listing everyone's sins alongside their names. We then find they start leaving, one by one. Oldest to the youngest. Maybe the moment they leave, maybe He just strikes out that name, and strikes out that name, and strikes out that name.

And while we read this as a story about them, we need to flip the mirror. I pray that we as church people, as religious people, aren't walking around with stones. Because the reality is every single one of us is guilty. We're all her. And I don't just mean that we have all sinned. I mean, specific to that sin. According to Jesus, by either our deeds or our thoughts, we're all adulterers. By definition, adultery means that you're sleeping with somebody that you are not married to. And you may say, "Well, I've never committed adultery on my wife." Alright, cool. But in Matthew chapter 5 verse 27, Jesus says, "You have heard that it was said, 'You shall not commit adultery.'" That's the seventh commandment. And you're thinking, "Cool. I'm good on that one, okay?" "But I say to you that everyone who looks at a woman with lustful intent has already committed adultery with her in his heart." Uh-oh.

Anybody want to be like, "Nah, not me"? Then look what He says. "If your right eye causes you to sin, tear it out and throw it away. For it is better that you lose one of your members than that your whole body be thrown into hell. And if your right hand causes you to sin, cut it off and throw it away. For it is better that you lose one of the members than your whole body go into hell. *And if your iPhone causes you to sin, throw it in the freaking ocean.*" That part is not in there, okay? I added one verse.

So adultery falls under the category of sexual immorality. The word in the Bible for sexual immorality is *porneo*. Sound familiar? This is any sex outside of marriage. And marriage, according to the Scriptures, according to God, is one man, one woman, for one lifetime. And so according to Jesus's definition of adultery, if you're looking at pornography, you're guilty. And He could drag any of us in there and say, "If you've ever commodified another person, not valued them for who they are but looked at them and thought about what you could get from them, because that's what you want, then you're stone-cold guilty of adultery." That's what we're talking about here.

I'm not talking about noticing whether somebody is pretty or handsome. That's not what this is. It's looking with lustful intent. And here's why Jesus makes such a big deal of it. I mean, He says, *"Gouge out your eye, chop off your hand."* Jesus is saying, *"This is extremely important. If you're watching pornography, I'm just going to tell you. It's killing your marriage. It's killing it. Your marriage won't last. It won't survive. It will kill the intimacy. And if you say, 'Well, I'm not married,' okay, then you were just pre-deciding that your future marriage is dead. And it is killing your ability for intimacy. And I'm not even talking about emotionally. I'm talking about physically."* Erectile dysfunction in guys thirty and forty years old right now is through the roof, and it's because of a pornography addiction when they're fifteen to twenty-five.

Jesus says to go to extreme measures. Giving yourself away to somebody who is not your husband is sexual immorality. And if you say, "Yeah, but we're married in our hearts." No, you're not. "No, we're married in God's eyes." Have you seen God's eyes? They're blazing red fire, okay, and He's not happy with it. I'm telling you. Taking something that is not yours is not manhood, that's boyhood. Boys take. Men serve. Men look at women and say, "You are so valuable. You are so valuable that I want to treat you as valuable. I'm tempted, you're awesome for sure, but you are so valuable that I am going to commit my life to you in the covenant of marriage, and that's what it takes to be able to be with somebody like you."

This is Jesus's standard. Now, this next one is really unpopular today. But hear my heart here. According to the Scriptures, same-sex romantic practice is in the sexual immorality category. No more or less than any other category. There will probably be a day when this statement is categorized as hate speech. But listen, just because you hate it doesn't make it hate speech. Even if you don't agree with me, just know that it comes from a place of love. I love you enough to not buy into everything the world is telling you. I love you enough to bring you the very Word of God. Because freedom is only found in one place: the Word of God. And the Word of God is the will of God. His Word is perfect in every way. It is a light to our path. It revives the soul.

We have a whole bunch of same-sex-attracted people that come to our church. Sometimes even as couples, and to them I just say, *I love you so much. The courage and humility that you have to put up with me week after week after week, I love you so much. Just hear this. I don't write the mail, I just deliver it. Please hear from my heart how much I love you and just want to share the Word of God with you. And what God has for you is better than anything in this world, because what you are really looking for is intimacy with Him. And what you're settling for is a counterfeit that will never satisfy.*

Every single one of us falls into the sexual-sin category. Now, let me just give you one little caveat. If you are in an abusive sexual relationship, that is not sin on your part. There is a power differential. Someone is exercising power over you. And that is not your fault. If this is you, please come to our church. Call us. Let us help you. We will start with the police. Okay?

The church should be the last place on the planet where some kind of abusive man or person in power could ever make it. The Gospel ought to just root that up and out. So that's not what we're talking about here.

Listen, times have not changed. This was common in the first-century church. Let me read for you a letter that Paul writes to the church in Corinth (1 Corinthians, chapter 6). "Or do you not know that the unrighteous will not inherit the kingdom of God? Do not be deceived." And then he gives a list—not an exhaustive list—of unrighteousness. "Neither the sexually immoral"—that's *porneo*—"Neither the sexually immoral, nor idolaters, nor adulterers, nor men who practice homosexuality, nor thieves, nor the greedy, nor drunkards, nor revilers, nor swindlers will inherit the kingdom of God."

To which you go, "Uh-oh." Especially you swindlers. I don't know what that means. And look at what he says next. "And such were some of you." That means that when Paul would go to the Corinthian church, the place was full of people who were sexually immoral, acting on same-sex desire, who were revilers and drunkards and swindlers and sinners and all of these things. "Such were..." Past tense. "But you were washed, you were sanctified, you were justified in the name of the Lord Jesus Christ and by the Spirit of our God."

In other words, that *was* you. It is not you. If you are in Christ Jesus, you have a new name and your name is not the old thing that you used to do. The old thing that you used to do is dead, and you have been renamed in the name of the Lord Jesus Christ by the Spirit of God. That's good news. Now skip down to verse 15. He says, "Do you not know that your bodies are members of Christ? Shall I then take the members of Christ and make them members of a prostitute? Never!" Because that's what was happening in the first Corinthian church.

People were sleeping with people who weren't their husband or wife. People were sleeping with a boyfriend, sleeping with a girlfriend. They would go to the temple and sleep with the temple prostitute and call it worship. And they had this false belief that "I can do what I want with my body. It's my body, my choice. I've given my heart to Jesus, but I'm going to give my body to the temple prostitute." To which Paul says, *Whoa. Don't you know that's not just a physical act? That's a spiritual union.* "Or do you not know that he who is joined to a prostitute becomes one body with her?" Paul tells the Corinthian church, *Sex is a supernatural gift from God that is supposed to be a picture and a reminder of the Godhead. One God in three Persons. God the Father, Son, and Holy Spirit, in a perfect submissive love relationship with one another, and though there is one God in three distinct Persons, there's still only one God.*

When a man makes a covenant with his wife for a lifetime, they come together, they consummate the relationship, and they become one. In God's economy, one plus one, in the covenant of marriage, equals one. And so Paul says, "Or do you not know that he who is joined to a prostitute becomes one body with her? For, as it is written, 'The two will become one flesh.' But he who is joined to the Lord becomes one spirit with him." So then here's Paul's advice, which is similar to Jesus's advice when it comes to sexual immorality, when it comes to adultery, when it comes to any of that temptation. *Flee sexual immorality. Period.* If you have ever failed when it comes to the area of sexual immorality, it just comes down to this. At some point you decided to flirt instead of flee.

The Forrest Gump translation is, "Run, Forrest, run." That's what this is. When you get to Ephesians chapter 6, the Bible says, "For we do not wrestle against flesh and blood" (6:12). This means when you come against the enemy himself, the Bible says it twice. *Stand firm against the enemy and his evil schemes* (6:11). This means that today, if you're walking to your truck and the devil is sitting in your truck, then you command him, "Get up out of my truck! That's my truck. God has authority over me, I have authority over my truck, get out of my truck." You stand firm against the enemy and his evil schemes. However, if you put this book down and walk outside to your truck, and your ex is sitting in the truck with that look in her eye, you run. Flee. Flee sexual immorality. "Every other sin a person commits is outside the body, but the sexually immoral person sins against his own body" (1 Corinthians 6:18).

Any and all sin separates us from God, and all sin is forgivable by Jesus at the cross, but there are categories of sin, and the Bible is saying, *"This one's different."* There's something about sexual sin that the enemy uses that brings more shame and condemnation than everything else. This is why you never hear Christians joke about sexual sin. Have you ever noticed you can joke about everything else? No couple has ever been sitting in disciple group and said, "Oh my gosh, my wife used to hook up with everybody. Tell them about spring break '82. This is hilarious." Nope.

Often, at the end of a service, someone will approach me and say, "I need prayer." And I'll ask, "About what?" They drop their head, avert their eyes, and start to tear up. "I don't think I can ever be forgiven of it." One hundred percent of the time they are talking about sexual sin. It's just different. Paul says, "Or do you not know that your body is a temple of the Holy Spirit within you, whom you have from God?" Listen to this: "You are not your own, for you were bought with a price. So glorify God in your body" (Ephesians 6:19–20). If you're sleeping with your boyfriend, if you're sleeping with your girlfriend, if you're sleeping with anybody outside the covenant of marriage of one man and one woman for one lifetime, you have taken your eyes off the Gospel. You are flirting and not fleeing. But more importantly, you don't know how valuable you are. Your value is found in the Gospel. God says, *You're not your own. I bought you with a price* (1 Corinthians 6:20). And the price that God was willing to pay for you was the blood of His very own perfect Son, Jesus Christ. That's how valuable you are.

After Jesus doodles in the ground He says, *"Alright. All the perfect people go first, and whoever isn't perfect, we can start playing the judgment game."* I think that's when they begin to understand. You see, here's the crazy thing. In that group of people, only One was perfect. Only One had the right to judge the woman and throw stones. But, in His mercy, He decides, *"I'm not going to throw any stones. I'm going to leave here, and one day, I'll climb up on a cross and pay the price for her sin and all of mankind's sin."*

Back to John 8. "But when they heard it, they went away one by one, beginning with the older ones." Why? Because the old guys know when to give up. The old guys are like, *"Yeah, He got us, man. He got us."* And so they drop the rocks one by one and file out. Think about this. I wonder if she heard the rocks fall. I wonder if every time the rock hit she flinched because she thought, *"Is that it? Is somebody throwing it?"* And one by one, a rock drops, and a rock drops, and a rock drops. And then Jesus was left alone with the woman standing before Him, eyeball to eyeball. And He said to her, "Woman." Incidentally, he refers to her the same way He did His mother at the wedding in Cana. "Woman." He addresses her with dignity. Respect.

Jesus treats this woman with dignity when these other men are using and abusing her for their own benefit. "Woman, where are they? Has no one condemned you?" Maybe she opens her eyes and she begins to look around. "No one." What's that next word? This is not a rhetorical question. She says, "No one" and then adds to it the oldest confession. "Lord." Which He is. Jesus is Lord.

Her word choice shows she's beginning to operate in faith, beginning to lean in to Jesus. Why? Because He just saved her life. *"Who here condemns you?"* I feel like she's lying on the ground, bracing herself for the impact of judgment and condemnation because she knows that she's broken the law and she's waiting to just get wiped out by rock after rock. And instead she gets run over by the Grace Train of our Lord and Savior, Jesus Christ. *"Who here condemns you?"*

It is the kindness of God that leads us to repentance. You might look at this and think she'll exit the temple and continue doing whatever she wants. Maybe. But I doubt it. Not after she's experienced the Grace of Jesus Christ. The Pharisees knew the law and were quick to constantly point it out. They told her she was guilty. Truth is, that's not what's going to change her. She knows she's guilty. Change comes after you've been run over by the Grace of Jesus Christ. I love this. It's so tender. She says, "No one, Lord." And Jesus says, "Neither do I condemn you."

Can we be honest for just a second? Anybody struggle with condemnation? Or am I the only one? Man, I struggle with it bad. Really bad. The enemy takes this area of my past, and he brings it up often. Usually, about three minutes before I step up to preach. He loves to point out every broken promise, every temptation I failed to flee from. It usually sounds something like, "Who do you think you are? How in the world are you a pastor? You still have the same struggles and temptations that you did when you were a teenager. You think you're progressing in your sanctification? I don't think so." Condemnation is the native tongue of the enemy. If he opens his mouth, condemnation is about to come out.

To this, Jesus says, "Who's condemned you?"

"Uh, nobody."

"Then neither do I condemn you." I told you in the last chapter that "condemnation" is a building term. It means unfit for use. It's what the enemy wants you to believe. When the enemy condemns you, he's saying, "I've evaluated your situation, and you are unfit for use." The crazy thing is that Jesus looks at the very same structure and declares that your body is His temple. You know what that means? The enemy slaps the condemned sticker on you, but if you are in Christ, Jesus rips that thing down and says, "No, no. When you put your faith in Me, I'm going to fill you with the Holy Spirit, and wherever the Spirit of God resides, that's called a temple."

When the enemy says you are unfit for use, Jesus says, "Shut your mouth, you liar. That body is my permanent address here on this planet." That's what He thinks about you. That's where your value is. He doesn't condemn you. Many of you feel shame and condemnation and you need to stand on the tracks and let the train run you over on its way to glory. You need to receive the Grace of Jesus. This is why none of us can ever get over the Gospel. When the enemy tries to define me by my scars, I tell him, "No. I am defined by the scars of Jesus Christ. It is finished. Yeah, I did struggle with that. Yeah, I did do those things, but that old me is dead. I have been crucified with Christ. It's no longer I who live, but Christ who lives in me, and the life that I now live, I live by faith in the Son of God who loved me and gave Himself up for me."

The enemy tries to label you "adulterer," but then Jesus comes along and shakes His head. "Nope. That's not what I'm calling her. I'm calling her 'daughter.' Why? Because that's who and what she is."

You see, only Jesus gets to tell you who you are, and so we have to consistently preach the Gospel to ourselves. Listen, I'm not alone here. Can we agree that the Apostle Paul was a Christian when he wrote Romans? When he gets to Romans chapter 7, he writes, *What is wrong with me? I want to do good, but I can't pull it off. Evil's right there with me. The evil things I don't want to do, I can't stop doing those things.* Does that sound like anybody else's walk? Yeah, mine, too. Then his conclusion at the end of Romans 7 is, *What a wretched man I am. Who would save a wretch like me?* Then, don't miss this, you get to chapter 8 verse 1 of Romans, and the answer is, Jesus Christ. Romans 8:1: "There is therefore now no condemnation for those who are in Christ Jesus." This is what Jesus is providing this woman. "There is therefore now no condemnation for those who are in Christ Jesus."

Some of you ask, "What's 'no' mean?" Well, honestly, it means no. None. Some of you respond with, "I believe in Jesus, and I know He forgives me, but I just can't forgive myself." I would just politely, lovingly, caringly say to you, "Who do you think you are? You think your standards are above the standards of a righteous and holy God? Or do you think the cross wasn't enough and you've got to help Him out a little bit?" Either one of those is a misguided view of who God is and how much He loves you, and how sufficient His Grace is for you.

We would do well to preach to ourselves, to constantly remind ourselves of the Word of Jesus, "Neither do I condemn you."

Most people want to just stop the story right there. "Woo, He won't judge me." But He doesn't stop. There's a semicolon there. That means, "Breathe on that for just a second." And then He keeps going. He says, "Neither do I condemn you; go, and from now on sin no more."

He's full of Grace, but He's also speaking the truth. Jesus is driving the Grace Train where there is no condemnation. Every seat is shame-free. But He's also not shying away from the truth. Truth is, she's living in sin. So, here's the truth train. *"Quit sinning. Go and leave your life of sin."* Just because He offers Grace does not mean He lowers the truth bar. He does not say what she is doing is not sin. He loves her enough to extend Grace and speak the truth to her.

We live in a world right now that says, "God is love, so do whatever you want." Have you met a parent who lets their kid do whatever they want? Doesn't work out well for either the kid or the parents. God loves her so much that He's looking at her and saying, *"If you continue down this lifestyle, it's not good for anybody. Not for you. Not your family. Not the other guy's family. It's killing everybody. Go and leave your life of sin."*

And listen. If you met a person who was malnourished, the way to cure them would not be gluttony. That's the world we live in. Woe to a society that calls evil good and good evil. The way to heal that person if they are malnourished is to feed them a healthy diet. And so when people are walking out of step with the way God created us to live, particularly when it comes to sex and sexuality, it's not good enough to just give them a sticker and say, "Do whatever you want to do." No. It's to give them a healthy diet of the Word of God to say, "God loves you, He died for you. He designed you. He has a purpose and a plan for you that's way bigger than you would ever know."

Jesus says to her, *"Now leave your life of sin."* And here's what's important. Pursuing a life free from sinning only works when you have an encounter with Jesus and experience His Grace. Because without it, guess what you turn into? Next thing you know you're walking around with a rock like a Pharisee. "I don't do that stuff. I don't do those things that you do." The reason that she's going to be able to have victory over sin is because Jesus saved her life when she knew that she deserved to experience the penalty for her own sin. Instead of experiencing that penalty, she experienced the reality that Jesus was going to be the propitiation for her sin, the payment that satisfies. There's no way you can get run over by the Grace Train of Jesus and not walk away completely different than when you walked into Him. The Grace of Jesus doesn't condemn. It changes us—from the inside out.

Here's the point. In Christ, we are to leave behind our condemnation and we are to leave behind our life of sin. Here's the reality. If you know Jesus and the Spirit lives in you, what is happening here is you are being invited by the conviction of the Spirit to daily repent, to daily take up your cross, to daily turn your back on your own sinful wants and desires, and once again remind yourself that Jesus came down on our level. He took the stones for us, and He does not condemn you, and by the power of the blood of Jesus we can turn this page differently and not continue in our life of sin.

Want to hear a crazy story? If it weren't true, it'd be tough to believe. In 1829, three men named George Wilson, Abraham Poteet, and James Porter robbed the Reading Mail Stagecoach in Pennsylvania.* Court records suggest George Wilson, age twenty-four, was unwilling and caved to the threats of Porter, the leader.

During the trial on December 6, 1829, Poteet testified that Wilson— who had a criminal record and had previously served time in prison— pointed a pistol at the driver, Samuel McCrea, and commanded him to stop or they'd kill him. An open-and-shut case. On May 27, 1830, Wilson and Porter were both convicted and sentenced to ten years for robbing the mail and given a death sentence for threatening the driver.

---

*https://www.reddit.com/r/AskHistorians/comments/zcbmkk/do_we_know_what_happened _to_george_wilson_the/?rdt=62409 (which is citing a contemporary newspaper account).

Awaiting execution, Wilson crossed paths with a prison warden whom he had known while serving a prior sentence. In a private conversation, a repentant Wilson expressed regret for his actions, his life, confessed his guilt, and asked for a Bible. Word spread of Wilson's change of heart, and several newspapers began looking into the matter, determining that Wilson had been manipulated by Porter. Only July 2, Porter was executed while a pardon was issued for Wilson.

Which he refused.

Wilson—who was serving his ten-year sentence—returned to court on October 21, 1830, and declined to accept the pardon. When the judge asked him why, Wilson said he had nothing to say and did not want to be pardoned. This raised a question the court had not dealt with before—while it could issue a pardon, could they require the pardoned to accept it? This legal question traveled up the ladder and landed at the Supreme Court, which determined that while President Jackson could issue a pardon, the court could not require the convicted to accept it. In order for the pardoned to walk free, he or she had to accept the offer. Or said another way, the pardoned was not actually pardoned until he or she agreed to and received the pardon for their actions. The legal battle continued while Wilson served out the remainder of his ten years in a hard-labor camp awaiting his execution, which never came.

But the story doesn't end here, and this is why it reminds me of the inexplicable Grace of God: While Wilson refused the first pardon, a second pardon was issued. Toward the end of his sentence, Wilson was pardoned again by President Martin Van Buren for all charges.

Which Wilson accepted this time.

I love this story for this reason—there is no limit to the Grace of God. But there is a condition: It must be received for the pardon to take effect. If you, in your past, have shunned His Grace, or taken it for granted, or stared at it with indifference, I want to encourage you, it's not too late. If you're in a rough spot, staring at bars of the prison of your own making, and you think you're too late for the Grace of God, that you didn't take Him up on His offer, that you've lost your one and only chance—I've got good news. You're not too late. There is no limit to His offer of Grace. And no expiration date as long as you are alive. All you have to do is cry out—and accept it while you have breath in your lungs.

Here's what you need: conviction. The conviction of the Spirit is like a warm blanket. It's an invitation. Here's how I want to close this chapter. Every single one of us, if we're honest, is just living in sin or at some point was living a life of sin. Living outside God's design. Sleeping with somebody not your spouse. Looking at pornography. *Porneo* is like the junk drawer of sexual immorality, and the enemy is crushing us with it right now. And by the Grace of God, we're busted, and while we may not be publicly busted, all of us know we are.

But God loves us so much that He would convict us of the sins in our life right now and the unconfessed sins of our past. Because when we confess them out loud to Him, we bring them to the light, and the enemy loses its stranglehold on us.

I want you to pray. Lay down your condemnation. Tell the enemy, "I am not who you say I am. Only Jesus gets to tell me who I am." The first thing you need to do is confess it to God. And none of us escape this. We all got it when it comes to this. If you're married, invite your spouse. Come to the altar together. Confess your sins one to another. Bring them to the light. There's freedom there. There's no freedom in darkness. Only chains. Husbands, if you're afraid, don't be. The enemy wants to kill your marriage, wants to steal the intimacy out of your marriage, wants to destroy your moral authority over your kids. That's what he's trying to do. And what the Spirit of God is trying to do is to make sure that His love for you overflows toward each other in that covenant of marriage.

If you're single, pray with a friend—preferably not the one you're sinning with. I'd suggest guys pray with guys, and girls pray with girls.

It's just safer. If you're a parent of a teenager, why don't you get on your face and pray against the enemy, because he's trying to kill a generation of young men and young women. I mean it. I've got two of them. They carry temptation around in their pockets, and he is trying to kill, steal, and destroy everything that God wants to do in their lives.

This woman was forced into the presence of Jesus, and that encounter changed everything. Nobody's going to make you pray, but pray you need to. Starting with confession. With repentance. The enemy does not want you to repent or confess, because when you don't, he can keep you in shackles of shame and a prison of your own making. You want to bust down the doors? Want to break some chains? Want freedom? Right now? It's available. Jesus Himself, right now, is inviting you. Come. Pray. Why don't you just come and experience some Grace?

I've written a prayer to help you along. But it's not the words that count. It's your heart. I'm just giving you a model to follow. Modify as you want.

This prayer has been printed and used before. I am borrowing this from my friend Charles's book *What If It's True?* I'm using it again here because I like it, it's really thorough, and because it's not only a great prayer but it's a great tool, to be used again and again. To come back to. Why? Because we as people have a tendency to sin sexually more than once.

Jesus, this hurts and I am ashamed but I want to confess my sexual sin. (Now, do it. One by one. Hold nothing back. Name it all. If you question whether you ought to mention that one, the answer is yes. Definitely. Take your time. Don't skip any.)

Father, having confessed, I repent. For each act. Forgive me. I don't want this anymore. Come lift this sin off of and out of me. You made my body to be Your temple, and I have defiled both mine and others'. Father, I am so sorry. Create in me a clean heart and renew a steadfast spirit within me. Cast me not from Your presence and take not Your Holy Spirit from me.

Lord, You made me a sexual person, but I've perverted myself. I want my sexual relationship with my husband/wife to be what You intend. I present my body as a living sacrifice to You. I consecrate my body, my sexual nature, to You. Lord, where I have harmed others by my words, thoughts, or deeds with regards to sex, I ask Your and their forgiveness.

Father, would You please cut me free—forever—from every unholy soul connection which was created through any and all of these acts. Cut my soul free from theirs and cut their soul free from any tether to mine. Father, I bless them in the name of Jesus. I give back to them the pieces of their soul that I've held in prison and ask You to give me back mine. Holy Spirit, please fill me and heal me in every place vacated by that tie. And please fill every person now free of me and return to them the part of them that I stole.

Lord Jesus, I thank You for offering me complete and total forgiveness. That You have wrapped me in a spotless robe of righteousness and that when you introduce me to Your Father, He sees His spotless Son and not my filthy rags. That said, Lord, I forgive all those who harmed me sexually or took anything from me. I release them from any anger or judgment. I tear up any IOU.

Father, I break every spiritual, sexual, emotional bond with anyone with whom I have ever had one and place the cross of Jesus Christ between me and that sin, declaring that You made a public spectacle of the author of that sin when You died on the cross (Colossians 2), that You render my enemy powerless (Hebrews 2), and that it was for this reason that You were made manifest so that You might destroy the works of the devil (1 John 3:8). Lord, if I've made any unholy agreements, I break them now in the name of Jesus.

Father, I ask that You would heal my relationship with my wife/husband, completely. I consecrate our sexual relationship to You to be what You determined. I invite You into our marriage and into our bed, and I declare and decree that my desire is only for my wife/husband.

Period. I desire no one else. He/She satisfies me completely and my eyes and heart desire no other. I thank You, Father, that my desire is for them and them alone.

Lastly, Lord, I speak Your Word over me; I declare it and agree with it—that it is Your blood that cleanses me from all unrighteousness. That You make all things new. That by one sacrifice, You have perfected forever those of us who are being sanctified. That You, Jesus Christ, are the end of the law for righteousness to everyone who believes. That I have been crucified with You and that it's no longer I who live but You who live in and through me, and the life I now live, I live by faith in You who gave Yourself for me. And that by Your blood and in Your name, my old man is dead. That You have declared me holy and when You present me to Your Father, He, because of You, sees me washed white as snow. In Jesus's name, amen.

Now, if you prayed that prayer, let me pray over you:

Our good and gracious Heavenly Father, Lord, we love You more than anything, and we know that our battle is not against flesh and blood. But we have an enemy that has methods, that has schemes, and one of his greatest schemes is in this area of sexual immorality. And Lord, I pray, I pray that You would root out any spirit of a Pharisee in this place, holding a stone of judgmentalism, and may we all drop them and understand that we are all sinners saved by Grace, and the reason, Jesus, that You came is to set us free. You did not come to condemn. You came to save.

And so, God, we claim that. And Spirit of God, I pray that You would re-preach the Gospel to every single one of us reading this book, that therefore now there is no condemnation for those who are in Christ Jesus. So, Lord, I pray that chains would fall off. I pray that years of addictive behavior would be broken because of an encounter with You. I pray that what the enemy used for evil, You would flip it upside down, it would bring us to a desperate place at Your feet, and we would experience the love and the Grace and the peace, the justice of You, and that we would know that when you said, "It is finished," it counted for this, too.

I pray marriages would be saved. Couples would be healed. Strongholds would be broken down, and we would no longer be slaves of fear but we would be children of God. We pray this in Jesus's name, amen.

Chapter 5

GRACE CLEANSES

Grace is not a contract. It's an inconceivable gift.

What's your greatest regret? The answer probably didn't take long to come up with. My regrets have a tendency to stay close to the surface and pop up when I least want them to. Usually right before I preach.

What about this one? What causes you the greatest shame? Same answer? Yeah, me, too.

When we sin against a holy God, He responds in us with conviction. It's His emotive response in us. Conviction is God-given, heart-piercing, sanctifying, and intended to lead us back to Him. The enemy, on the other hand, responds with guilt and shame, and his intent is to use them as a wedge to separate us from a loving God.

Here's what I mean. Go with me to Psalm 51.

We're going to be talking about sin. Particularly sexual sin. And you might ask, "Well, didn't we just cover that in the last chapter?" Yes, but stick with me. There's more. If you remember, Paul says this in 1 Corinthians 6: "Every other sin a person commits is outside the body, but the sexually immoral person sins against his own body." This means sexual sin is just different. It doesn't mean it's unforgivable. Please hear that. It is. Absolutely and completely. Remember, "It is finished." It just means it dings the soul at a different level.

Now you should know I've been praying like crazy that today, right now, chains would fall off as you read this. Marriages would be saved.

Forgiveness would be poured out. Shame would be gone. And that freedom and healing would reign. That God would create in us a clean, new heart, because if the tomb is empty, anything is possible.

Now, for those of you who really don't struggle in this area, hold tight. I'm going to walk us through a true story in which the sin was sexual but the resulting prayer is a model of repentance for any sin. For all of us.

Here's what you need to know—we're all sinners. Fact. Given that, we all need to walk in daily repentance. I'm wanting to put a prayer in your hand, in your heart, that will be a lifelong model of what repentance sounds like. I use it often.

So, here we go.

The subscript of Psalm 51 says this. It says, "To the choirmaster. A Psalm of David, when Nathan the prophet went to him." This puts a date stamp on this psalm. We know exactly what was going on when David wrote this. And just to be clear, it says, "After he had gone in to Bathsheba." Well, that's a little graphic, isn't it? He wants us to know this is for real. This wasn't an emotional affair. This wasn't like they were texting each other. It wasn't a little bit of flirting. This is what was going on.

If you back up to 2 Samuel chapter 11, I want to look at the multiple steps in the life of David that lead to this infidelity. It's not just a one-time thing. There was a decision that led to a decision that led to a decision that led to destruction, and that's the way sexual sin goes. You see, it is our direction, not our intention, that determines our destination.

Can I get a witness? You should probably underline that.

Your marriage is on a path, and it's going somewhere, and it never ends up anywhere awesome by accident or mistake. In 2 Samuel chapter 11, the Bible says, "In the spring of the year, the time when kings go out to battle, David sent Joab." If you take notes in your Bible, write the Greek word "Uh-oh."

That's not any good. David's the king. Joab is not the king. This is the time when the kings did what kings do, and kings are supposed to go to war, but David abdicates his responsibility, and he sends somebody else instead. Note to self: It's a scary thing when men begin to abdicate responsibility.

Listen, men are like flatbed trucks. They just drive better when they're carrying a load. I hope you know that's true. If they've got a little extra time, a little extra margin, a little extra energy, a little extra change, then it is not good. It is not good at all. *And so he sends Joab and his servants with him and all of Israel, and they ravage the Ammonites and besiege Rabbah, but David remained in Jerusalem.*

Not going to war was the first step toward his downfall. Coach Lee, the guy who led me to Christ, used to say this: "If you don't want to fall down, don't walk in slippery places."

David put himself in a slippery place, and it gets worse. Verse 2: "It happened, late one afternoon, when David arose from his couch." The most dangerous thing on the planet is a lazy man. When you get pent-up energy, you aim it at the wrong thing. I'm telling you, it's what gangs are full of. It's what prisons are full of. It's what strip clubs are full of, men who are not providing and protecting and being the prophet, priest, and servant king of their home and community. When he's supposed to be at work, he's lying around on his couch.

"It happened, late one afternoon, when David arose from his couch and was walking on the roof of the king's house." Notice, this was not his first time. The king had been on his roof before. The king knew what he would see from his roof. The way it worked, he didn't live in a neighborhood like we do. The palace was at the highest place in the City of David, and when he stood on top of his palace, he could look down on all of his subjects, on all of the other homes, and I think he knew what he was going to see. And so he was walking on the roof of the king's house, and he saw from that roof a woman bathing, and the woman was very beautiful, which immediately took David from lazy to looking. This is step number two.

Now listen, there's a difference between look and lust. You, as a human being, can appreciate that another human being is pretty or handsome or whatever the word is, but when that look transfers to an intent to objectify somebody else for your own benefit, you have now moved from observation to sinful lust. This objectification is what David is doing. He's watching Bathsheba take a bath. This is the moment David clicks the link to the porn site.

Verse 3: "And David sent and inquired about the woman." This is step number three. He's going to set up an encounter. This isn't a look anymore. Now he wants to meet her. Let's make this very practical. Darling, this is when you're getting ready in the morning, putting on your makeup, and you ain't thinking about your husband. You're thinking about your boss. This is when you adjust your gym time because you know that girl's there, and when she laughs at your dumb jokes, it makes you feel better about you. This is when that girl that you dated way back in high school twenty-five years ago, when you were all slim like Tarzan, sends you a little private message in your social media, and instead of blocking her immediately, like the devil of hell she is, you just shoot it back with a not-so-innocent "Hey, girl, what's up?"

And your response is "Ain't no big deal. I read through the whole Bible. It didn't say anything about text."

David sent and inquired about the woman and then, the Bible doesn't say who it is but somebody speaks up and says, "Is not this Bathsheba, the daughter of Eliam, the wife of Uriah the Hittite?" This is David's chance. God loves David so much He would put somebody in his sight. *Whoa! Hold on. You know who she is? She's married to another dude, David. You know this?*

This unnamed voice is the Spirit of God coming in, and going, "Hey!" This is the Holy Ghost saying, "Back up, Terry. Put it in reverse." That's what this is.

Remember in the last chapter when we talked about 1 Corinthians 6, where Paul told us to flee? Any time any of us have ever failed sexually, it's because, at some point, we didn't flee. We flirted. Every single time that's what happens. And when the Bible says to flee sexual immorality, that word, in Greek, for sexual immorality is *porneia*. Sound familiar? That word is a junk drawer for all sexual sin. Let me reiterate, according to the Bible, any sex outside of marriage, which is one man and one woman for one lifetime, is sexual sin.

Do you see the steps David's taking? Or, not taking? He's lying on his couch, doesn't go to war, walking around the roof. "Who's that? Go get her for me." And then somebody pipes up, "Whoa! Are you sure?"

Proverbs, written by Solomon—David's son—is a book full of wisdom, and there are three chapters back to back to back in which an older guy is trying to warn a younger guy about these decisions that lead to death and destruction in your own life. I can't think of any other place in the Bible that dedicates three full chapters in a row to warn us about a particular sin. In Proverbs chapter 5, this older guy is warning the younger guy and he says this: "For the lips of a forbidden woman drip honey" (Proverbs 5:3). It's like, "Hey, bro, I know it's sweet at first. I know it makes you feel good when she gives you compliments and you're thinking, 'Nobody at home gives me compliments.' It's sweet as honey when she laughs at your dumb jokes, tells you how awesome you are. Because you think to yourself, 'She really gets me.' Yeah, she's going to get you, but it don't mean what you think it means."

"But in the end, she is bitter as wormwood" (5:4). It's a trick. "Sharp as a two-edged sword" (5:4). Listen to this: "Her feet go down to death" (5:5). Do you see the path language here? "Her steps follow the path to Sheol [hell]" (5:5). Brother, listen to me, she ain't flirting with you. She's trying to kill you, and she doesn't even know it. She does not ponder the path of life. Her ways wander, and she does not know it. It's one step at a time, and all those steps only lead to one place. Hell. You want to experience hell? Then follow her where she's leading. Follow him where he's leading. I mean, you can ask a whole bunch of people at our church, and they will tell you it has destroyed their lives. I'm not here to beat you up. I'm not here to make you feel bad about you. I'm here to love you enough to just share the warning from Scripture.

When you get to Proverbs chapter 6, verse 27, the old guy asks the young guy, "Can a man carry fire next to his chest and his clothes not be burned?" The fool thinks, "Yeah, man, I can do this. This is different. We're in love." Or, "Well, I know, but…we're married in our hearts." That's not a thing. You realize that? You're just making that up. You're either married before God in a covenant, or you're not married. If that's you, if you're taking something that's not yours, you're not ready to be a husband. And listen, darling, if you're the daughter of the King, the only person who should get to touch you is somebody who commits their whole life to you—before God. That's how valuable you are. Otherwise, you're carrying fire.

"Or can one walk on hot coals and his feet not be scorched?" (Proverbs 6:28). The answer is no. You cannot. I know you think you can. That's why this man's the fool. My friend Jeff Kopp told me one time the three most dangerous words you can ever say are "I got this." Because, the truth is, no you don't. David said, "I got this," and some unnamed person spoke up and said, "Um, boss. No you don't. She's married to Uriah the Hittite."

By the time you get to chapter 7 of Proverbs, the older guy says to the younger guy, "I have perceived among the youths, a young man lacking sense" (Proverbs 7:7). When you flirt with sexual immorality and don't flee from it, you lack sense. That's Hebrew for you're dumb as a bag of hammers.

Then it says this in verse 8: "Passing…" I think this is the key verse to understand these three chapters. "Passing along the street near her corner, taking the road to her house." You talk to anybody that's ever blown their life up sexually and what they will tell you is they would give anything to back up to this decision. At some point, they're walking down the road, and they haven't actually sinned yet, but they notice. They give that look, and there she is, saying, "Come on. Why don't you come down here?"

And you begin to think, "I could take a couple steps down this corner. I mean, I've looked through the whole Bible and nowhere in the Bible does it say, 'Thou shalt not turneth a corner.' I mean, it's just a lunch. What's the big deal? It's just a few pictures. It's not porn. It's just Instagram. It's just one DM. All I'm going to do is just check on her, see how she's doing." At some point, you made a decision that made a decision that made a decision that leads to destruction. You set fire to you.

By the time you get to verse 21, it says this: "With much seductive speech she persuades him; with her smooth talk she compels him." Then in verse 22, he's being facetious: "All at once he follows her." Everybody knows it's not all at once. It may seem like it happened all at once to everybody else, but not to the fool. He didn't just blow up his marriage in a day.

"All at once he follows her." And I love this. This is the description: "As an ox goes to the slaughter." I don't know if you ever slaughtered something before, but it's not pretty.

The ox walks into the shoot and he thinks, "I'm big. I'm bad. I'm hairy. I'm tough. I got this." And yet, he's seconds from a bullet to the brain. The author of Proverbs gives another illustration that I like even more: "Or as a stag is caught fast till an arrow pierces its liver" (7:22–23). You ever liver-shot a stag? Well, I have. And for the record, I shoot a Mathews bow because I'm a massive fan of Matt McPherson and everything he does in and for the Kingdom of God. Not to mention, his bows are just awesome.

I hunt a lot. Primarily I bow hunt, and the bows are so good these days. They produce so much energy and push the arrows at superfast speeds—over 330 feet per second. Often—and I've seen this a lot—the arrow will pass through the animal so fast that the animal doesn't know it's been hit. They raise their head because they heard a strange noise, and then after a few seconds, they tumble over. Lights out.

Here's what the Bible is saying. Every single person that flirts with sexual immorality, every dude who's got that little hidden porn stash, every guy taking advantage of one of God's daughters, every one of God's daughters giving herself to some boy who only wants the privileges of manhood but not the responsibilities of manhood, you're a dead man walking. The arrow has already passed through.

A bunch of you reading this right now just want me to show you the line. "Pastor, why don't you just show us the line. Like, how far is too far? What's okay and what's not okay, because if you could just show us the line, then we would know what to do and what not to do."

Here's the problem. That'll never sustain you, because the moment you say, "Alright. That's the line," you'll cross it. Human nature wants to see how close we can get to the line without going over the line. And the moment you approach the line, you start thinking, "Well, how far can I go over the line and still manage the consequences? How far can I go and still get back to good?" And after you cross it, nothing but carnage in your wake, you look behind you and think, "How in the world did I end up here?" This is how you got your last speeding ticket. You pushed until the blue lights behind you told you that you'd pushed it too far.

Any time you hear about some Christian failing or falling, especially when it's some famous pastor, there was a series of steps. A progression downward. They flirted. They did not flee. They approached the line. Crossed the line. And then when we all read it in the headlines, somebody asks, "Pastor, what happened? How could that happen?" Truth is, he took his eyes off Jesus and somewhere along the way, when the Spirit of God came to him and said, *"But isn't that Bathsheba and she's married to Uriah the Hittite?"* he didn't listen. He said, "I got this." And he didn't. None of us do.

If you have sinned sexually, that's what happened. If you've been sinned against sexually, that's what happened. If you were the adulterer, that's what happened. If you're living in a raging porn addiction, that's what happened. If you're hooking up, that's what happened. Every single one of us is just a few steps away from destruction, and anybody who regrets the things they've done would say, "I wish I could go back to that corner and make a different decision." This is the warning that the old guy gives.

And so David gets this warning. *"David, isn't she married to somebody else?"* But David didn't listen. He pounded his chest and said, *"I got this."* In 2 Samuel 11, verse 4, it says, "So David sent messengers and took her." Game over. "And she came to him, and he lay with her. (Now, she had been purifying herself from her uncleanness.) Then she returned to her house. And the woman conceived, and she sent and told David, 'I am pregnant.'"

There are a lot of commentaries that suggest this meeting was not consensual. Women in this culture weren't even second-class citizens. Not to mention, David was king. What's she going to say? He has absolute power over her. The Bible does not specifically call it rape, but it very well could have been. Having crossed the line, David now thinks he can clean up his own mess, so he comes up with a plan to cover it up.

He calls for Uriah, the husband. *"Go get Uriah. Bring him home."* They bring him home. David calls him in. *"Bro, you're the man. Appreciate you fighting for the country and because I appreciate you so much, we're going to throw a party at your house, and then, as a reward, you get to sleep in your bed. With your wife. Tonight. Deal?"* But David has just one problem. He picked a man with absolute integrity. To honor his men, who are all fighting out in the field, he sleeps on the ground. Not with his wife.

David then tries to liquor him up to get him to do it, but he still won't do it, so David calls his boss, the general, and says, *"Put Uriah on the frontlines. Then attack the Ammorites. Get as close to their castle as you can, and then when Uriah is exposed on the front, everybody just kind of back up."* It's a massive betrayal of one of his most loyal soldiers. It's murder. Uriah dies on the battlefield.

Verse 26: "When the wife of Uriah heard that Uriah her husband was dead, she lamented over her husband. And when the mourning was over, David sent and brought her to his house, and she became his wife and bore him a son. But the thing that David had done displeased the

Lord." David thinks he's gotten away with it, but after thirty years of ministry, I've learned this—nobody ever gets away with it. Because God knows. God sees. And God judges every one of us. What's crazy is that it's the kindness of God that leads us to repentance. It's God's kindness that convicts us of sin.

David doesn't listen. You and I read this and think, "How could the man that wrote the psalms, a man after God's own heart, trainwreck his life like this?" The truth is every single one of us has the ability to absolutely trainwreck our lives, our families, our work, and our witness through sexual immorality.

Billy Graham had a rule that I've adopted. As of late, it's brought criticism. Some have even claimed it's toxic. I don't care. I love my wife. Dr. Graham never traveled alone. Never walked into a hotel alone. Never met alone in a room with any woman other than his wife. Some would say that's extreme. Okay. Great. I'm extreme. And I love my wife.

The world says it's abnormal to live like Billy Graham. You want to know what normal is according to the world? Normal is broke and divorced and depressed. You can have normal. The Bible says pride comes before destruction and a haughty spirit before a fall. I don't want either. I want to walk in humility. Like Billy Graham. Like Jesus commands.

When you get to chapter 12 of 2 Samuel, a year has passed. David thinks, *"Whoo, all good. We got this."* "And the Lord sent Nathan." Nathan's going to call David out. Do you have some Nathans in your life? Do you have anyone who can call you on the carpet? Tell you the truth about you? I sure do hope you have some people in your life and they love you more than they love what you think about them, and that they are willing to have the hard conversation with you. Do you have a Nathan? I know some of you are reading me and thinking, "Yeah, you." Okay. Thanks, but that's not enough. You need truth-telling people in your life who are not afraid to ruffle your feathers.

Nathan comes to David, and he's going to confront the king on his sin, but he's the prophet and David is the king. How exactly does he bring that up? But what he does is brilliant. He approaches it this way: *"Hey, boss, I need some help."* Then he makes up a story.

"There are these two people that live in your kingdom. One guy's rich, one guy's poor. The rich guy has sheep and herds and lambs aplenty, but then there's this poor guy. He's got one little baby ewe lamb, and he doesn't even treat it like a lamb. He treats it like his daughter. He named it and sings it songs and lets it live in the house and gives it birthday presents. And then one day, the rich guy had a friend come over for dinner, and instead of taking one of the many lambs or sheep that he's got all over the place, he goes and he takes the one little baby lamb from this guy who loved it and he slaughtered it and he ate it. What shall we do?"

David is ticked, man. Verse 5: "Then David's anger was greatly kindled against the man, and he said to Nathan, 'As the Lord lives, the man who has done this deserves to die, and he shall restore the lamb fourfold, because he did this thing, and because he had no pity.' Nathan said to David, 'You are the man!'"

Or, as the King James Version says, "Thou art the man."

One of the problems that we as believers have is that we use the Bible to diagnose everyone else's problems except our own. We use it like binoculars to probe other people's lives but seldom use it as a mirror to our own. Here, Nathan is holding it up as a mirror to King David and the reflection is ugly, and David knows it.

Verse 9: Then Nathan, on behalf of the Lord, says, "Why have you despised the Word of the Lord, to do what is evil in his sight?"

A few years ago, I was standing in my kitchen having a robust dialogue with one of my children, who had not made wise decisions. Somewhere in the conversation, I raised my voice. "What are you doing? If you would just listen to me, your whole life would be awesome. You are so blessed. If you would just do what I say, everything would be awesome…"

And about the time those words left my mouth, the Spirit of God said to me, "Tell him again, Dad."

So I did. Louder. "Listen to me. I'm your dad. I love you. And if you'd just do what I tell you to do, your life would be so much better, and you would avoid so much pain."

And God said, "Tell him again." So, I was about to open my mouth a third time but thought, "Oh, wait a minute. I don't think we're talking about him anymore." Truth is, I'm a lot more like David than I want to admit. But I'm not alone. You are, too.

Nathan continues, "Why have you despised the word of the Lord?" Verse 10: "Now therefore the sword shall never depart from your house." In other words, *I will forgive you of your sin, but I will not rescue you from your consequences.* And for the rest of his life, and his kids' lives, his family is jacked.

Then in verse 13, David responds. He has no defense. And this shows his heart and how quick he is to repent when confronted. He simply says, "I have sinned against the Lord."

How do you respond to conviction? Can I just be honest? Little therapy for me. I get so defensive. I have elders whose job it is to help me follow Jesus better, and they are supergood. They are supernaturally gifted at pointing out all my problems. And whenever they do, I want to respond with, "Whoa. Hold on. Let me give you some reasons why it's not that big of a deal. Okay? Oh, you want to talk about the speck in my eye? Funny you brought it up because you got a log in yours, and I know more verses than you…" I know it's bad. It's actually worse than you think.

But not David. Maybe this is why he's a man after God's own heart. He immediately just repents. "I have sinned against the Lord." And then look at Nathan's response: "And Nathan said to David, 'The Lord also has put away your sin; you shall not die.'" Literally, "put away" means passed over. What? How's it that easy? That's not fair. Is that fair? Doesn't he have to do something more than that? "I have sinned against the Lord." I mean, is this it? What a scandal of Grace. How in the world could David do such atrocious things and then Nathan, the prophet of God, says to him, *"The Lord has passed over your sin. You shall not die"*?

Well, I'm glad you asked. All of that was just a preamble to the meat of this chapter. Now let's move on to the main point.

Psalm 51: The story recounted in 2 Samuel 11 and 12 is the objective reality of what happened before David writes Psalm 51. Psalm 51 is the subjective appropriation of the objective reality of the Grace of God in the life of David. I know that's a lot. Let me break it down—Psalm 51 grew out of David's sin.

Just in case you're a little slow on the uptake, let me just be clear here. We are all David at this point. Every single one of us has sinned against the Lord, and so here's what David does. He responds with Psalm 51:1, "Have mercy on me, O God." He offers no excuses. As a Jesus follower, this should be our posture. Do you take your sin serious enough or do you think, "Well, I'm not that bad"? Every single one of us is much, much worse than we thought. We're not good people. There's no such thing. There was only one good man, and we killed him. His name is Jesus. We're bad. Born under sin. And straight up, we deserve death. David knows this, and yet he asks for mercy. Mercy means not getting what we deserve, and how in the world can God save a murdering, unfaithful rapist? The answer? Just like he saves me and you. By His mercy.

David continues, "Have mercy on me, O God, according to your steadfast love." The Hebrew word for "steadfast love" is *hesed*. It's one of the most beautiful words in the Bible, and we don't really have one word in English that does it justice. We need several to really define it.

Hesed is maybe better defined by a word picture of a nursing mom. When the baby cries, the mom lactates in response. The cry of the baby is met by exactly what the baby needs. Not only the milk, but arms wrapped around us. Breath on our face. A whisper in our ears. And when we cry out, "Have mercy on me, God," our cries stir in God this steadfast love that is produced in Him to meet all of our needs. That's what he's talking about here.

"According to your abundant mercy blot out my transgressions" (Psalm 51:1). Notice what David does not say. He does not say, "From now on,

I'll try harder, God." That's not what he does. He says, *"I need you to do for me what I can't do for me. Wash me thoroughly from my iniquity and cleanse me from my sin."* Notice that God is the active agent here. "For I know my transgressions, and my sin is ever before me." No excuses, just confession.

And then he says, "Against you, you only, have I sinned and done what is evil in your sight." To which we all think, wait a minute. I mean, Uriah thinks you sinned against him because he's dead. I bet Bathsheba's mama thinks you sinned against her, so what is he talking about? Here's what he's saying. All sin is a sin against God. We can sin against one another. We can hurt one another, but every time we sin, it is always a sin against God.

Remember in the New Testament, in the Gospels, where Jesus is teaching in a house and these four buddies bring a paralyzed man on a mat and they can't get in the house, so they climb up on top of the roof and dig a hole and then lower the paralyzed man down through the roof. And Jesus looks at the guy, and the first thing He does is say, "Your sins are forgiven" (Matthew 9:2). And the religious people are thinking, *"Who does He think He is? Only God can forgive sins."* Ding, ding, ding. Winner, winner, chicken dinner. The reason that Jesus could say "Your sins are forgiven" was because everything that man had ever done was against Jesus.

You don't get to forgive sins that aren't against you. For instance, let's say a few minutes ago, you got in a fight with your spouse. Or boss. Or whatever. Anyway, there was a fight and you said horrible words to each other. Maybe you threw a vase or something. And then, knowing you messed up, you call me and tell me all about it.

How weird would it be if I said, "I forgive you"?

You'd scratch your head. "What do you mean *you* forgive me? We sinned against each other. Not you. What business do you have forgiving us for our sins against one another?"

This does not mean you shouldn't ask forgiveness. You should. But primarily, you have sinned against God. Every single sin is always against Him.

This is what David is saying. *"Against you have I sinned."* Then he goes on to say, "So that you may be justified in your words and blameless in your judgment." In other words, what David is saying is, *"If you damn me to hell, you would be doing the right thing."* This is a humble posture. Verse 5: "Behold, I was brought forth in iniquity, and in sin did my mother conceive me." Now, I know some of you have grown up in a generation where your kindergarten teacher told you that you were a snowflake and you were a rainbow and you're puppy's breath and you're a Skittle. Well, look here, Skittle. She lied to you. Yep. I'm sorry to break it to you, but your kindergarten teacher's a liar, too. Every single one of us, especially me, is a crooked, wretched, depraved, blackhearted sinner. Born this way. And this is what David is saying.

He continues, "Behold, you delight in truth in the inward being, and you teach me wisdom in the secret heart" (Psalm 51:6). This is crazy. He's saying, *"God, You're even going to use my own sin to teach me some things about Your character and nature that otherwise I wouldn't learn."* Then he says, "Purge me with hyssop, and I shall be clean" (51:7). At worship services, the priest would dip hyssop in blood and sling it on people. Think about that. Imagine that kind of service. On the Day of Atonement, they would dip the blood of a lamb and sling it on the people, so they went home with blood on them. Imagine getting blood on you at church. You'd think, "This is intense."

Without the shedding of blood, there's no forgiveness of sin. If a house was deemed unclean, once it was consecrated and made clean, they would take hyssop and blood and they would mark it on the outside so everybody knew it was a clean house. The blood cleansed the house. And so David says to God, *"God, I need You to do that for me because I can't clean me up. Wash me and I will be whiter than snow. Let me hear joy and gladness. Let the bones that you have broken rejoice."* In other words, David is claiming, *"Because of Your mercy and steadfast love, even though I have sinned and deserve death, You're not done with me."*

And, even if you've done some stuff you never dreamed you had the ability to do, He's not done with you either. "Hide your face from my sins, and blot out all my iniquities." You see, here's what David knows. David knows Exodus 34, and in Exodus 34, God tells Moses these two truths about what happens when we sin, and they seem to counter against each other. In Exodus 34, the Lord passed before Moses and He proclaimed, "The Lord, the Lord, a God merciful and gracious, slow to anger, and abounding in steadfast love and faithfulness, keeping steadfast love for thousands." That's just who God is.

And then listen to this. Look at this next verse. When sin happens, there are two options: "Forgiving iniquity and transgression and sin, but who will by no means clear the guilty." Well, how in the heck are those two things simultaneously true? And I think David is proclaiming, *I want to be on the forgiving iniquity and transgressions side, not the by no means clear the guilty side.* How is that simultaneously true? How can you simultaneously forgive sin and make the guilty pay?

Short answer? The cross of Jesus Christ.

At the cross of Jesus Christ, for anyone who would put their faith in Christ, the payment for our sin is poured out on Jesus, and He makes the payment and we get credit for His righteousness, and we are forgiven of our sin. This is the scandal of Grace. So the way that David is saved, the way that David's sins are passed over almost a thousand years before Jesus walks the Earth, is described by Paul in Romans chapter 3: "For all have sinned and fall short of the glory of God" (3:23). That's David. That's you. That's me. "And are justified by his grace as a gift, through the redemption that is in Christ Jesus, whom God put forward as a propitiation by his blood, to be received by faith." That's how we are forgiven, by putting our faith in Jesus.

But what about David? David hadn't even heard of Jesus yet. I'm glad you asked. Paul says this. "This was to show God's righteousness, because in his divine forbearance he had passed over former sins. It was to show his righteousness at the present time, so that he might be just and the justifier of the one who has faith in Jesus" (Romans 3:25–26).

Let me explain. Because of God's justice, all sin must be paid for. Because of God's mercy, He delays the payment. This is how David makes it to heaven. Actually, this is how you and I make it to heaven today. Why? Anybody sin this week? And here you are. But the Bible says the wages of sin is death, because if He did not delay payment, you'd be a greasy spot on the surface of the Earth. Because of God's justice, all sin must be paid for. Because of God's mercy, He delayed the payment. And because of His Grace, He made the payment on our behalf. He is the Just and the Justifier.

Back in the day, David puts his faith in the coming Messiah. David puts his faith in the One who would be pierced for our transgressions. See Psalm 22. David wrote that one, too. David knows that there's going to be a messiah, a lamb that comes, and His shed blood would count for you and me and David. And because of that shed blood, you and I and David are credited with righteousness. In David's case, it is because he has placed his faith in the coming Messiah. Another way to say it is this: What we know by name, Jesus, he knew by faith, and that's how he was forgiven.

But David doesn't stop there. He keeps going. After he says, "Cleanse me and wash me. Make me whiter than snow," he prays, "Create in me a clean heart, O God, and renew a right spirit within me" (Psalm 51:10). *God, I need to be different. I need you to change my wants and change my desires and do something for me in here that I can't do for myself.* You see, it's not enough for me to be sorry. I need to be different. This is not works-based righteousness. This is evidence of the goodness of God transforming David's life. I think it's right here that David is run over by the Grace Train. How do we know? Because if you've ever been run over by the Grace Train, it changes everything about everything about everything for everyone who would believe.

What I mean is this: If you got run over by a train, there's no way you would look like you look now. You'd be a bit disheveled, probably missing a limb, maybe bleeding from the nose and walking with a limp. You would be different. So how in the world can you encounter the infinitely greater power of the good news of the Gospel of Christ, be run over by it, and then remain unchanged? It's impossible. So you and I don't need to just be forgiven. We need to be different. Changed. From the inside out. "Create in me a clean heart, O God, and renew a right spirit within me. Cast me not away from your presence, and take not your Holy Spirit from me" (Psalm 51:10–11).

It's by Grace you were saved, and it's by Grace you stay saved. Contrary to popular opinion, you can't lose your salvation, because you didn't save you. Jesus did. Then David says, "Restore to me the joy of your salvation, and uphold me with a willing spirit" (51:12). *"God, could you just remind me of the joy I had for You when I first was forgiven because I've taken my eyes off of You and I got them fixed on this girl over here and it messed me all up. Restore unto me the joy of my salvation."*

I've read this psalm a bunch in the last thirty years, but as I was working on this chapter, I noticed something I'd never seen. There's not one mention of sex. Not one mention of murder. Not one mention of lying or cover-up. Why? Because those are all just symptoms of the problem, and the deep problem is sin.

Then David goes on to say, "Then I will teach transgressors your ways, and sinners will return to you" (51:13). In other words, *"God, You are going to use this in my life for ministry. You're going to use my mess for ministry. You're going to use this misery to share the message of the good news of Your steadfast love."* He says, "Deliver me from blood guiltiness, O God, O God of my salvation, and my tongue will sing aloud of your righteousness. O Lord, open my lips, and my mouth will declare your praise."

You know what this means? Forgiven people worship.

Remember the woman in the Gospels who was a "woman of ill repute." She was a prostitute. Forgiven by Jesus. He's having a dinner with religious people, and she knows that she's been forgiven by Him, so she walks into the room uninvited. She anoints His head and His feet with oil. She begins to weep over Him. She breaks open an alabaster jar, and what happens? It changes the atmosphere in the entire house where the religious people are replying, *"Who is this touching you?"* Jesus waves them off. *"I'll tell you who it is. She's been forgiven much; therefore, she loves much"* (Luke 7:47).

Every Sunday, I have a perspective of the people of God that is different than most. From where I stand, I get to watch people's response to the Gospel. And let me tell you who worships. Forgiven, repentant people worship their faces off. And it's beautiful.

Then David says, "For you will not delight in sacrifice, or I would give it; you will not be pleased with a burnt offering. The sacrifices of God are a broken spirit; a broken and contrite heart, O God, you will not despise" (51:16–17). In other words, rote religious activity does not move the heart of God. Just singing all the songs and doing the things that you always do, because that's what you've always done, does nothing. Only a daily broken and contrite heart, pouring itself out in confession and repentance, moves the *hesed* heart of God.

Martin Luther said, in the first of his ninety-five theses, that the life of the believer should be that of daily repentance. Maybe this is why Jesus says to pick up our cross daily. Maybe I'm talking about you. Maybe you're one of these people. Maybe you're reading this book and you're thinking, "You know, I sort of skimmed over the last chapter because it got a little too close to home. But I've done some stuff. And that stuff is weighing heavy on me and I'd like to be free from it. From the guilt and shame. From the regret." The remedy is simple. You need to say, "Have mercy on me, God. Wash me. Create in me a clean heart."

Let me bring this closer to home—a lot of you picked up this book and you're faking your way through life. And in truth, the fake you is doing just fine. You wear a mask so no one knows the truth of you. And no one will ever know if you just turn the page or put this book down. But what if this is your moment? What if God is literally standing next to you? Whether in the prison cell, subway, office, coffee shop, or bed, what if He's just waiting for you to bring it to Him? You can sit there with a stiff upper lip and remain unchanged. You can take all your stuff to the grave. Or you can take it to His cross and dump it at His feet with a broken and contrite heart crying out, "Have mercy on me, oh God."

I pray God is going to use this message right now to save your marriage and save your future, but like David, you need to cry out to Him: "Lord, I need help. Have mercy. Cleanse me. Wash me. Forgive me. Change me. Create in me a clean heart. Restore to me the joy of Your salvation."

Oh, and by the way, Psalm 51 worked. Here's what I mean. In 2 Samuel 22, David is going to write a song that's also recorded in Psalm 18. I know it's backward in our psalms, but this means Psalm 51 has already happened. Listen to some of the words that this adultering, lying murderer writes down. David says, "The Lord dealt with me according to my righteousness; according to the cleanness of my hands he rewarded me" (Psalm 18:20). Wait a minute. Does David have clean hands? No. "For I have kept the ways of the Lord, and have not wickedly departed from my God" (18:21). This brother needs clinical help. What's wrong with him? Who is he talking about? "For all his rules were before me" (18:22). Are you sure? How about the one about don't murder? How about the one about don't sleep with people who are not your wife? Those are two that come to mind, David. What are you talking about?

"And his statutes I did not put away from me. I was blameless before him, and I kept myself from my guilt. So the Lord has rewarded me according to my righteousness" (18:22–24). Anybody reading this right now want God to reward you according to your righteousness? According to the cleanness of your hands? Here's the key. "With the merciful you show yourself merciful" (18:25).

What is David doing here? Theologically, David is walking in what we call the imputed righteousness of Christ. Somehow, supernaturally, by the spirit of God, David knows what Paul is going to write to the church in Corinth. When Paul says, *God made Him who was without sin to be sin for us that we would be made the righteousness of Christ* (2 Corinthians 5:21), David knows this. He knows that when God sees David, because of his faith in the coming Christ, God does not see his past sin. He does not see his mistakes. He doesn't see his adultery, his affair, the murder. He sees the imputed righteousness of Christ. Therefore, he can say, "I stand blameless before God, before the God of mercy."

Can you imagine walking in that kind of freedom? We spent a good bit of time in chapter 3 talking about the prodigal son. I won't rehash it all here, but I want to mention two things about the nature and character of a God who stares a long way down the road, then runs to us when we return and covers our face in kisses. One of the things about this picture that I just can't get over is the dad, running to the boy. First-century Jewish men didn't run, especially if you were a landowner, because you've got to hike up that robe, show all that man thigh.

He humiliates himself in front of everybody and grabs the boy. Gets to him before anyone else. You know why? Because Deuteronomy says if you've got a rebellious kid, then the elders should just throw rocks at him until he dies. The dad knows this. So he waits, and waits, and waits, and then when he sees a speck in the distance, he launches himself off the porch, covers the distance like Halley's comet, and wraps his arms around him. The father covers the son because the dad knows if the elders start throwing rocks, they'll hit him first. The father will gladly take the blows meant for the boy.

Then after he's wrapped him up, a shield wall between the boy and the rock-toting elders, the Bible says he kisses his face. Literally, in Greek, he fills up his face with kisses. That's not one little peck. Think about it. Think how unclean the boy is. How much he stinks. He's been feeding pigs.

But the father's not finished. In his Grace, he does four things. He gives him a ring to reclaim him. He gives him his shoes so that he'll know he's his son. And he throws a party for him. But then there's this: He says, *"Go get my robe."* Why? Because the boy's a mess. Nowhere in the Bible does it imply that the boy cleaned up before he came to his dad. It's straight from the pigpen to Dad's house, and so when everybody sees the boy, they see a mess, and he says, *"Go get my robe."* The robe would have been perfect. Spotless. And he wraps the perfect, spotless robe of righteousness around the boy, so when anybody sees him, they don't see the filth. They see the father. This is a picture of imputed or shared righteousness.

This is the Grace of the Father.

Can you imagine walking in that kind of freedom? David did. It worked for David. How about you? You can be free right this second from a lifetime of sin and shame and regret. The Bible says in James chapter 5, "Is anyone among you suffering?" (James 5:13). Man, some of you are suffering a guilty conscience, shame, condemnation. For some of us, it's things we have done. For others, it's what's been done against us. Or to us. James continues, "Let him pray. Anyone cheerful? Let him sing praise. Is anyone among you sick?" Normally, when we go to James 5, we talk about physical sickness and healing, but the Bible says that hope deferred makes the heart sick, and some of you feel like because of your divorce, because of your affair, because of your abortion, because of whatever, fill in the blank, your sexual sin, some of you feel like you're hopeless, but if the tomb is empty, there's hope for you.

Is anyone among you sick? Some of you have a sick heart. Based on the evidence of David, God can heal you. Here's his last bit of instruction, James 5:15: "And if he has committed sins..." Let's be honest. That's all of us. It's every single one of us. "And if he has committed sins, he will be forgiven. Therefore, confess your sins to one another and pray for one another, that you may be healed" (James 5:15–16).

A bunch of us are like David. We sinned back in the day, and we think hiding it allows us to get away with it. In fact, there's a bunch of you who are married right now, and when you were not married, you were dating. You were sleeping together, and you thought, "Well, you know what? We made it and we got married." And you've never addressed that thing, and you need to confess that to the Lord. Husbands, you need to repent to your spouse and before the Lord: "I didn't do it right. I took what was not mine." Or to the wife, "I gave myself to somebody who had not committed themselves to me yet. And I repent." Or maybe it's a sexual sin or an affair, an adultery or something that even happened against you, and the enemy tries to use it, even though it's not your fault. Maybe it was abuse against you, and the enemy uses that harm against your soul to tell you you're broken. You're dirty. You're condemned.

I'm not suggesting you sinned in that experience, but it's wounded you. It's dinged your soul and there's shame around it. Maybe you don't want to talk about it. Let's bring that to the Lord. Offer it up. Let Him heal the wound.

"Jesus, this hurt me and I'm still hurting. Will You please take it away…" When we come and we confess our sins and we pray for one another, the Bible says we'll be healed. Why? Because therefore, now there is no condemnation for those who are in Christ Jesus. So I want to do that. And for anyone hearing the whispers of condemnation of the enemy, particularly in this area, then let's just pray and silence the enemy.

Pray with Me

Our good and gracious Heavenly Father, God, we love You more than anything and we thank You that You loved us. And God, this is love, not that we've got to get ourself all fixed and straightened out to be presentable to You, but You loved us by sending Your Son, Jesus Christ, as the propitiation, the payment that satisfies for our sin. God, I pray against the whispers of the enemy right now of doubt, of condemnation, of pride, and I pray that we would be a people with a broken and contrite heart and we would come before You saying, "Have mercy on me, God. Create in me a clean heart." I pray that we would walk out of here and the chains would be gone. Addictions would be broken. Marriages would be saved, and freedom would reign in the name of Jesus. Lord, I ask that when the enemy whispers his lies of condemnation, You would remind us of Your truth. We are not defined by our scars from the past. We are defined by Jesus's scars from the cross. We are no longer dirty or broken or unfit for use or defiled. We have been wrapped in the perfect and spotless robe of righteousness of our Heavenly Father. Lord, I pray that, like David, You would use our message to point people to the message of the good news of the Gospel of Jesus Christ. God, we thank You that You have always been in the habit of using even our self-inflicted pain as a platform for Your glory. As we experience that scandalous Grace in our lives, I ask that You would lead us to pour out our gratitude to You. We pray this in the good, strong name of Jesus Christ, our Lord and Savior. Amen.

Chapter 6

GRACE FOR THE OUTCAST

*The singular thing that separates the Gospel of
Jesus Christ from every other world religion
can be summed up in one word: Grace.*

could explain, but let me just dive in. This will make sense in a minute.

John chapter 4, verses 1–2: "Now when Jesus learned that the Pharisees had heard that Jesus was making and baptizing more disciples than John (although Jesus himself did not baptize, but only his disciples)..."

You know why Jesus didn't baptize? Because He just wanted to remove Himself from the comparison trap. It does not matter who baptized you. It matters in whose name you are baptized. "He left Judea and departed again for Galilee. And he had to pass through Samaria." Underline the words "had to." Here's the problem with this. It says He had to pass through Samaria. No, He didn't. Because, in the cultural context of the day, Jews would have walked around. It was a six-day journey around and a three-day journey through. There was tension between the Jewish people and the Samaritans. They hated one another. You've got to seriously hate some people to add three days' walking to your journey. The hatred was cultural, ethnic, religious, all mixed into one.

In the thousand years before this, the Israelites disobeyed God, so God removed His hand of protection and turned them over to the Babylonians. Nebuchadnezzar and the Babylonians came in and scooped up almost all of the people and took them into what we call the "Baby-lonian exile." Those who remained, what we call "the remnant," lived in the northern kingdom. Throughout time, they began to intermarry with people who believed differently than they did. Pragmatically, this meant they took a little bit of his religion—the Yahweh worshipping—and they took a little bit of her religion, and mixed it all together. And then they came along and said, "You know what? We're going to cut this whole section of the Bible out and we're only going to believe the first five books of the Bible called the Pentateuch." In today's language, we call this a "cult." They took what they wanted to believe, and molded it into what worked for them, while keeping some of the same language and artifacts of the faith of the fathers.

Years later, Nehemiah shows up to rebuild Jerusalem. And when this group of Jewish people who had intermarried with other non-Jewish people offered to help, Nehemiah refused because they had been unfaithful to God. This caused a rift between the Jews and the Samaritans. In response, the Samaritans started making their own rules about where and how they would worship. By the time Jesus arrives in Samaria, a few hundred years have passed, and the Jews and the Samaritans hate each other. So much so that the Jews call the Samaritans "half-breeds," which is a word that has no place in the church. We—every single person on planet Earth—are an image-bearer of God, and every single person is fearfully and wonderfully made, knit together in their mother's womb. God thought each of us up, individually, so we're not breeds. He gave us the right to become His children for anyone who would believe in Christ. Co-heirs with Christ. He doesn't say anything about us being half of something.

Jesus could have gone the long way around but chose not to because He had a divine appointment with an image-bearer of God: a woman at the well. Culture told Him not to, and ethnicity told Him not to, and religion told Him not to, but His Father told Him He had to. And so He did what His Father told Him to do. In fact, if you keep reading in John, you'll get to John 5:19. It says, "So Jesus said to them, 'Truly, truly,

I say to you, the Son can do nothing of his own accord, but only what he sees the Father doing. For whatever the Father does, that the Son does likewise.'"

This means Jesus had to pass through Samaria. Which begs the question—what do you have to do? What is God telling you to do that you're not doing? Is it the mission field? Giving generously? Witnessing to the person in the cubicle next to you? Forgiving the person who hurt you or abandoned you or betrayed you? What is He telling you to do that you haven't done? When God calls us to do a thing and we make those steps toward that thing, there will always be an exit ramp that says, "Go around Samaria." And then there's that narrow way of a step of obedience that God has said, "Come on, keep coming this way." My point is this—listen to the whispers of what He is telling you. And by faith step in that direction.

"So he came to a town of Samaria called Sychar, near the field that Jacob had given to his son Joseph. Jacob's well was there" (4:5–6). We'll come back to the significance of that well. "So Jesus, wearied as he was from his journey, was sitting beside the well. It was about the sixth hour" (4:6). Here's what John wants you to know—Jesus is fully God. In the beginning was the Word, and the Word was God and the Word was with God. And the Word became flesh and dwelt among us. And that Word is Jesus, who is 100 percent man and 100 percent God.

When He walks into Sychar, He's tired, thirsty, and needs a place to sit. So He sits in a place that His culture would tell Him He shouldn't sit, and He begins talking to a woman His culture would tell Him never to talk to or with. You should let that sink in—I don't care where you are or what you've done, Jesus is not above sitting down and talking with the least of us. He's not "above" us. He's "with" us. It's literally what His name means. Emmanuel. God with us.

The sixth hour means it's about noon. "A woman from Samaria came to draw water" (4:7). If you turn back one chapter in John's Gospel, you'll remember Jesus recently had a one-on-one conversation with Nicodemus. These two people could not be more opposite. Nicodemus came at night, the woman comes during the day. He's a man, she's a woman. He is a Pharisee, the teacher of Israel. This means he is highly respected, he's got lots of bling, he's got lots of notoriety, he's got lots of power. She's got nothing. She's a nobody from nowhere who's done nothing right in her life. And guess what? Jesus gives her the same audience that He gave to Nicodemus. You know why? Because she's not a breed. She's an image-bearer. And He fashioned her from the dust of the earth. He thought her up. She matters. A lot.

And so a woman from Samaria came to draw water, and Jesus said to her, "Give me a drink." Now in the Greek it's supposed to be a tender request. Like, "If you don't mind, could I maybe have a drink or something?" That's kind of what He's saying. "(For his disciples had gone away into the city to buy food.) The Samaritan woman said to him, 'How is it that you, a Jew, ask for a drink from me, a woman of Samaria?'" (4:8–9). She realizes this is scandalous. It's not supposed to happen.

But that's the thing about the Grace of the Gospel. It's scandalous.

John, the Gospel writer, goes on to explain, "For Jews have no dealings with Samaritans." Literally in Greek that phrase "no dealings" means "mixed uses." In other words she says it is culturally inappropriate for Him to drink out of her bucket, because they're not supposed to share from the same cup. Also, there's more going on here than first meets the eye. First of all, she's drawing water at noon. Which tells us a lot about her. In the first century it was the role of the children or the women to go get water in the morning. First thing. While it was still cool.

So why is she showing up in the middle, hottest part of the day? Well, here's the problem. One thought is that she avoided the well early in the morning because all the other townswomen were there, and she was sick of being the subject of their gossip and taunts. This suggests she's probably an immoral woman and doesn't want to be around these people. She's sick of the condemnation.

Secondly, not only do Jews not talk to Samaritans, but in the first century men didn't talk to women like this. It was a divorceable offense for a single man to talk to a married woman.

And then not only that, in the Old Testament the well was a significant place. In the Old Testament, Abraham's servant found his son Isaac's wife at a well. Jacob met his wife at a well. Moses met his wife at a well. And I know what some of you people are thinking: "Where's that well, Pastor?" But Jesus does not mind breaking down religious traditions to get to His people. He doesn't mind breaking gender boundaries, cultural boundaries, ethnic boundaries, religious boundaries, and moral boundaries to sit with this woman whom everybody tells Him He's not supposed to be talking to or with. A friend of mine, Pastor Bryan Loritts, says it this way: "The Gospel compels us to strange relationships." This is not an excuse to sin but rather an encouragement to love the otherwise unlovable.

And so Jesus wastes no time. He jumps right in. He says, "If you knew the gift of God, and who it is that is saying to you, 'Give me a drink,' you would have asked him, and he would have given you living water." Underline the words "living water." Jesus always teaches on two planes, a physical reality and a spiritual reality, and the physical always points to the spiritual. She thinks He's talking about H_2O, and He's talking about a supernatural thirst quencher.

We see this often in the life of Jesus. He is the Lamb of God who takes away the sin of the world. He is the greater Moses who can cure your snake bite from the inside out (see Numbers 21). The hand-washing rites of purification are no longer needed, because He's going to bring the new wine and transform you from the inside out. After His death and resurrection, His very Spirit is going to dwell in us, making us His temple. This is what He's saying over and over and over. And now He is saying, *I am the one that will quench your thirst.* Or, better yet, *I am better than Jacob's well.*

Verse 11: "The woman said to him, 'Sir, you have nothing to draw water with, and the well is deep.'" Once again, it goes right over her head. She's not tracking. And yet God is so patient with His people. Then it starts to click in, and she asks this question. *"So, where do I get that living water? Are you greater than our father Jacob? He gave us the well and drank from it himself, as did his sons and livestock"* (4:11–12).

What's very interesting is that Jesus happens to meet her at Jacob's well, because the parallels between her life and the life of Jacob are undeniable. You see, Jacob was on the run from God for basically his entire life. In fact, Jacob's name means "heel grabber or deceiver," and the reason that he was named that is he had a twin brother. His twin brother was named Esau, and in the Old Testament they would name you what you are, or what you were going to be, and so the first kid comes out of the womb and they name him Esau, which means "hairy." And then the Bible says that the second kid, Jacob, was grabbing onto his heel, as if he was trying to get out first, so he could get the blessing of the firstborn. Heel grabber, or deceitful one, or trickster is what "Jacob" means.

And then he lives up to that name. He tricks his brother into selling his birthright, and tricks his dying father so he can receive the father's blessing. And so when Esau gets mad, Jacob goes on the run. And he runs from his home, he runs from his family, he runs from his brother, and ultimately he's running from the Lord. And one night he lies down in a place called Paddan Aram. He puts a rock on the ground, he lies on the rock, and God gives him a dream, and he sees the stairway of heaven. And then, he's still on the run, and then later God calls him back to that place. And when he gets back to that place, Jesus walks him down and, in my opinion, he wrestles with the pre-incarnated Christ. The Bible says, *I have come face to face with God and I did not die* (Genesis 32:30). But because he didn't quit, Jesus dislocates his hip, and for the rest of his life he never walked the same again. He was run over by the Grace Train. But before He leaves, He changes his name from Jacob, "deceitful one," to Israel, "one who wrestles with God."

Judging by the conversation and the time they meet, this woman has been running away from God for maybe her entire life. But Jesus doesn't care. He chose this time. He chose this place. He rerouted His life to meet with her. Face-to-face with her. And like He did with Jacob, He's going to wrestle her in this conversation, and when He's finished, she's going to walk away and never be the same. So she says to Him, "Are you greater than our father Jacob?" (4:12).

Verses 13–14: "Jesus said to her, 'Everyone who drinks of this water will be thirsty again, but whoever drinks of the water that I will give him will never be thirsty again. The water that I will give him will become in him a spring of water welling up to eternal life.'"

What He is saying is this: If you continuously go after the temporary things of this world, you will always be dissatisfied, but He offers satisfaction. Jesus is saying, *You keep coming back to the same temporary wells, but I am offering you satisfaction and security that the temporary things of this world cannot offer.* And before we look too harshly at her, we would do well to realize that every single one of us has a tendency to do this. This world only offers three wells: the pride of life, lust of the flesh, lust of the eyes. That's it. In my church, we have a lot of names for these. One of their names is the merry-go-round of normality. This world spends billions of dollars a day to get you to take your seat on the little hobby horse on the merry-go-round of normality and just shut up and play your role.

To just wake up, eat something, go to work, sell something, come home, eat something, drive something, watch something, go to sleep, again and again and again. And the biggest prayer of your life is *thank God it's Friday.* Here's the truth—if you're only living for the weekend, you're not doing this thing right. God has created you for so much more.

At first it's fun. You climb on that wooden horse and think, "Oh look, I've got the shiny one with the unicorn horn." But do ten years on the merry-go-round of normality, which only leads to the cul-de-sac of stupidity, and you realize it ain't that merry. Sooner or later, you'll think, "Is this it?" "Is this all?" And Jesus is saying, "No, darling, this ain't it.

This will continuously leave you thirsty, but I will quench your thirst forever and ever and ever."

For some of us it's the pride of life. That's our go-to. We're just trying to win the approval of people. If I could just get her to like me, or him to call me back. If I could get enough likes and posts. Maybe even a blue check. If I can just get enough people to think highly of me, then I would be fully and finally satisfied. Trust me, the applause of man will never be enough. You'll just keep coming back dissatisfied.

Some of us are sucked in by the lust of the eyes. We see some stuff and we think, "I know what I need, I need me some stuff. If I could just get me some more stuff then I'd be fully and finally satisfied." This is the cul-de-sac of stupidity. Not because stuff is stupid, but because we are stupid. Shiny things never satisfy. The first lap around you think, "If I could just get a new house, move into that neighborhood, get some new pants, get that kind of car, another half bath," whatever the thing is, we think, "then I'll be satisfied." The problem is that when we get the thing, it doesn't satisfy, and we think, "I have an idea. I'll get another thing. A different thing. I just need newer stuff." Which is us taking another lap in the cul-de-sac. It happens to every single one of us.

The third well is the lust of the flesh. Meaning I want to feel a certain way. It could be anything from pornography to popcorn and everything in between. It could be a relationship with somebody you think is going to fulfill you. Going to complete you. Or you think you're going to find fulfillment and satisfaction at the end of a bottle. Or drugs. Or you could pour yourself out in the gym trying to sculpt the perfect body. You begin to think, "If I could just hit my ideal weight, then I'd be happy." Have you met people at their ideal weight? They ain't happy. They want your cheesecake, and you want their abs. Truth is, you can't have both. To the over-forty crowd, can I get a witness?

Jesus is saying, *"You're seeking satisfaction and security in the things of this world and they'll just never provide it."* Part of the reason He's telling us this is because your insatiable soul can only be satisfied with an everlasting God. Because you were created as an image-bearer of Him. And only He satisfies. Why do we continuously go back to the temporary things of this world when we were created for eternity and we have eternity in our hearts that only the eternal God can fill? Jesus is saying, "I have that for you."

When God created the very first man and He breathed into him the Spirit—or *ruach*—of God, and man opened his eyes, he was face-to-face with his Heavenly Father. The first time he breathes in, he knows at the heart level, "This is what I was created for. Communion with Him." This is what He is saying to her. The engine of your soul was created to run on the fuel of a relationship with Jesus Christ. So Jesus says to her, *"This is what I'm offering you."* And the woman says, *"Sir, give me this water so that I will not be thirsty or have to come here to drink… to draw water"* (4:15).

One time when I was in high school I was doing door-to-door evangelism. I know people don't do that anymore, but I did. I had my Lord's Gym shirt on, and I was doing the survey thing for a Fellowship of Christian Athletes camp, and I knocked on this door, and this lady opened the door. I think she was running a little bootleg daycare, because there were kids running everywhere. And she had this look on her face like she was a bit overwhelmed. Didn't quite know what to do or why I was standing at her door. There were diapers and snot and tears everywhere. She opened the door, and I was standing there with my little survey, and I said, "Can I tell you about the peace I found in Jesus Christ?" She looked over her shoulder then back at me, and she said, "Yeah, you can." The look on her face said, "You're offering peace?" And so I said, "Uh-huh, I know Him." Five minutes later I was praying with this lady to receive Christ.

If I'm coaching Jesus in His evangelism tactics, when she says, "Sir, give me this water," it's game on. I'd be coaching, "Jesus, it's time to close the deal. Close your eyes, bow your head, and pray. Admit, believe, confess, receive. Bam! This is it right here. The dotted line. Get her to sign up. Get her into a baptism class. Boom, she's in."

But Jesus is Jesus, and I am not. He doesn't do what I would have done. Jesus says to her, "Go call your husband, and come here." Now, again, if Jesus had invited me to be His evangelism coach, I'd step in with this advice: "Hey, Son of God, come here real quick. Alright, listen… Son of Man, I know You're the second person of the Trinity co-equal with the Father, and all things were made by You, through You, for You, and to You. I get all that and I know that You know the very thoughts she has before she can ever articulate them. But I don't know if you read to the end of the story, bro, she ain't real proud of her marital situation right now. So, why are You bringing that up? Look, we're saved by Grace through faith, so let's just get her in and then we'll walk her through sanctification. But we don't want to miss this moment. They don't come around too often. Let's just get her in a disciple group and surely somebody from her disciple group's going to be like, 'Honey, who are you living with? I've seen your Facebook page,' and then we can talk about that then. Because here's the thing, You're going to mess up the whole deal if you bring this up here. We can deal with all of that later." But Jesus says, "Go call your husband, and come here." The woman answers, "I have no husband." And Jesus says, "You're right in saying 'I have no husband'; for you have had five husbands, and the one you now have is not your husband. What you have said is true" (4:16–18).

Back up a second—Jesus is sitting at the well with this lady talking about living water and she says, *"I'll take some. Where do I get this living water?"* Ultimately, I think Jesus is saying, "Hey listen, I know you want a quick fix and easy satisfaction. Maybe a little easy believism where you pray a prayer and check the box, but that's not what we're talking about." Here's why I think He does this. Because to be partially known is to be unknown, and you cannot be fully loved if you are not fully known. Jesus prompts her to go get that thing that most embarrasses her. The thing that causes her shame. The thing that has driven her to be here, alone, in the middle of the day, to avoid everybody, because she's tired of the whispers and the label. When Jesus tells her to go get that thing, He is telling her, "I am not ashamed of you. And the thing that you are most embarrassed by is the very thing that I will die for and to free you from."

Let me ask you—what are you trying to keep from Jesus? What are you most embarrassed about? Ashamed of? You think He doesn't know about it? Here's the thing, fight the devil in the dark and you're going to get your tail kicked. So drag him and it into the light. Jesus is saying, "Go get that thing and drag it out here into My presence." When you bring it to the light, Jesus fights on your behalf. Because what begins to happen is the enemy lies to you and wants you to think you are defined by your wounds. Your scars. But it's not true. Not true at all. That's a lie from the pit of hell. We are defined not by our scars but by His. Jesus looks down from the cross and the nails tearing the flesh and says, "You are now defined by Mine. By these stripes you are healed."

C.S. Lewis says it this way. In *Mere Christianity,* speaking on behalf of Jesus, he says, "Give me all of you. I don't want so much of your time and so much of your talents and money and so much of your work, I want you, all of you. I have not come to torment or frustrate the natural man or woman, but to kill it. No half measures will do. I don't want only to prune a branch here and a branch there, rather I want the whole tree. Hand it over to me, the whole outfit, all of your desires, all of your wants and wishes and dreams, turn them all over to me. Give yourself to me and I will make you a new self in my image. Give me yourself and in exchange I will give you myself. My will shall become your will, my heart shall become your heart."

Jesus is pointing out that the Gospel is not just fire insurance. The offer is freedom. Freedom in this life. Freedom in the next. While the Gospel does keep us out of hell when we die, it also allows us to walk in the freedom that Christ has purchased for us on the cross. And so He says, *"Go get your husband. Go get the sin that has defined you. Go get the thing that gives rise to the whispers. Go get the thing that embarrasses you the most."*

Here's the lesson for us—the fake us is doing just fine. We are all really good at faking it. Wearing masks that disguise the real us. But

Jesus came for the real you and He invites you to bring it all to Him. All your baggage, all your sin, all the stuff you're ashamed of. Right up to the foot of His cross. And I know what you're saying: "Oh, oh, Pastor, no, we are not supposed to talk about that around other people. You know what they'll think of me."

The enemy wants you to believe that when Jesus died on the cross that He died for some sins, just not that one. That one is too far. To which Jesus shakes His head. "Nope. Go get that and bring it here to Me. Go get your affair. Your porn addiction. Your eating disorder. Your depression. Your substance abuse. Your drinking too much. Your drinking alone and trying to hide it." Go get the thing that the enemy wants to keep you broken under, and Jesus says, "Bring it to Me." What is the thing in your life that you have tried to hide from Jesus? Which is silly if you stop and think about it. Because He knows all things.

To each of us, Jesus says, "Listen, I already know. And I am not ashamed of you. I put shame to death at the cross when I said, 'It is finished.'"

Jesus looks at her and says, *"Go get your husband,"* and the woman says, *"Sir, I perceive that you're a prophet"* (4:19). You think? He just read her mail right there. When the Spirit of God starts noodling around in deep-down places, we all want to deflect. Which she does with a theological question. Happens all the time. She says, *"Alright, hold on a minute. Can we talk about something that has nothing to do with me? Let's talk about that for a while."* "Our fathers worshiped on this mountain, but you say that in Jerusalem is the place where people ought to worship" (4:20).

Often when I talk to people about Jesus and it starts to get real and He starts to deal with the real wounds, they deflect. "Whoa, whoa, let's talk about something else." One time, coming back from training pastors in East Africa, we connected through Amsterdam, and this girl sat next to me. Didn't take long to figure out she was in Amsterdam doing some shady stuff.

So this is how I roll on an airplane. Here's my evangelism strategy. On average, I preach every Thursday and Sunday. This means every two or three days I've got to prepare a sermon. If I've got a long flight, I can write multiple sermons. So, I sit down, pop out the Bible, and look at the person next to me. If they don't want to talk about it, I lean into my Calvinism and think, "Nope, it's not their time and so God bless them." And I get to work. But if they want to talk, or they open a door—"Sir, I perceive you are a prophet"—then I'm all in. All right, all right, all right. So on this flight I got my Bible out and she said, "You actually believe that?"

"Yup, I do. You wanna talk?"

She had no place to start, so I started with creation. I told her that she was created as an image-bearer of God and that her very first parents breathed the breath of life into her and the reason there's nothing in this world that could satisfy is because only the eternal God can satisfy. And as I was talking, you could tell the Gospel was doing what the Gospel does. It started working. She started to get real teary, and then she realized this was going to cost her whole life. The offer is free, but the condition is surrender. So here came the deflection. She started asking about dinosaurs and about a man alone on an island who never heard the Gospel. And then she started talking about why the church hates LGBTQ people. So I said, "Okay, first of all, God loves everybody, and so should the church. I know we don't, but we should. We're working on it. But let's cover something. Are you LGBTQ?" "Nope." "Okay. Are you a paleontologist?" "No. I am not." "Are you a sociologist looking for the lone man on the island?" "I am not." "Okay, so how about we talk about what we're just talking about right here."

This is what this Samaritan lady is doing. "Hey, can we talk about mountains?" And Jesus is like, "Or, why don't we just keep talking about this living water that I'm offering? Because in reality what's happening in your life, darling, is you're not just coming to this well, but you're going from man to man to man to man looking for satisfaction and security and I am the only

Man that will be able to bring that to you. Can we talk about that?" Jesus immediately zeroes in and brings it right home. "Woman, believe me, the hour is coming when neither on this mountain nor in Jerusalem will you worship the Father. You worship what you do not know; we worship what we know, for salvation is from the Jews" (4:21–22). Jesus is full of Grace and truth and He gives her both. *You're wrong, I'm right. Now, let's get back to it. The hour is coming and is now here when true worshippers will worship the Father in spirit and in truth, for the Father is seeking such people to worship Him.*" Look what He says. The Father's not seeking worship, He's seeking worshippers. He's not looking for a concert, He's seeking a congregation of sons and daughters. He's not looking for a performance, He's looking for a movement of people that would be a house of prayer.

Here's what He's saying: "I came on a rescue mission for you. Yes, for you. It's why I'm sitting here while everyone around us is whispering, 'Why are You talking to her?' And I don't care what they say. I walked through all of that to get to you." The Father is looking for people who will worship Him in spirit and in truth—with your whole heart and enthusiastically. And some of you reading this need to worship God in spirit. You need to take your hands out of your pockets, and move your mouths when we do the singing part. When your team scores, you go nuts and dance around, and yet when Jesus scores a victory for all eternity, you stand with your hands shoved into your pockets. Does that make any sense?

We have a young man named Cade who sits front row in our church. Cade has special needs, and he is also a worship leader for us. Cade likes to jump up and spin around. He dances with delight, and I love it. He is uninhibited. And when he does, he helps lead us in worship. And every time he does, he looks to his dad for his approval, and his dad puts his hand on his shoulder and gives him a fist bump. That's worship. And it's beautiful.

When we worship, we look to our Dad for approval, and through the blood of Christ, He puts His hand on our shoulder and gives us a little fist bump. That's worshipping in spirit and truth. That doesn't mean you just do crazy for crazy's sake. We are rooted in the Scriptures because you can't rightly love God without right thoughts about God. Jesus is saying, "God isn't looking for mountains. He moved mountains so that I could come here and be face-to-face with you. He's looking for you to worship Him that way." He goes on to say, "God is spirit, and those who worship him must worship in spirit and truth." And the woman said to him, "I know that Messiah is coming (he who is called Christ). When he comes, he will tell us all things."

I wish you knew Hebrew so that you could understand the power of this next line. It would blow your dentures out. Seven times in the Gospel of John, Jesus makes "I am" statements. Seven is the number of completion, and "I am" is the covenant name of God. He says things like, "I am the bread of life." "I am the way, and the truth, and the life." "I am the resurrection and the life." "I am the good shepherd." The reason the "I am" statements are such a big deal started way back in Exodus chapter 3, and because Exodus is the second book of the Bible, we can be pretty confident that the Samaritan woman was well acquainted with God's covenantal name.

Moses encounters God through a burning bush and God says, *"Go tell Pharaoh to let my people go."* And Moses says, *"If they ask who sent me, who shall I say sent me?"* And God says, *"You tell them that my name is I Am That I Am"* (Exodus 3:10–14). This is how we translate it in English, or I Be What I Be. Literally in Hebrew it's called the Tetragram, it's just four letters. In English we pronounce it "Yahweh." In Hebrew, when you say it, it's supposed to sound like inhaling and exhaling. *Yah-weh.* In short, the God of the universe is saying, "When I'm in a covenant with you, I am as close to you as your next breath."

The woman says to Jesus, *I know the Messiah, the Christ is coming* (4:25). By the way, if you're new to Bible study, Christ is not Jesus's last name, it's His title. He is the anointed one. He is the Lamb of God who comes to take away the sin of the entire world. He is the substitutionary atoning sacrificial Son. He is the serpent crusher that the Old Testament talks about. He is the suffering servant. Jesus looks at her and says, *"The great I Am is here to pursue you"* (4:26).

As Jesus finishes speaking, the disciples return and marvel that He's talking with this woman because He's breaking down all the barriers. But no one challenges or questions Him. And so the woman left her water jar and went away into town and said to the people, "Come, see a man who told me all that I ever did. Can this be the Christ?" (4:29).

Notice what Jesus does in this interaction. Jesus reaches in, shines a light on the thing she's most ashamed of, and then removes the shame and condemnation. How do we know? She runs into town and declares, *"I met a man who knows everything I ever did."* And they're thinking, *"We all know what you did. You should be ashamed of it."* And she declares, *"Nope, that's not how this works."* We all know John 3:16: *For God so loved the world He gave His only begotten Son*, but remember, it keeps going to 3:17: *For God did not send His Son into the world to condemn the world, but to save us through Him.*

"They went out of the town and were coming to him" (4:30). Think about it. The first evangelist to the Gentiles is a woman with a shameful past. Which makes her a perfect disciple. God takes this woman's life, which is a mess, and uses her mess to share His message of God's redeeming love. And so He keeps going. "Meanwhile the disciples were urging him, saying, 'Rabbi, eat.' But he said to them, 'I have food to eat that you don't know about'" (4:31–32), and the disciples missed it. So the disciples said to one another, *"Anybody give him something to eat? Has anyone brought him something to eat?"* And Jesus said to them, "My food is to do the will of him who sent me and to accomplish his work" (4:33–34).

The most satisfying thing you can do is just do what He says. And you have no idea what hangs in the balance. Just be obedient and do what He tells you to do. Jesus continues, "Do you not say, 'There are yet four months, and then comes the harvest'? Look, I tell you, lift up your eyes, and see that the fields are white for harvest. Already the one who reaps is receiving wages and gathering fruit for eternal life, so that sower and reaper may rejoice together. For here the saying holds true, 'One sows and another reaps.' I sent you to reap that for which you did not labor. Others have labored, and you have entered into the labor" (4:35–38).

In other words, there's just one team, and it's all Team Jesus. You have no idea the part you might play in changing somebody's forever if you'll just be faithful to do what He's told you to do. Verse 39: "Many Samaritans from that town believed in him because of the woman's testimony." What was her testimony? *"He told me all that I ever did."* She just told her story. *"This is what I did. This is what He did."* "So when the Samaritans came to him, they asked him to stay with them, and he stayed there two days. And many more believed because of his word. They said to the woman, 'It is no longer because of what you said that we believe, for we have heard for ourselves, and we know that this is indeed the Savior of the world'" (4:40–42).

I would ask you—who needs to hear your story? Some of you respond with, "Yeah, but mine's a mess." Maybe. Welcome to planet Earth. We're all a mess. God is a master at taking the mess and sharing His message. It's what He does here. "After the two days he departed for Galilee. (For Jesus himself had testified that a prophet has no honor in his own hometown.) So when he came to Galilee, the Galileans welcomed him, having seen all that he had done in Jerusalem at the feast. For they too had gone to the feast" (4:43–45).

Here's the deal. This woman is sitting at this well and she encounters Jesus Christ. We don't get a lot of info on how she got there. We do know she's had five failed marriages and now she's living with a guy who is not her husband, and we don't know if she's been abused or we don't know if she's an adulterer, but either way there's some serious sin going on in here. And I can guarantee you this, her plan A was not to be at this well at noon for the rest of her life to avoid all the people. But

I can also guarantee you this, that what the enemy intended for evil, God intended for good. And the Father set up a divine appointment with His Son to meet her there and to lean in and to say, *"Go get your husband, because the things that you have done are no longer going to define you, but what I'm going to do on your behalf at the cross, that's what's going to define you."*

The enemy wants you to believe that your wounds and your scars define you. Your bad choices. But Jesus turns that on its head. He says, *"My scars and my wounds tell you who you are."* Here's the point: Fake you is doing just fine. Every one of us is really good at masking our pain. Our mess. Our lives can be falling apart, but when we walk into church or the gas station, and bump into somebody we know, we lie our faces off. We smile and tell them, "It's good, bro." Or worse yet, the church response, "I'm just blessed and highly favored." No. I'm pretty sure you're not. It seems like your life's falling apart.

Here's the truth—all of us are more wicked than we ever imagined and more loved than we could ever perceive. This is the inconceivable Grace that pours from the cross. All of the things that we're ashamed of, and all the things that we did and are done to us, try to label us and condemn us. Sometimes the whispers are all we can hear, but only Jesus gets to tell us who we are. And despite all the shame we wrap ourselves in, Jesus says, "It is finished" (John 19:30). "There is therefore now no condemnation for those who are in Christ Jesus" (Romans 8:1).

Jesus says to the woman, *"I know your past. I know everything. Everything that you're trying to keep hidden. But let's do this—why don't you give it to Me and let Me take it to the cross. I'm going to die for those very things so you don't have to. Give Me the things that bring death, and I'll give you My life. Deal?"*

Maybe it's that abortion. Maybe the enemy is telling you that you can never be forgiven. But that's a lie from the pit of hell. When Jesus died on the cross for your sin, for anybody who would believe, when He says, "It is finished," it counts for every sin. And for some of you it's your porn addiction. And if you're wondering why I'm bringing that up after spending the last two chapters talking about sexual sin, it's because it's a stronghold for men (and rising among women) and sometimes they need a two-by-four to the head to bring it into the light. If this is you, the enemy has a grip on you. It's as if there's a power outside of you that is compelling you to do things that you promised you wouldn't do anymore.

Or maybe it's that substance abuse, and you've got it hidden. Pretty well covered. You hide drinks. Stash them away in different places. Or maybe it's that affair. Maybe it's the thing that busted up your marriage. Maybe it's that eating disorder. Those times when you excuse yourself to stick your finger down your throat. Maybe it's that depression. Here's the crazy thing about depression for the Christian. Most of us don't have a category for it because we think we're supposed to be immune from depression. You read Paul's letter to the Philippians from prison and he says, "Rejoice in the Lord always; again I will say, rejoice" (Philippians 4:4). Or he says, *I have learned the secret of being content in every situation* (Philippians 4:12), and you're anything but content. Compared to the rest of this world, you tell yourself you should be the happiest person on the planet. You've got this house and cars and jobs and people who love you and all of that, but every morning you can't make happy turn on. You feel like, what's wrong with me? And Jesus says, *"Go get that and bring it here to Me."*

Or maybe it's that image. All your girlfriends think you have it all together. They do. They think you're a great mom and yet at the house you scream and yell things at your kids and you're so ashamed of what comes out of your mouth. Bring that failing business and bring that failing marriage and bring that insecurity and bring that self-harm and bring that hopelessness and bring that loneliness and bring that doubt because God didn't answer the prayer the way you thought He should have answered the prayer. Jesus says, *"Go get that and you bring it here to Me. You drag it out of the darkness and you drag it here into the light."*

Why? In Matthew 11 Jesus gives this invitation. He says, "Come to me, all who labor and are heavy laden" (Matthew 11:28). Let me tell you what's a real heavy burden—carrying around sin and shame that you don't need to be carrying around anymore. It'll wear you out. Jesus says, *"Bring it to Me, and I will give you rest. Take My yoke upon you and learn from Me, for I am gentle and lowly in heart, and you will find rest for your soul."* You cannot harness up the light yoke of Jesus when you're carrying around the yoke of the slavery of shame in your life. To all of that, Jesus says, *"So, go get it and bring it here to Me."* Peter says, "Casting all your anxieties on him, because he cares for you" (1 Peter 5:7). But don't cast it like a rod and reel, where you throw it out there and then reel it back up to tote all week. He means throw it away from you with everything you have.

How do you do this? You say, "Jesus, at the foot of Your cross, I need You to take this, because I can't tote it anymore." And He says, "I died that you don't have to. Here, let Me have it. Your sin, your shame, your guilt, all of it. Just drop it right here."

Here's how I want to end this chapter, and it's dangerous. If you can get on your knees, it'd be a good idea. It shows submission. Surrender. Now, open your closet door and click on the light and tell Jesus, "This is what I don't want You to know about me. This is my sin. This is what I'm ashamed of."

And tell Him all of it. Remember, you can't tell Him anything He doesn't already know. And you're not telling Him for His benefit. You're telling Him for yours. The telling will begin to set you free.

Pray with Me

Our good and gracious Heavenly Father, God, I thank You and I praise You that You invite us just as we are to come to You. And I thank You that You love us far too much to leave us that way. And

Lord, I pray that like Jacob walked away and he walked differently after wrestling You face-to-face, and like this woman walks away from this encounter with You at the well and she was free of condemnation, Lord, I pray that every single person that would believe in You today, God, would walk away from this wrestling match with You and they would be free of shame and free of condemnation, because therefore now there is no condemnation for those who are in Christ Jesus. It is for freedom that You have set us free. May we walk in that freedom. May we walk in a manner worthy of the Gospel of Jesus Christ. May the cross be the reminder that we have all been outed. There is no reason to hide. Jesus knows it all and chose to give His life for our ransom in spite of our past and even current struggles. Lord, allow us to walk in the kind of freedom that a son or daughter walks in.

God, I pray against the whispers of that lying enemy right now. He's got no place in this house, he's got no place in the mind of the believer. And Lord, I pray that You would shake us up, You'd shake up our religion, You'd shake up our tradition, You'd break down every single wall to come and get Your children to worship You in spirit and in truth. And so, Lord, I pray for freedom, I pray where the Spirit of the Lord is there will be freedom. We pray it in Jesus's name. Amen.

Chapter 7

GRACE FORGIVES

*Grace rolls away stones and raises dead
people to life.*

We know that Jesus is the Sovereign, Savior, King of the cosmos, but in order for us to know Him, know the Father, and know what we are being saved from and saved to, Jesus would teach and preach. And when He did, He told stories. Parables. The word "parable" comes from two Greek words that mean to cast alongside of. This means Jesus would take a complex concept, like the Kingdom of God and forgiveness, and He would cast that alongside things that people could understand. Just common everyday stories. Like fishing or farming. That kind of thing.

In Matthew 18, Jesus tells a parable about forgiveness, which we all need and need to offer. Much of what I've written thus far has dealt with what you do when you sin. Like repent. This chapter deals with what you do when somebody sins against you. C.S. Lewis says this about forgiveness: "Everyone thinks forgiveness is a lovely idea until they have something to forgive." Can I get a witness? Have you been sinned against? Our culture wants you to forever stay the victim. The Gospel helps you unlock the secret to living the victorious life of forgiveness.

Whenever I am the one doing the sinning, which is most days of my life, I always want to lean into the Grace of God, but whenever I am sinned against, then I really want to stand on the justice of God and say, "Get him, God." Just being honest. Now, let me warn you, the beginning of this chapter is going to be fun. Second half, not so much. Because when you talk about real forgiveness, very few people actually manage it. So, lean in with me here, and let's ask God to do some soul work in you that could change your life forever. And I'm not talking about the sweet by-and-by or one day when you die. I'm talking about doing some stuff today. Some stuff left undone in your soul because you have not done the Gospel-driven work that God would have you to do. So I dare you to lean in.

With that in mind, go to Matthew chapter 18, which is one of the greatest sermons on what it means to forgive. To help us understand what forgiveness actually is. You see, most of the time, when people think about forgiveness, they think about feelings, and because your feelings haven't changed, you think that you haven't forgiven somebody. We'll see if that's true or not. We pick it up in verse 15. Jesus says this: "If your brother sins against you…" Now, that's not a very big if, is it? I mean, it should just be, "When your brother sins against you…" because let's just be honest. If you're alive on planet Earth and you're around people, they're going to sin against you. Want to know why? Because we're all sinners.

Some of you have been looking for the perfect group. Perfect community. Perfect church. Perfect people who get you. And you have yet to find them. Why? The problem isn't other people. At least not entirely. The common denominator in every group you find yourself in is you.

When somebody sins against you, one of the first questions to ask is, "Is this my brother or not?" In other words, has this person surrendered their life to the lordship of Jesus Christ? I don't know why, but in the South, the church expects a lost world to act like Jesus is their Lord when they never claimed He was their Lord. Lost people act lost. Why? Because they're lost. So, the reality is, if somebody who is not a follower of Jesus sins against you, the primary conversation that you need to be having with them is not about their sin against you, but their sin against the almighty God. And not just about your individual forgiveness of them, but God's ultimate forgiveness of them at the cross. In other words, it's not just a reconciliation conversation between the two of you. It's got to be rooted in their reconciliation with God the Father. Not by what they do, but what Christ has done for them. If the person who sins against you is not a brother, a believer, then the primary conversation you need to have is that of evangelism first. Not forgiveness and reconciliation.

On the flip side, if it is your brother, another Christian, and he or she sins against you, the next question that you have to ask is, did they actually sin against you, or did they just get on your nerves? Because them getting on your nerves is not a sin, as much as we might want it to be.

I looked through the entire book of Proverbs trying to find one proverb about getting on somebody's nerves, and it's just not there, which means it's very, very important to know the Word of God. You've got to know the difference between your own personal preferences and the precepts of God, but when your brother sins against you, here's what Jesus says to do. He says, "Go and tell him his fault, between you and him alone" (18:15).

If you'll just do this, it'll change your life forever. Talk *to* and *with* people instead of *about* them. Gossip is not forgiveness. So, talk with people. Go to them. Don't tweet them. Don't DM them. Don't TikTok them. Don't Facebook them. Go to their face. And sit down. Any conversation that is serious or sensitive should be had face-to-face. Honestly, almost nobody actually does this, and I know this because people come to me for counseling. By the way, I would highly recommend you not come to me for counseling. I'm not a good counselor. A little too direct. If you do come to me, the first thing I'm going to ask you about a problem with another person is: "Have you talked to this person?" I'm astounded at the number of times people reply, "No. I thought I'd tell you, you'd tell God, and God would get them." That is not how this works.

Some of you are spending a lot of time praying about something like this when, and I mean this reverently, you need to quit praying and start going. As in, go to that person and have a conversation. Now, most of the time when I actually do Matthew 18 and go talk face-to-face with somebody, it doesn't go the way I think it will in my imaginary conversations. By the way, if you're wondering who you should talk to, who you need to forgive, just ask yourself who you're having imaginary conversations with. The person that just popped up on the back of your eyelids is the person you need to forgive. When I go to that person and I confront them with whatever it is, I almost always get some information that I didn't have in my imaginary conversation, and I almost always end up going, "Oh, well, I didn't know that," and it changes everything. And so Jesus is saying, *"Sometimes, reconciliation can happen this quickly. So go tell him his fault between you and him alone. And if he listens to you, you've gained your brother."* Verse 16: "But if he does not listen, take one or two others along with you, that every charge may be established by the evidence of two or three witnesses."

This is not like an intervention, and this is not "You all hold him. I'll get him." That is not what this is. This occurs when a mature, faithful Christian, an objective third party, steps in, hears the grievance, and helps point out the blind spots. Not only in your brother, but also in you. Which is also why you need a disciple group. Trusted Christians with whom you have deep, abiding relationships so that, when there is something that you cannot handle on your own, you can go to those folks, and they can help you with this reconciliation. And you need them before you need them. You don't need to wait. Waiting until you need Christian friends to begin developing Christian friends is like beginning your retirement account when you retire. Guess what? You will not have a retirement account. You will have a problem. And if you find yourself in a situation that you need some help resolving and you don't have people to go to, it's because you did not begin to build that bank before you actually needed that bank.

What Jesus is saying here is, *"You get some trusted, mature, objective, third-party folks to come and help you."* Verse 17: "If he refuses to listen to them, tell it to the church." Now, He does not say, "Tell it to the church service." He doesn't mean the weekend thing you attend, okay? It's not like, at the end of the service, you stand up and start pointing out one another's sin. Quite honestly, many churches throughout church history have done that. They've brought people in front of the church service and called out their sins and kicked them out. This is not what it means. He's talking about bringing it to the leadership of the church. He says, *"If he refuses to listen, then tell it to the church."* This means bring some pastors, bring some elders, bring some deacons, bring some folks of spiritual authority who can bring the Word of God into the situation to bring about reconciliation. "And if he refuses to listen even to the church, let him be to you as a Gentile and a tax collector."

Throughout church history, a lot of people have taken this to mean "If you sin and you don't repent, then we're kicking you out of our church," and they have done that. Hear my response to that: Jesus is kinda Jesus-juking us with this. How did Jesus treat the Gentiles and tax collectors? He loved them. He rolled out the red carpet for them. He went to the cross and died for their sins. This is how you treat the unrepentant Christian. Now, do you put them in leadership? No. Are they elders? No, but do you roll out the red carpet and offer them the same Gospel that Christ on the cross offers you? Yes. Yes. And yes.

And then in verse 18, He gives a little commentary. He says, "Truly, I say to you, whatever you bind on earth shall be bound in heaven, and whatever you loose on earth shall be loosed in heaven." This is a really, really big deal. In other words, your earthly relationships have an eternal impact. Remember the great commandment is to love God and to love one another or to love people. Then He goes on to say two of the most misquoted verses, or really quoted-out-of-context verses, in the whole Bible. He says, "Again I say to you, if two of you agree on earth about anything they ask, it will be done for them by my Father in heaven" (Matthew 18:19). Now, a lot of prosperity guys like to quote that verse to justify praying for cash, money, and prizes. But Jesus is not talking about a Cadillac here. He's praying for a reconciled relationship.

And then the next one: "For where two or three are gathered in my name, there am I among them" (Matthew 18:20). This is not a worship verse. This is a verse about reconciliation. Here's what He is saying: Our horizontal relationships are so important to God that any time two people, with Jesus in the middle, get together, to give and offer forgiveness in the name of God, no matter how broken and no matter how damaged that relationship is, God can and does get involved in a supernatural way. That means there is not one relationship that could be so fractured by sin that the Grace poured out at the cross could not put that thing back together. In other words, if the tomb is empty, then anything is possible, even reconciliation. Amen?

Verse 21: Peter speaks up. Why? Because anytime there's dead air, Peter is going to open his mouth. And Peter comes up and says to Jesus, "Lord, how often will my brother sin against me, and I forgive him? As many as seven times?"

What you've got to understand here is Peter is trying to show off. He's trying to display his level of maturity. *"I am the greatest disciple of all. Lord, people sin against me often, as You probably know, and how many times should I forgive them? Up to seven times? Because that feels awfully generous on my part."* He is trying to be Super-Christian with a big "F" on his chest for "faith" and his cape just fluttering in the wind.

Here's why I say this. Do you know what the standard in the Old Testament is for forgiveness? Do you know how many times you're supposed to forgive? According to the Old Testament? According to the law? Zero. Forgiveness is not an Old Testament value. The Old Covenant demanded justice. You get what you deserve. Eye for eye. Tooth for tooth. Death for death. But then Jesus starts talking about forgiveness, and Peter asks: *"What about seven times?"* Jesus's reply probably surprised Peter. A lot. Verse 22: "I do not say to you seven times, but seventy-seven times." The ESV translates it "seventy-seven" times but literally, in Greek, it's "seventy and seven." You'd have to know Greek to understand this, but what Jesus is doing here is really hyperbole. The language we would use is "a bazillion." It's not even a real number. It's the number of completion times the number of completion with a zero on the end of it. To infinity and beyond. That's what he's saying.

Here's how we know it's not seventy-seven, and here's how we know it's not seventy times seven, 490. Husbands, if Jesus really meant 490 times is the limit on which we forgive one another, then when you got married, about seven months into your marriage, your wife would come to you and say, "Baby, uh, I know the Bible says, 'Love keeps no record of wrongs,' but you're on number 488. So, you got two more, and then it's over." So we know it's not that.

Every time I think about this, it reminds me of college. I was training these two guys in the gym who were dental students from Iraq. (At one point in my life, I spent way too much time in the gym.) They wanted to meet American girls, and they thought if they worked out and got muscles, they could meet American girls. Add to this the fact that they had money and I did not, and I knew how to work out and they did not. Turned into a great partnership. Somewhere in there I gave them a Bible and they gave me a Quran, and we tried to convert one another between sets. One day, I was talking to them about their nutrition: "Boys, you all got to eat some protein. We're talking chicken. Steak. Eggs. As many as you can." I said this on a Friday. They responded, "How many eggs?" I shrugged. "I don't...Man, eat, like, a hundred eggs. Okay?"

In my head, I'm thinking seven, but maybe this exposes the difference between Dillon, South Carolina, and Iraq, because they took it literally. On Monday, they came to me in the gym. Bloated—looking like they're each carrying a basketball in their stomach. They can barely move. I said, "Whoa! For the sake of Pete, how many did you eat?"

"One hundred."

"What? Why?"

"You told us to. To build muscle."

"Bro...I didn't mean actually eat a hundred eggs. Oh, man. Yep. You're never going to meet an American girl."

In other words, Jesus is saying to Peter, *"How many times have I*

forgiven you?" And Peter responds, *"Well, let me count 'em up. One, two…*
A lot," and then Jesus tells a story.

Now, what is brilliant about this story is this story is going to be about
finances, but He's not talking about finances. Part of the reason I think
He talks about finances is to keep everybody's attention, but, remember,
the whole time, this story about finances is not about finances. It is about
forgiveness, and in it Jesus is destroying the many misperceptions about
forgiveness. He is helping us think about forgiveness in a way that we
can get our mind around so that we can actually make the decision to
forgive instead of being ruled by our feelings.

Verse 23: Story time. "Therefore the kingdom of heaven may be compared to a king who wished to settle accounts." Underline that. "Settle
accounts." Apparently, forgiveness is like settling accounts with his servants.
Verse 24: "When he began to settle, one was brought to him who owed
him ten thousand talents." Underline the words "owed him." And when He
says, "ten thousand talents," everybody listening to this story immediately
realizes this is just a story. This can't be an actual event because a talent is
twenty years' wages. So, this brother owes him ten thousand times twenty
years' wages. Today, this would be a trillion dollars. I added it up. If you
take the Duval County median income, it's, no joke, a trillion dollars. In
fact, when Jesus gives this story in the first century, that was more than
the GDP of Israel. So, no individual human could actually own that much
money, and it would take this brother two hundred thousand years to make
this much money. So, the moment everybody hears this, their mindset is,
"Okay, this is just a story," because there's no way any one person could
have this much debt. So, he owes him ten thousand talents.

Verse 25: "And since he could not pay, his master ordered him to be
sold, with his wife and children and all that he had, and payment to be
made." Remember, Jesus is talking about forgiveness. What He is saying
is, *"When somebody sins against you, they have created a debt–debtor rela-*
tionship, and they owe you something, and in order for you guys to be square,
they have to pay you back." When you are sinned against, a debt–debtor

relationship is created. And in order for the balance to be returned to zero, the account must be "settled." We even use these words in our English language. If somebody does you wrong, you'll say, "I think you owe me an apology."

Verse 26: "So the servant fell on his knees, imploring him, 'Have patience with me, and I will pay you everything...'" To which we respond, "No, you won't. You can't. You'd have to work two hundred thousand years in a row to pay this guy back. It's impossible for you to pay him back," but the servant still says, "Have patience with me, and I will pay you everything."

Verses 27–28: "And out of pity for him, the master of that servant released him," and here it goes, underline this, "and forgave him the debt. But when that same servant went out, he found one of his fellow servants who owed him a hundred denarii." Which is about ten grand. About four months' wages. It's still a ton of money, but the brother has the ability to pay him back. "And seizing him, he began to choke him, saying, 'Pay what you owe.'" Verse 29: "His fellow servant fell down and pleaded with him, 'Have patience with me.'" Now, pay attention: he uses the same words that the first guy used. "Have patience with me, and I will pay you." Verse 30: "He refused and went and put him in prison until he should pay the debt," which means he'd never be able to pay his debt, because they don't pay you a lot when you're in prison.

Verse 31: "When his fellow servants saw what had taken place, they were greatly distressed." It makes no sense to them from the outside looking in. "How could this be? Bro, you just got forgiven. A trillion dollars. And now this guy owes you ten thousand dollars and you throw him in prison? We thought that, given what you just experienced, when you saw that guy in the street who owed you money, and he told you, 'Man, I'm so sorry. I'm working on paying you back,' we thought for sure you would respond, 'You know what? Don't worry about it. I have recently been forgiven a debt I could not repay in ten thousand lifetimes, so you don't have to repay me the debt that you owe me.'" The servants are thinking that because the first debtor had been forgiven so much, he would easily extend Grace toward the second debtor. Not so.

"And they went and reported to their master all that had taken place. Then his master summoned him and said to him, 'You wicked servant! I forgave you all that debt'" (18:31–32). Now, that is the definition of forgiveness: "I forgave you all that debt." "'Should not you have had mercy on your fellow servant, as I had mercy on you?' And in anger his master delivered him to the jailers…" (18:32–33). In Greek, the word translated here "jailer" is tormentor or torture. "…Until he should pay all his debt." End of story. And here's Jesus's one-line commentary on forgiveness. Remember, He's answering the question that Peter asked. *How many times am I supposed to forgive?*

Verse 35: A very scary verse. And do not tone down Jesus's words. "So also my heavenly Father will do to every one of you, if you do not forgive your brother from your heart." To be clear, Jesus is not saying that if I forgive, then I open myself up to be forgiven by God. This would then mean that by your good work, you can save yourself. You can't. You cannot earn your salvation. He's saying it the other way around. He's not saying that forgiveness earns forgiveness from God. He's saying that our forgiveness is evidence that we have been forgiven by God. Once we are, we do. Forgiven people forgive people. It's just the way it works.

Here's the point. Forgiveness is not a feeling. Forgiveness is the willful decision to cancel someone's debt against you because, at the cross, Jesus canceled our debt. Or the redneck way I would say it from Dillon, South Carolina, is, "If you ain't given it, maybe you ain't got it." That's what Jesus is saying. Scary verse. How in the world could God look at you and cancel all of your debt, and then we look at someone who's sinned against us and not forgive them?

It's usually at this point where, in your mind, if you're being honest with yourself, you're thinking, "Yeah, but listen, man, that's easy to say, but you don't know what happened to me. You don't know what he did to me. You don't know what she did to me. You don't know how much money it was. You don't know the number of times they betrayed me. Abused me. Took advantage of me. Over and over and over."

You're right. I don't. I get it. I'm not suggesting the sin against you is not a big deal. It's a really big deal. The sin against you is such a big deal, Jesus had to die for it. But here's the truth: Any Christ follower who does not offer forgiveness has taken their eyes off the cross. Anybody who withholds forgiveness has Gospel amnesia about the forgiveness they have received. Unforgiveness is keeping you from the abundant life that God has called you into.

When we hold on to forgiveness and we don't release that forgiveness and we don't forgive those who have sinned against us, it always turns into bitterness, which goes into resentment, which begins to build walls against people who want to love you. Then, you can't give and receive love like God intended you to, and before you know it, you live a life full of fear, and fear is the bully that keeps you in the corner, that will not allow you to walk in faith that God has called you to walk into.

Forgiveness is hard work. It's a process. It's a willful decision to cancel someone's debt against you. It's not a haphazard comment where you flippantly say: "You know what? I forgive him. Now, don't ever mention their name around me again because that stirs something up in me..." If you're still stirred up, I question if you've really forgiven them. You might have, but you need to check yourself before you wreck yourself. Which is what unforgiveness does. It wrecks us. It's the poison we drink thinking it'll kill somebody else.

If you have the guts to follow through and actually forgive somebody, I promise you the enemy is going to stir up all kinds of emotions in you. You know why? Because if the enemy can get you to disbelieve your forgiveness on the horizontal level, it'll be the way that he tries to dismantle your understanding of your Gospel forgiveness on a vertical level. In other words, you'll begin to doubt how in the world the forgiveness thing works, and forgiveness is at the heart of the Gospel. If you begin to say, "I can't even forgive this person of one sin. How in the world can the almighty God forgive me of all of my sins?" Amen? Thank God. Thank God Jesus is our Lord, and our feelings are not our lord. You see, forgiveness is a choice, and people say this dumb stuff, like, "Well, you just got to forgive and forget."

No, that is so dumb. No, you need to forgive and remember that you forgave. Because how do you forget something like that? I mean, especially if somebody has really sinned against you. You don't just get over it. You get over the flu, but you don't get over abuse. It just becomes a part of your story, but by the character and nature of God, He can redeem some of the worst things that ever happened to you and redeem them for His own glory and goodness. So you forgive, and you remember—you remember that you have forgiven.

Often, when we forgive we think: "Well, it's not fair. I mean, if I forgive them, they're going to get away with it." But to withhold forgiveness is to try to punish somebody else, when all it does is put us in a prison of our own making. It's like trying to kill the rats in the house by taking rat poison yourself. That's just not how it works. Here's the hard truth—to forgive is to set the prisoner free and then learn that the prisoner was you.

Forgiveness is the decision. Forgiveness is a process. A tough one. Maybe the most difficult thing we ever do as people. Forgiving folks who don't deserve it. Which is exactly what Jesus did and does to every one of us who believe. Few people are willing to go through the Gospel-driven work required to forgive. One of the reasons that people don't forgive is because they believe that if they do, they will have to let go of the excuse that explains their bad behavior. If you actually forgive them, then are you going to have to reevaluate why you drink so much? Or take the medication that wasn't prescribed to you? Or why you continue to say those awful things you say to them and about them? As long as you hold on to that unforgiveness, you feel you are justified abdicating all responsibility for your bad behavior.

Secondly, forgiveness is not necessarily reconciliation. It may lead to that one day, but there are some relationships that you should never get back into. Never go back to. If you have been abused physically, sexually, emotionally, God never calls you to go back into that moment and subject yourself to that again somehow in the name of Grace. Absolutely not. But even still—and I know this is really hard to hear, but that makes it no less true—God calls us to forgive them just as He has forgiven us. Forgiveness is unilateral. Reconciliation takes two parties, and it has to be safe and healthy for both. And I know you think, "But they don't deserve forgiveness." Right, but neither do we. God didn't wait until we got our act together and then forgave us. He extended the forgiveness to us first. The extent that you have been forgiven should be the extent to which you forgive, and if you don't forgive, your only option is bitterness.

What Jesus does in this parable is brilliant. This is why He is the master teacher, the storyteller. In this parable, this story on the finances, He actually gives us the process by which we are to forgive. I dare you to do this on this page. Write it at the bottom. Identify who has hurt you. For some of you, the moment you read "forgiveness" on the first page of this chapter, somebody's name or face came to your mind. They hurt you. They stole from you. They lied to you. They slandered your name. They broke a promise to you. Step one is to identify who hurt you. Honestly, a lot of Christians have a hard time doing this if somebody they love sins against them, but you have to settle accounts.

Then, there's a group of you reading this who, if you're honest, you look in the mirror, and you're thinking, "I don't know, man. Somehow, something's wrong with me. I wake up every day, and the slightest little thing just sends me over the top. I have the shortest fuse. I've got this low-grade frustration everywhere I go, and as I look back on my life, I think the problem is me." Then, you should write "Me" right there. Because you hurt you. You have been your own worst enemy. You've broken promises. You lied. You've stolen. You've burned every bridge of every relationship you've ever had, and now here you are, and the good news of the Gospel is that Jesus forgives all sins. Even the sins you committed against you that you have not forgiven you of. Think about it. What makes you so special that you can't forgive you? Jesus has.

I have added a debt ledger here to help you walk through the process that Jesus lays out. It will be very important for you to walk through the process. If you are like me, you'll be tempted to skip over this part of the book. If your heart is holding on to unforgiveness, then I can't urge you enough to do the work and fill out the debt ledger. This is not an exercise to skip over or quickly skim through. The freedom of your very soul is on the line.

Who sinned against me?	What have they taken from me?	What emotions does this cause in me?

The next thing you need to do is identify what they owe you or what they've taken from you. And then you take it to the next step and say, "And what feelings are associated with their actions against me?" A lot of us downplay this part: "Listen, man, I have repressed that stuff for so long. It's not that big a deal. I've let it go."

To say, "That thing is just not a big deal. Don't worry about it," is to look at the cross of Jesus Christ and say, "You're wasting your time. You didn't need to do that." Who among us would say that? No one. Sin is a really big deal. Including when we sin against ourselves. Because for all of it, Jesus had to die on the cross. And so who hurt you? What do they owe you? What did they take from you? And what kind of feeling was associated with this?

Here's what I mean. Some of you have someone in your life who sinned against you, and if you're honest, and if you could talk to them right now, you would say, "You know what? You owed me safety. You owed me protection. God put you as an authority in my life and you didn't do it." It could be a dad. A teacher. A coach. Or an aunt and uncle. Somehow they leveraged their authority to abuse you—to do things to you that have jacked up your entire life, and you want to tell them, "You owe me my childhood back."

For some of you, it's a business partner. Years ago, you all started together, and you had ideas, writing on napkins, and if you're honest, you were the smart one. He was just there, and then, before you know it, he gets kind of shady, and a couple deals go down. Now, your ideas have turned into cash, and, somehow, he's got the company, and you're not even there anymore, and your heart is screaming, "Bro, you owe me my dream. You stole money. You stole my business."

For some of you, it's your kid. Maybe not your little kid, but maybe your grown kid, and you're feeling, "You owe me. I raised you right. I'm not perfect. Nobody's perfect, but we did the best that we could do. We gave you everything you needed and a whole bunch of what you wanted. We raised you in the church, and, yet, the moment you could, you used us, you abused us, you turned your back on us, and you now make me feel like somewhere between a neglecter and an enabler, and you blame me for everything wrong with you. You break your promises, you use us over and over, and your mama cries herself to sleep every single night over you. Sometimes, when you call, I just wanna hang up." You say, "You owe me."

For some of you, it's your ex. And because you've never forgiven your ex, you can't move on in your next relationship, and it's hosing up all of your relationships because you think, "You know what? You owe me. You promised. You promised in front of God and an entire group of people. You promised that you would never leave me or forsake me, in good times or bad, whether rich or poor, in sickness and in health, and then in one moment, you turned your back on me and us and Him, and now you're somewhere else with someone else, and I feel like you threw my heart in a blender and jacked up my whole world. And not only that, you stole the opportunity for me to tuck in my own kids, and the thought of somebody else doing my job has just ruined me."

Do I need to go on?

Ultimately, sin is an act of rebellion against God, and sin, all sin, must be paid for. God will never look at sin and say, "No big deal. Don't worry about it." Sin is a very big deal to God. This is why God made Him who was without sin to be sin, so that you and I might become the righteousness of God—in Him. You and I carry a debt ledger in the back pocket of our hearts. On it we've scribbled the names and sins of those who have wounded us. I want you to think about that ledger like a legal document that you would take before the court of the Almighty Judge of the universe and flip through the pages. "See, God, they owe me. They have done me wrong." Truth is, you're right. They have. No argument there. You have proof. Proof that you have been sinned against. But here's the thing—because we do have access to the throne of God Almighty, we have a decision to make. We have two choices: We can either cancel the debt, or not. And while you're thinking about that, I want you to remember what kind of throne we approach. The writer of Hebrews said, "Let us then with confidence draw near to the throne of grace, that we may receive mercy and find grace to help in time of need" (Hebrews 4:16). It's a throne of Grace. And we are in need. The wound in our chest is proof.

I am going to highly encourage you to lay that ledger down at the feet of the King and cancel the debt. Tear up the ledger. But you say, "How? That means they just get away with it?" No. You're just giving them up to God to let Him do with them as He would. You're letting Him exact His justice and giving up the right to exact yours.

If you decide not to lay it down, not to tear it up, let me tell you what's going to happen:

It will ruin you forever. You'll never be able to walk in the freedom that Christ purchased for you because it's like a ten-thousand-pound anchor dragging you down, lodged deep down in your soul.

Here it is: Cancel the debt and walk in freedom. Or hold on to it and live in a prison of your own making. Freedom or slavery. Your choice. I mean, if you are going to hold on to it, you might as well blow it up really big. Laminate and frame it. Post it somewhere prominent in your life. I'd suggest your living room or in your office. And point to it often. Tell everyone you know about it. "See, there's Ted. He is the reason that I'm so jacked up. It's not my fault." Sounds crazy, right? Almost as crazy as not forgiving when you have been forgiven of all.

Can I just be honest with you? That person who owes you can't repay you anyway. You can't go back to your childhood and get those years back. You can't go back to your first marriage and get that back. You can't go back to those days and get back what was taken.

But because Jesus canceled all of our debt, we have the ability, through the blood of Jesus, through the power of the Holy Spirit, under the love of God, standing on the authority of the Word, to say, "You know what? You're forgiven. I cancel your debt. I cancel your debt." And so I would encourage you, after you spend the time creating this debt record, if you are going to decide because of the Gospel power in your life to cancel the debt, then cancel it. Do something with it. Tear it up. Throw it away. Burn it.

In my church, we had a girl who had been abused. She wrote a debt ledger that would just crush you, so she built a coffin and put it in it. She dug a hole in her yard and buried it and put a tombstone on it. Here's why this matters: The moment you do that, the enemy is going to bring up all of these feelings to try to convince you that it didn't actually work. The reason she did that was so that anytime the enemy reminded her of what happened in the past, she could take the enemy to the graveyard and point. "Nope. I didn't forgive and forget. I forgave, and I remember. What do I remember? I remember that the debt has been canceled. Those people don't owe me anything anymore because Jesus paid it all."

Another guy in our church wrote an extensive debt ledger, and he carried it around with him for a while, couple of weeks, and then, finally, he got to the point where he was ready to say, "You don't owe me anymore," and he burned it and put the ashes into an urn. And because he's a surfer, he paddled out at the pier and sprinkled out the ashes of his debt ledger so that whenever the enemy tries to bring up all of these feelings, he just paddles out, and he reminds the enemy and he reminds himself that the forgiveness of God is just lavished upon him wave upon wave upon wave.

I dare you. I dare you to identify who hurt you, to identify what they owe you, what was their sin against you, and what feelings are associated with that so that you realize the debt. Write it all down. Every detail if you need to. Then, by and through the power of the Holy Spirit, lay that ledger down at the cross and say out loud, "I forgive you. I cancel the debt. Forever." Give them to God and release them from owing you.

Here's what this means: Years from now God might do a Gospel work in that person, and that person that hurt you so deeply might show up, fall on their knees, and beg your forgiveness, genuinely, and from a pure heart. And if that were ever to happen, because you already forgave them, you could say, "No, no, get up. You don't owe me an apology. You don't owe me anything. I have forgiven you."

The reality, the truth, is this: If you do this, you're going to experience all kinds of emotion. Wave upon wave. Some of you are going to feel like throwing up. Whatever the emotion, bring it to the Lord, and bring it to the Lord, and bring it to the Lord, and remind yourself that forgiveness is a willful decision to cancel the debt. It's a decision of your gut. Over time, not necessarily overnight, your feelings will begin to line up with the decision to forgive. You see, when you bring that thing to the Lord, you bring it with the same kind of intensity that it's stirred up in you.

Do you know why I know that? Because the Holy Spirit of God inspired people like David to write down some crazy prayers in the Bible. Check out Psalm 139. If this wasn't in the Bible and you prayed this in my prayer group, I would be like, "I don't think you can come anymore. That's crazy."

Psalm 139 is a very popular chapter in our church. We pray it a lot. I pray Psalm 139:14 over my daughter every single night: *Dear God, I praise You because I am fearfully and wonderfully made. Your works are wonderful. I know that full well.*

When you get down to verse 17 of this chapter, David says this. "How precious to me are your thoughts, O God! How vast is the sum of them! If I would count them, they are more than the sand. I awake, and I am still with you." Isn't that sweet?

Next verse, "Oh that you would slay the wicked, O God! O men of blood, depart from me! They speak against you with malicious intent; your enemies take your name in vain. Do I not hate those who hate you, O Lord? And do I not loathe those who rise up against you? I hate them with complete hatred; I count them my enemies."

Next verse, "Search me, O God, and know my heart!"

This brother has some issues. But guess what? Me, too.

I think this is why the Lord gives us this parable on what it looks like to forgive. To forgive is not about the feelings associated with it. To forgive is to cancel the record of debt. Why? Because they deserve it? No. In *The Weight of Glory*, C.S. Lewis says, "To be a Christian means to forgive the inexcusable because God has forgiven the inexcusable in you." So, how does that happen? In 1 John, John tells us this: *Oh, what manner of love the Father has lavished upon us that we should be called children of God* (1 John 3:1). Do you know what that word "lavish" means? It means God did not just put enough of His love on you to cover you. He lavished His love. Filled you all the way up. It's oozing out of your ears. And He puts some more in another bucket of love and another bucket of love and another. Like, love's just going anywhere, everywhere.

That word "lavish" is like what my daughter Reagan used to do with the water in the bathtub. She was very tiny. But somehow when I walked into the bathroom after she'd taken a bath, she had lavished the water all over the bathroom. It was like a wet Saint Bernard came in there and just shook off. I would think, "How did it get on the top of the mirror?" It's just everywhere, and God's love and forgiveness for us is heaped upon us and heaped upon us and heaped upon us so that, as we have been forgiven and loved by the almighty God, it spills out over into the people that He places in our lives. You think, "How is that possible?"

Here's how. It's rooted in this knowledge, and this is where the rubber meets the road. If the almighty maker of heaven and earth decides to open my debt ledger, the one I've accumulated over my life, and identify what I owe Him or what I've taken from God, through my rebellion and sin and pride, it would be a very long list. Much longer than I could ever atone for or repay or do anything about. I'm bankrupt. Couldn't pay for my own sin in ten thousand lifetimes. And when God looks at that, He has every right to be angry with me. To take it out on me. To exact justice on me. To eradicate me from the earth.

And don't think for a moment that my sin against Him is not a big deal. It's a huge deal. How huge? Let me point you to dead Jesus hanging on the cross. That's how huge. My sin did that. The wrath of God—which I stirred—was satisfied through the shed blood of His own Son who—because He loves me and lavished His Grace upon me—made payment on my behalf.

Here's the thing—don't miss this—most of this chapter has been focused on sin. Why? Because without a true picture of the ugliness of your own sin, it's difficult to truly understand the infinite nature of the manifold Grace of God. You'll stand at the station and watch the train pass by. But if you know the depth of your own need, if you see your sin clearly, you'll respond when the conductor hollers, "All aboard." Which Jesus does when He says, "Follow me."

This is the freight train of Grace. Paul says this in Colossians 2:13–14: "And you, who were dead in your trespasses and the uncircumcision of your flesh, God made alive together with him, having forgiven us all our trespasses, by canceling the record of debt that stood against us with its legal demands. This he set aside, nailing it to the cross."

So, why do we forgive? We forgive because Christ forgave us. Now, if you're not a Christian, and you have not experienced the forgiveness of God, I don't intend to be mean here, but I don't think that you're very well equipped to forgive other people. You haven't experienced being run over by the Grace Train, so your forgiveness of someone else is really just a pragmatic thing for you. And, just being honest, forgiveness is always better than unforgiveness. If you have not surrendered to the lordship of Jesus Christ and experienced the lavish love of the Father poured out at the cross by His Son, and if you have not experienced the words of Jesus when He pushed up on His nail-pierced feet, and He says, "It is finished," then the Spirit of God does not dwell in you, and I don't really know how you cancel the debt that people owe you. On the flip side, if you have experienced the forgiveness of Christ, I'm not saying it's easy, and it might still be a daily struggle, but I don't know how you can withhold it from other people.

Forgiven people forgive people. It's just what we do.

If there is somebody in your life and you know that you need to cancel the debt, then use the debt ledger. Begin that hard work of filling out the debt ledger. Don't be in a hurry. The Lord never is. When you've finished, you have a very important decision to make. Will you cancel the debt? Reminder: If you are in Christ, all of your debt has already been canceled.

Pray with Me

Our good and gracious Heavenly Father, God, we thank You and we praise You that we don't forgive people because they deserve it, just like we didn't deserve it and You forgave us. Lord, I thank You that forgiveness is not even wrapped up in what we feel about it. God, I pray that, over time, You would line up our feelings with our Lord and the decision to cancel the debt. Holy Spirit, would You do a work in us, that we could never, ever, ever, ever do on our own? And, God, I pray that You would use some of these most painful experiences ever to be a tangible expression of the Gospel of Jesus Christ to men and women that, though they do not deserve to have their debts forgiven, they're going to experience that, and, God, the reason we can do this is not because we heard a teaching or not because we're going to fill out a graph, but the reason we can do this is because Jesus paid it all. Help me be someone that extends forgiveness to the extent that I have been forgiven. I pray this in the good, strong name of Jesus. Amen.

If you need or want to pray with someone, we have folks at our church who'd love to pray with you. Call our Care Team: 904-685-6722.

Chapter 8

GRACE IS SLOW TO ANGER

When you are run over by the Grace Train of Jesus, He changes everything about everything about everything—forever.

If you and I were scheduled to have lunch at noon and you walked in at twelve-thirty saying, "So sorry man, I know I'm late, I just got run over by a train," I'd probably think to myself, "Okay... It's possible." But if that actually happened, truth is you probably wouldn't have to tell me. I would be able to see it. There'd be physical evidence, proof, that a train actually ran you over. Your hair would be messed up. Shirt tail untucked. Might even be a few broken bones. Or maybe an arm or leg missing. The human body cannot compete with the power of a train. At all. In a one-to-one game of chicken, train wins every time. So, if you sat down in the booth, looking like you just walked out of a *GQ* ad, I'd wonder if you were telling me the truth.

The same is true in our walk with Jesus. If we have been run over by the Grace Train, there will be evidence in our life. We will be different. People might not be able to put their finger on it, but there will be a visual difference between the person before the Grace Train incident and the person after the Grace Train incident. Jesus says that saved people act like it. His exact words are "The tree is known by its fruit." The Bible knows nothing of the fruitless Christian. If you were dead in your sins, screaming down the highway to hell, and Jesus in His mercy snatched you out and transferred you from the kingdom of darkness into His Kingdom, you'd look different, sound different, act different.

Look at it this way: If you were walking up to the gallows, staring at the noose, and a man stepped in front of you, put the noose around his own neck, and motioned to the executioner to kick the lever, how often would you tell the story of that man? Sing his praises? Would you ever stop telling people about the one who saved you? Of course not. You'd name your children after him.

When Jesus pours His Grace upon us, we can't help but be different. It's as natural as the law of gravity. Why? Because we're not the people we used to be, and we don't have to do the things we used to do. And one of those things is expressing anger. For those of us who have wrestled with anger, or maybe even used it to our advantage and benefit in our younger years, anger is the antithesis of the Grace of Jesus. It's His Grace that prevents us from experiencing the anger, or wrath, of God. So before we end this book, let's talk about anger. Specifically, let's talk about yours. And mine.

I've heard it said that anger is like the pin on a grenade being pulled. What I want to do in our time together in this chapter, through the Word of God and the power of the Holy Spirit, is ask Him to help us put the pin back in. Simple enough?

Anger's a really big deal. The Bible specifically mentions anger more than two hundred times. Extended periods of anger raise your heart rate and raise your blood pressure. It releases adrenaline, which, when it enters the bloodstream, can lead to cardiac arrest. Anger will shorten your life, it clouds brain function, it lowers your immune system, it increases your risk of stroke by more than 50 percent. According to a recent Gallup poll, right now the world is sadder, angrier, more worried, and more stressed than ever in the history of Gallup polls. Anger is considered the primary cause of roadside accidents; aggressive driving causes 66 percent of traffic fatalities, 37 percent of aggressive driving incidents involve a firearm, and half of drivers who find themselves on the receiving end of road rage respond with, you guessed it, road rage.*

Anyone struggle with anger? I know what you're thinking right now. You're thinking, "I might need to leave this chapter open on my father-in-law's coffee table."

Here's the crazy thing about anger—Christians don't get angry. We get frustrated. Know what I mean? We get aggravated. So if you're not sure this chapter is for you, I've come up with a couple little tests to help you out:

You might have anger issues if every time you call your kids' names, they flinch.

You might have anger issues if you refuse to judge people, but you just constantly think, "How could they be so dumb?"

You might have anger issues if you would never yell but your exhale sounds like a city bus letting out its air brakes. Sssss.

You might have anger issues if you are undefeated in both the past events that you replay in your mind where you remind and convince yourself you were right and the imaginary conversations that you wish you had or that you intend to have.

You might have anger issues if people often ask you, "What's wrong?" and your answer is, "It's just my face."

You might have anger issues if they know you by name at Home Depot for your frequent visits to buy drywall and spackle.

You might have anger issues if you regularly use your husband's toothbrush to clean the toilet. (Gretchen gave me that one. That scares me.)

You might have anger issues if you're afraid to put your church's bumper sticker on your car.

And you might have anger issues if Little League umpires cower every time you show up at the field.

---

*https://www.safemotorist.com/articles/roadrage/#:~:text=66%25%20of%20traffic%20fatalities%20are,likely%20to%20exhibit%20road%20rage.

Anger often sits just under the surface waiting to rear its ugly head. One of the real problems of anger is that we think it's our problem to deal with, but the truth is that our anger impacts others, especially those we love—starting with our children. Can I get a witness?

A dear friend of mine, a fellow pastor, who loves the Lord with all that he is, and someone I look up to as much as anyone, called me. I could hear the pain in his voice. He's a godly man. Great husband. Great dad. Great friend. All the things. But to say he can be a little edgy would be an understatement. Doesn't take much to set him off. (I asked his permission to tell this story.) I picked up the phone, and he said, "Hey, I need to confess something serious to you." Whenever a pastor says that to me, I think, "Oh, no, did he disqualify himself? Did he sleep with someone not his wife? Steal money? Murder somebody?" None of the above. He said he was pulling onto JTB, a highway here in Jacksonville, with his family in the car with him. And Jacksonville, like every major city, has city planners who decided to connect two parts of the city with a highway but didn't plan very well. They failed to account for more people, because this particular stretch of road goes from four lanes to two lanes back to three and down again to two in a very short distance. And while this is happening, drivers and their cars are fighting exits and on-ramps that seem to come in at all the wrong places. If you look on Google Maps, this section is always red. Well, my dear friend, who will remain unnamed for the protection of the innocent, pulls onto the highway when somebody pulls in front of him and slows down. He grips the steering wheel, nostrils flare, vein pops out on his throat, and he's managing to keep his mouth shut and keep it all bottled up and not say what he's thinking when, out of the mouths of babes, his sweet, innocent daughter, strapped into the car seat in the back, shouts, "Move over! What is wrong with these people?"

My friend hears this and thinks to himself, "Oh, no, not only do I have an anger issue, but I am passing it along to my kids."

I told him, "Bro, that's no big deal." And he said, "It's a really big deal. I've got to do something immediately because I don't want to pass on a generational curse to my kids." As we unpacked it I realized he was spot-on. One of the things we thought about is how will our kids ever understand the love of God if all they ever see from their earthly dad is anger? Even if it's not anger addressed at them. When the slightest little thing sets us off, it can teach a younger generation that God is just waiting for us to mess up so He can lose His stack and crush us with His thumb. But that's not who He is.

Here's the thing—being angry is not the problem. It's what we do with it. Jesus says be angry, but don't sin, and don't let the sun go down on your anger. Now, some people interpret that to mean don't go to bed mad. I don't think that's what that means unless you go to bed at five-thirty p.m. This means we need to keep short accounts with one another. Because if you don't keep short accounts, if you don't address this quickly, then what happens is we give a foothold to the devil. That's the NIV version, and I like that version because it shows us that unresolved anger turns into bitterness. Which is a foothold that allows the enemy to yank you around. And if you want to kill this in your own life, then confess it to another. Out loud. Multiple times, if need be. I thank God for my buddy and his sensitivity to the Lord that he would pick up the phone and call me.

Now let's unpack what James says about anger. In James, chapter 1, we're going to begin in verse 19. It starts out this way: "Know this." This is an imperative. James wants you to know something. He is signaling from the get-go that we should pay attention to what he's about to say.

In case you're new to Bible study, James is the half brother of Jesus. Mary was their mother. Think about that. James saw Jesus grow up. Walked around in His shadow. And it was not until the resurrection that James put his faith in His brother as God. As the Lord and Savior. Let me ask it to you this way: How many of you have a brother? What would it take for you to be convinced that your brother was the Savior of the world? James was not convinced until the resurrection of Jesus. But

James, post-resurrection, believes that his older brother is the Messiah. And then he writes this letter. It's the oldest letter in the New Testament. Which means it was written first.

"Know this" is a transition verse that connects back to verse 18: "Of His own will he brought us forth by the Word of truth, that we should be a kind of first fruits of his creatures." James is reiterating that you and I are a kind of first fruit. In other words, when you get saved and put your faith in Jesus, that faith will always produce fruit. Why? Because a seed has been planted inside of you that will sprout, grow, and produce fruit. James is very practical, and he's going to describe the symptoms of the Gospel-infected life. Why? Because if you don't have any symptoms, you may not have been infected with the Gospel. That's where he's going. He is not saying that you do these works to earn your salvation. He's saying, because of your salvation, you will be driven by Grace to get to work. You can't not. You have to.

Then he's going to address who he's talking to. "Know this, my beloved brothers." So, before he gets to activity, he wants to start with identity. He's saying, *"Listen. Before I tell you what to do, I need to make sure you know who you are."* My beloved brothers. Let me ask you this. Do you know who you are? And if you don't, that's probably why you're so angry. Because anger can oftentimes be the response when we're confused or when we're lost or when we think we're the center of the universe and all of the cosmos is supposed to revolve around us. So he starts with who we are. And we can't know who we are until we know whose we are. You should let that sink in. Ownership produces identity. And if you are in Christ Jesus, He owns you. You are His son or daughter. That's your starting point. No amount of sin disqualifies you or changes that. See Romans 8. But that's another book.

I already told you that the most important thing about you is what you think when you think about God. But what's the second most important? I think it's this: What do you think God thinks when He thinks about you?

Let's take them one at a time. The first most important thing about you is what you think when you think about God. If you think He's always angry at you, then you're always going to try to perform so that He won't be mad at you. If you think He is distant, then you will be distant. If you think that God loves you, then you can respond in love. The first, most important thing is this: What do you think when you think about God? The second most important thing is this: What do you think God thinks when He thinks about you? And your answer reveals a lot.

James answered the question. Here's what God thinks when He thinks about you: You are My beloved. That's a powerful word to be called. We don't use that word much. But God inspires James and also John to call His children beloved. If you break down the etymology of that word in English, it means this: Be loved.

And when He says beloved, He's saying that He loved you fully and finally at the cross. That God demonstrated His love for us in this, that while we were yet still sinners, Christ died for you. The cross was and is and will forevermore be how He demonstrated His love. Not in our circumstances, but at the cross.

First John, chapter 4, says this: *And this is love. Not that we love God but God loved us and sent His Son as the propitiation for our sin.* Remember, "propitiation" means a payment that satisfies, which means that if you are in Christ, He cannot be dissatisfied in you. Think about that. He's not disappointed in you, He's not dissatisfied with you. He knew exactly what He was getting when He purchased you with the blood of His own Son, Jesus Christ, and when He looks at you, He does not see the filth of your life that you bring to Him. He sees the righteousness of His Son wrapped around you like a father wraps a robe around his son.

Not only is it a title—"Beloved"—it's also a verb. Be loved. If we had any concept at all of how much God loves us, then that's how we would treat people. Some of you are angry because we just don't know how loved we are. Because we think God allows us into His presence based on our performance. And the better we perform, the closer we can get. Which is *skubalon*. He loves us because He loves us and He invites us in. All the way. Period. The reality is that loved people love people. Safe people make people feel safe, forgiven people forgive people, hurt people hurt people, and wounded people wound people.

So before he gets into what to do with your anger and how to handle your anger, James first wants you to know who you are. And you are beloved. But he doesn't stop there. It gets better. Then he says "brother." Not beloved random individual who has asked Jesus Christ to enter your heart all by yourself. No, no, no. And by the way, while you're not saved by the church, you are saved into a faith family. In the church, we are brothers and sisters. All of us were beggars. Now we're heirs. That should make all our heads explode. The Bible says we are to love one another. Lone rangers are lonely. And they have no one to love. This means you cannot do this thing called "following Jesus" solo or on your own. God saved you, and He saved you into a family. So, if you're not in a church, get in one. Besides, the enemy will always attack the solo before the herd. His chances are much, much better.

Now that we know who we are, he's going to get on to some action. James says this: "Let every person be quick to hear, slow to speak, slow to anger; for the anger of man does not produce the righteousness of God. Therefore put away all filthiness and rampant wickedness and receive with meekness the implanted word, which is able to save your souls" (James 1:19–21). He says, be slow to speak, be quick to hear, and slow to anger; for the anger of man does not produce the righteousness of God.

Alright. Can I just be real? Listen, if you need your pastor or favorite Christian author to have it all buttoned up and tied up, this ain't your book, and my church ain't your church. Okay? Just go back to wherever you came from because, confession time, I suck at this.

I don't even like to say the word "suck" a lot in church and certainly not in a book, and when I do Gretchen gets on to me, but I can't think of a better word. When I read this Scripture, I go, "Uh-oh." Because I'm telling you, if you've got to have a black belt in order to teach the topic, I'm not allowed to teach on this one. There are a few topics I feel pretty good about. Evangelism, worship, follow me as I follow Jesus. I'm good on those. This one? Not so much. This one is accompanied by a big, fat "uh-oh."

One time I was taking this personality exam, one of the thousand I've taken. My elders love them some personality exams. So I'm sitting in my living room and I'm answering all the questions. Which, by the way, never make sense to me. Like, "Would you rather kick a baby or stab a puppy?" I'm like, "What?"

Every time I take one, without fail, they all say the same thing about me. But whatever. I'm submitted to the elders, and they tell me to take it, so I take it. One time I was sitting there, minding my own business, taking the test, Gretchen walked in and she said, "Hey, what are you doing?"

"I'm taking a personality exam."

And she just went, "Huh…"

And the way she said it was kind of like this smug little smirk. Like she knew something I didn't.

So I barked back, "Huh? Whoa. Time out. What?"

She responded—and pause, you got to give me a little grace here—she said—get ready—"All they're gonna do is give you a new word for a-hole."

That's what she said. That's my wife. Describing me to a T.

I know. I would never talk that way. Alright? I don't use that kind of language. Pray for her. It's a heart issue.

But so help me, that's what she said. Verbatim. But here's the thing. Confession time. It's true. I'm a D, I'm red, I'm dominant, I'm a driver, I'm a whatever. Remember StrengthsFinder? The test that found your strengths? My number one was "competition." C.S. Lewis says competition is the greatest sin, the greatest example of pride. Got it. Guilty. That's my best strength. I'm winning at sinning.

So here's why I bring it up. Because these days we—and I include myself in this—can use all these tests to justify our bad behavior. "Well, I'm an eight so we should expect that from me." No, we should expect one another to love God and love one another as Christ loved the church and gave Himself for her. That's what we should expect. These tests are not a justification for our grumpiness or our anger or the unsanctified places in our lives. Here's the truth of all of us: We pull out our personality exam to excuse what the Bible would call sin. My Myers-Briggs type is J-E-R-K. I can't help it.

According to the Bible, nobody gets to excuse sin. Matter of fact, we're commanded to repent for it. James says, *Let every person be quick to hear, slow to speak, slow to tweet, slow to comment, slow to repost, slow to like, slow to dislike, slow to...* Okay, maybe I added a couple. James is saying slow down. Because all of that only leads to this: anger.

More confession time. I've been in ministry for thirty years, on staff at the local church for thirty years. In the last two or three years, I've never seen people more angry. Not slow to speak, not quick to listen, but very quick to email, very quick to tweet, very quick to send nasty emails to brothers and sisters. We are talking covenant members in my church.

Let me just give you a warning. If you send me a nasty email, here's what I'm going to do. I'm going to call you and make you read it to me, because I can't read your tone in email. So, just know I'm going to call you and say, "Hey, would you please read me your email?" Don't believe me? I have. Many times. Too many people to count. Not because I'm itching to get into it. Not because I'm wanting to put somebody in their place. And not because I'm above reproach. I'm not. The elders call me on the carpet all the time. But because Matthew 18 lays out the process for confronting a brother, and clicking "send" on a tirade is not it.

A year or so ago, I got two emails in the same day. The first said, "I'm leaving this church because of masks." The second one said, "I'm not coming to that church because you don't make everybody wear masks." And I know these people, so I called them both and asked them to read their emails to me. "I just need you to read it to me because I know you but I can't hear your voice in it."

Honestly, I think a part of it could be, especially as disrupted as our world has been over the last few years with riots and political craziness and pandemics and everybody arguing about everything, if you sit at home and turn the news on, another city's burning down and you sit there and think to yourself, "Well, I'm gonna burn some stuff down, too." We're tired of all the hatred, but producing more of it is not the answer. James speaks into this and says, *"Mm-mm. Mm-mm. That ain't the answer. That ain't gonna work."* So let me ask you this: Are you quick to listen and slow to speak, or are you quick to defend and slow to understand? Oh, is that too close to home? Because oftentimes the stuff beneath anger is just defense and control. All of which is rooted in fear.

Verse 20: Now he's going to tell you why. "The anger of man does not produce the righteousness of God." James says you can get angry. In fact, you're going to get angry. Which is comforting to those of us who do. But then he specifies—and I'm so glad he does this—he specifies a type of anger. The anger of man does not produce the righteousness of God. Our anger is a dominating emotion. That said, there are no bad emotions. Emotions are a gift from God so that we can navigate this thing called life. Emotions are a tool to be used by God's people to navigate life, and they make terrible decision makers. And anger can have a tendency to take over all of the other emotions. Particularly this anger of man.

Anger typically rises up when you have unmet expectations. One of the ways to look at this anger of man, according to James, would be what we would call unrighteous anger. This gives us two types: righteous and unrighteous. Oftentimes, if you really dig down into it, the reason that you're angry is because people are not worshipping at the idol of you. They are not doing what you expect or expected them to do. The question is not: Do I get angry? The real question is: How do I respond when I get angry?

One of the things that we as sinful people love to do is excuse our actions and put the blame on somebody else. We got it honest, from Adam. "This isn't my fault, my words aren't my fault, my actions aren't my fault." Why? "Because you made me angry." If you've ever said that, I've got some terrible news for you. The only thing that can come out of you is what is in you. From the abundance of the heart, the mouth speaks. If anger is coming out of your mouth, then according to Jesus, anger is in your heart.

I've used this analogy before. Take any water bottle. What's inside? Water. Right. It's just water. And if I take the lid off, then shake it, squeeze it, and cause trauma to the bottle, the only thing that can spew out of there is what is in there. And so, if anger comes spewing out of you, it is because there is anger deep down in there. And unrighteous anger is like smoke to a fire. It is a warning signal; it is not good. Your check engine light is flashing.

How many of you, if your check engine light were flashing, would cover it with tape so you couldn't see it? Would that make any sense? Of course not. Your engine's going to blow. Something is wrong inside the engine block and you need to take it apart and find the cause so that it doesn't erupt into a ball of flames. If you don't deal with your anger, it will deal with you, and not in a positive way. And the dangerous thing about anger is that oftentimes, we convince ourselves that all of the problem is out there somewhere. We point our finger: "It's your fault, it's not my fault, you made me angry." But the Gospel demands a different approach. The Gospel demands that we first look in the mirror and say, "What's wrong with me? What is the plank in my eye?" Unrighteous anger is rooted in control, which is just a manifestation of the deeper problem, which is fear. I don't trust, I'm afraid, I feel unbalanced, and so I'm going to take over.

Now, watch this—and this is important. The Bible says that we are to be slow to anger. This is important. It doesn't say *don't be angry*. It says be *slow to anger*. I think what James is doing here when he says to be slow to anger is he's actually referencing what God said about Himself in Exodus chapter 34 when He revealed Himself to Moses. Moses said, "Show me your glory." And God said, *"I am the God of mercy. I am the God that is slow to anger and I am the God of love."*

The Hebrew word for "slow to anger" literally is translated "long nose." That's right, long nose. The Hebrew people believed that anger started deep down, in what we would say is the gut. They would say the bowels. And it would work its way up and make your heart beat fast. Then it would get to your neck and make your veins pop out. And then eventually, when it got to your face, your nostrils flare, and you snort like a horse. And then God says, *"But when it comes to you, I make sure My nose gets longer and longer and longer so that anger's got a long way to go before it ever makes it out to you."* It's a word picture.

James is saying, *"So we need to be like the Lord. Slow to anger."* Not no anger and not blow-up anger, but slow to anger. There is a way to be assertive and even aggressive without sinning in anger. Ephesians 4:26 says it this way: "Be angry—" If you stop reading right there you might think, "Well, I'm nailing that part." But keep reading. It says, "Be angry and do not sin." So is anger a sin? Apparently not. "Be angry and do not sin; do not let the sun go down on your anger, and give no opportunity to the devil." In the NIV, that's "Do not let the sun go down while you are still angry, and do not give the devil a foothold."

Here's what this means. If you've got some anger building up in you, you better resolve it very, very quickly. Because what begins to happen is unresolved anger will begin to ferment in your life, and fermented unforgiveness is bitterness. And bitterness is a foothold, an opportunity, for the devil. Here it says, give no opportunity. That word is *topos* in Greek, and it means a room. When you've got some unresolved anger in you, you're inviting the devil himself to come and be a tenant in your life, to live rent-free in your mind. Let me just ask—do you want the devil in your house? In your heart? In your relationships? With your children? Of course not. No one does. But when we don't deal with our anger quickly, then we open the door to a room. That's what happens.

When I read this, "give the devil a foothold," it reminds me of growing up with my younger brother, Russ. I'd be minding my business, sitting at the table, reading the Bible and praying, and, without provocation, he would come up and smack me in the head and then bolt to his room, at which point I would go tearing after him, because I wanted to lay hands on him and pray for him. It was very Pentecostal. So I'd chase him down about the time he reached his room, and he knew if he could get the door shut, he had me. I couldn't get in, and he'd just wait me out because I'd get bored, but if I could get one little toe in between the door and the frame, I had him. One little toe. Because eventually, I'd wiggle my whole self into the room, put my hands on him, and we'd pray about his sinful ways. I didn't have to get my whole self into his room. Just one little toe. It was only a matter of time. What started as a foothold led to an all-out invasion.

That's what the enemy wants to do with you. He doesn't care what you're mad about. He'll capitalize on anything. He just needs that little sliver. He wants you to be angry and sin, and he wants you to make sure you hold on to it for a long time and let the sun go down over and over and over so that he can take up residence in your mind and in your heart and in your house and in your relationships. That's what he wants to do. Paul goes on to say, a couple verses later, "Let no corrupting talk come out of your mouths, but only such as is good for building up, as fits the occasion, that it may give grace to those who hear" (Ephesians 4:29). And then he goes on to say a couple verses later, "Let all bitterness and wrath and anger and clamor and slander be put away from you, along with all malice. Be kind to one another, tenderhearted, forgiving one another, as God in Christ forgave you" (Ephesians 4:31–32).

Bottom line: Be angry and don't sin. You can be angry and not sin. Don't believe me? Jesus got angry, and He was totally sinless. In John 2, Jesus walks into the temple and finds money changers charging exhorbitant prices for sacrifices, or selling blemished sacrifices. Probably both. Let me explain briefly: In Deuteronomy chapter 14, God says, *All right. When you come into the temple, here are the sacrifices required on these certain days. But I get it. Some of you live a long way away, and you can't get a goat all the way from the backside of the desert to here, so here's what you do. Sell your goat at home and then when you get to the temple, we'll have some goats for sale.* This was how God set it up. But when the people would show up, the vendors at the temple would be charging ten times as much for the goat at the temple. The problem was not that they were selling stuff in the temple. The problem was that they were using God's name, using God's command, to take advantage of God's people. And the priests' job was never that the people serve them. The priests' job was to serve the people.

Jesus walks in the temple, eyes the situation, and He's angry. So what does He do? He sits down and methodically makes a whip. Which means what? He's slow to anger. He did not immediately react to the situation, but He did respond. He responded appropriately. He drove the cheats out of His Father's house. That's righteous anger. I can imagine He walks in, takes a look around, sits down, and fashions a whip. You ever made a whip? I've never made a whip. I've been whipped a lot, but it was a belt. My dad never made an actual whip. He just had this one Indiana Jones move where he'd unbuckle and fling that sucker out, and it would make that whipping noise. I'm still triggered by it.

Now take a look at the disciples as Jesus makes a whip. "Hey, boss, whatchu doing?"

Jesus nods. "I'm about to show you what I'm doing." Then He cleans house. Righteous anger always results in righteous action. He didn't just feel a thing. He did something about it.

So are there things that you should get angry about? Yeah. You should get angry about the things that anger God, like the mutilation of children these days in the name of health care. You should get angry about that. You should get angry about the taking of innocent human life in the womb and calling it a right. You should get angry about that. You should get angry about the trafficking of boys and girls and the

most vulnerable people around the world. You should get angry about
that. You should get angry about corrupt governments helping themselves while people starve to death. You should get angry about that. You
should get angry about any injustice against any image-bearer of God.
You should get angry about that.

But while this was Jesus's response and it was right and there was
no sin in it, it was not the norm. In all of Jesus's life it happened one
time, or maybe two times. We read about it in Luke 19 and Matthew
21. Some theologians think these accounts are talking about the same
incident, and some think it was two different events. But at most, it was
two times in all thirty-three of His years. This is not like every other
Tuesday, Jesus made a whip and went around whipping people. And by
the way, if this is your go-to Bible story, you have lost the narrative of
God's redemptive plan for all of human history. This is not the norm.
What was Jesus doing? He was defending the glory of God and the
dignity of God's people in a very violent way.

The Bible says from the days of John the Baptist until today, the
kingdom of heaven is forcefully or violently advancing, and violent men
take hold of it. Paul said it this way to the Romans: "Therefore whoever
resists the authorities resists what God has appointed, and those who
resist will incur judgment." (Romans 13:2). And, in my book, some of
the most evil resisting the authorities are the individuals who abduct
and traffic the innocent. At The Church of Eleven22, as part of our
womb-to-tomb initiative, where we believe every person is of value from
conception to grave, we support ministries who work with local law
enforcement to rescue the most vulnerable among us who are being traf-
ficked and bring swift and legal justice to the traffickers who profit off of
and exploit them. We believe it is the heart of God to rescue them from
that horror and restore them to the freedom He desires and intends for
them. Tim Keller, God rest his soul, says in *The Healing of Anger*, "In its
uncorrupted origin, anger is actually a form of love." This means anger is
love in motion to protect what you love the most. Repeat: Anger is love

in motion to protect what you love the most. The question you should ask yourself when you're angry is, what am I protecting or what am I defending? What Jesus was protecting and defending here was the name of God, the glory of God, the people of God. His Father's house. The reality is if you ask that question, "Why am I angry? What am I protecting, what am I defending?" most often the answer is "I'm trying to protect me, my comfort, my reputation, my ego." Let's just call it like it is.

We get angry when the whole world is not bowing down to us. What are you doing when you lose your mind online? What are you doing when you give your spouse the silent treatment? Here's what you're doing. You are protecting your own ego. The fundamental question is this: Do you trust God? And when we lose it, when we vent unrighteous anger, your answer is "Nope. I don't trust that He's got this thing under control." The key is this: Do you trust that He will either cover it with His Grace or confront it with His justice? Because that's what He'll do.

Again, confession time. Man, if living were as easy as preaching and writing, I would be a rock-star Christian. I'm telling you. But as I was studying this and writing this and letting the Word of God do its work in me, I felt convicted. A lot. A continual slideshow of people began rolling across the backs of my eyelids. You ever read the Bible and began to feel like your Bible was reading you? And it just won't quit? I've sent out texts all week saying I'm sorry. To employees, former employees, and the people who share my last name. Because here's the thing, here's the question I'm wrestling with. Lord. I'm a believer, I'm a Christian. I have the Paraclete, the Holy Spirit, the Helper, planted deep within me. And I do the Christian stuff. I read my Bible. Some might say I'm a pro at it. I do it all the time. I pray hard. Sing with my hands up. I'm in church a lot. Surrounded by godly people. I'm doing all the things, and the Spirit of God in me is producing fruit: love and joy and peace, patience, kindness, goodness, gentleness, and self-control. All of those are like anti-anger fruits. And yet, here's the truth of me that I don't want you to know: I'm always just one breath away from anger.

What is wrong with me?

I've learned that I'm not alone. How in the world are our children ever going to believe that their Heavenly Father loves them if their earthly father is mad at them all the time? Paul wrestled with the same thing. He didn't speak specifically about anger, but in Romans chapter 7, Paul asks this question: *What is wrong with me?* And after he has unpacked the Gospel for six and a half chapters, Paul says, *I don't understand what is going on in here. In my heart and mind. I want to do the right thing, and the wrong thing is right around the corner. There's a whole bunch of things I promised I would never do again. I'd never raise my voice again, I'd never yell again, I'd never say those words again. I promised I would never do those things again and it seems like the more I promise, the more they come out of my mouth. What is wrong with me?* His conclusion? *What a wretched man I am. Who could save a wretch like me?* Amen. Can I get a witness?

Which then leads him to this: Praise God for Jesus Christ. Praise God for the Gospel of Jesus Christ. Which leads to the greatest chapter in all of the Bible in Romans 8:1, which says, "There is therefore now no condemnation for those who are in Christ Jesus."

There's an ancient Native American proverb. A wise man, a chief, is sitting with this reporter, who asks, "How, how did you get so wise? How did you get so honorable? How do you have such great character and morality?" And the chief says, "Oh, I don't. Inside of me are two dogs fighting every single day. There's a good dog and there's an evil dog and they are at war fighting every single day." And the journalist asks, "Well, which one wins?" And he simply says, "The one that I feed."

I get it. I really do. Inside of me I'm really into the Jesus thing. I'm all in on it. And inside of me on a daily basis there is a war. A war. And even though I know theologically Jesus has already won the war, I'm still fighting. And I know. I've read to the end of the book. Good news, spoiler alert. We win. And yet, if I don't feed the good dog, if I don't feed the Paraclete, the Spirit of God, if I don't make sure that I take every thought captive, if I don't pay attention to my emotions and know that even my emotions are submitted and subjected to the lord-ship of Jesus Christ, then in one second I can be acting in the flesh and acting a fool. So you say, "All right. Well, Paul, so what do we do?" James answers it this way: paraphrasing, he says, *Alright. Here's what you're going to do. When it comes to anger, you're going to have to take off some stuff and put on some stuff. That's what you're going to do.*

He says, "For the anger of man does not produce the righteousness of God. Therefore put away all filthiness and rampant wickedness" (verses 20–21). You see, when you're angry and you're ruled by your emotions and it's the anger of man, then you're not protecting the glory of God, you're not protecting the people of God, you're not protecting your fam-ily, and you're not protecting vulnerable people. You're protecting your ego, and you're protecting your reputation, and you're protecting your comfort. And when you're in this place, you know what you can do? You can say some filthy wicked things, can't you? That's what James is saying. Unrighteous anger will lead you to say the filthiest things to the people that you're supposed to love the most, and it'll cause you to do some of the most wicked things that you didn't even believe you had in you. And so he says you better put away all of that and receive. That's right: Receive.

You need to take off those things. This is kind of like Lazarus com-ing out of the grave and Jesus says, *"Take off those grave clothes."* Because that kind of anger and malice and filth and wickedness, those are dead people's clothes. They don't belong on you anymore. You have to take those things off. And instead, you put on, you receive this gift of Grace with meekness.

If you've ever heard me preach, then you know that the word "meek" does not mean weak. It doesn't. In Greek it means a bit-bridled horse. It means controlled strength. Anger is not a thing that is just going to disappear. It's not a problem to be solved. It is an emotional power, where you need to hand the reins over to another master because our flesh can't handle it. That's what it is. That's what it means to be meek. It sounds like this: "Lord, I need help. I ain't got this. I get these emotions, I get these things that happen. Maybe it's partly the way I'm wired. I'm sure it's the sinfulness of my flesh because I want the world to bow down to me. And when these things happen, what am I gonna do? I need to receive, by Grace, this gift, and I need to be meek. I need to hand the reins to you and say, 'Lord, would you please help me direct this anger to the right place?'" So we receive with meekness the implanted Word of God. We've got to make sure that the Word of God, the voice of God through His inspired Word, is always louder than the voice of us in our head.

Do you realize you're the most influential person in your life? You know why? Because nobody talks to you more than you. You ever talk to yourself? All the time. Do you realize that if I talked to you the way you talk to you, you wouldn't allow me to be your friend? Nobody's broken more promises to you than you. Nobody's lied to you more than you. Nobody's betrayed you more than you. James is saying, *Okay, so you struggle with anger? All right, everybody welcome to Earth. Now, put off the filthiness. Put off the wickedness. And let's slow this train down, all right? And then you're gonna receive His Grace with meekness, and hand Him the reins to your life.* The implanted Word of God is not just an external record of God's work on the planet. It's also a thing. It's like a seed that gets planted inside of you, and it begins to do some stuff that a talk from me can't do, man. That's what it does. It produces fruit.

We have got to allow the Word of God to be louder than the crazy things that we tell ourselves or the crazy things that we hear from this world. And you've got to believe God's Word even more than you believe your own feelings. Again, there's no such thing as bad feelings, but your feelings will lie to you. You know this. "If I can just say this filthy and wicked thing, then it'll hurt them and then I'll feel so much better… right?" Not one time ever.

Receive with meekness the implanted Word, which is able to save your soul.

The Bible talks about anger more than two hundred times. Here's Proverbs 14:17: "A man of quick temper acts foolishly." You ever had anger lead to dumb decisions? You know what the Bible means in the Old Testament when it calls you a fool? It means you know better and you do it anyway. Simple is the person who just doesn't know. The fool is a person who knows and does it anyway.

Proverbs 15:1 says, "A soft answer turns away wrath, but a harsh word stirs up anger." How many of you know the phrase "It isn't what you say, it's how you say it"? If you find yourself saying, "What's wrong? All I said was…" you should memorize Proverbs 15:1. It's not just the words, it's the tone that you're singing it in. A harsh word stirs up anger, a soft answer turns away wrath. Proverbs 14:29 says, "Whoever is slow to anger has great understanding, but he who has a hasty temper exalts folly." Have you ever said something that maybe you shouldn't, then calmed down and thought, "I wish I could take that back"? He's saying, pump the brakes, slow down.

This is Proverbs 15:18: "A hot-tempered man stirs up strife, but he who is slow to anger quiets contention." You can't be responsible for anybody else, but you are responsible for your responses. And when we slow that thing down, we can slow down the rage in somebody else. Proverbs 16:32: "Whoever is slow to anger is better than the mighty, and he who rules his spirit than he who takes a city." Proverbs 19:11: "Good sense makes one slow to anger, and it is his glory to overlook an offense." What most people do is overreact to an offense.

Please know this: Anger can lead to overreaction. And we are addicted to being offended today. Offense is a choice. It's a choice. You get to decide if you're offended or not, and our culture is addicted to being offended. Most of us walk around with a notebook just waiting to write down all the offensiveness we feel. "Oh, I can't believe you'd say that to me." Okay? What you do with an offense is up to you, but this is the Bible's response to an offense: *Love keeps no record of wrongs and love is not easily offended* (1 Corinthians 13:4–5). So the mature person who is slow to anger overlooks an offense.

Ecclesiastes 7:8 says this: "Better is the end of a thing than its beginning." I love that. It ain't how you start that matters, it's how you end. And the patient in spirit is better than the proud in spirit. Be not quick in your spirit to become angry, for anger lodges in the heart of fools. Anger is not an event. And what happens when you don't deal with anger—this is what Paul is talking about in Ephesians chapter 4— when you don't deal with anger and you don't deal with unforgiveness, then it begins to ferment and it creates a bitterness in your heart. It is impossible to simultaneously have bitterness in your heart and the peace of Jesus in your life. They just don't coexist.

When something ferments, it stinks, and it'll get you drunk on emotion instead of having the peace of Christ that transcends understanding and the Spirit of God guarding your heart and mind in Christ Jesus. Matthew 5:22 says this: "But I say to you that everyone who is angry with his brother will be liable to judgment; whoever insults his brother will be liable to the council; and whoever says, 'You fool!' will be liable to the hell of fire." Jesus says if you even hate in your heart, you're as good as a murderer. This is a really big deal. As man thinks, so is he.

Ephesians 4:31 says this: "Let all bitterness and wrath and anger and clamor and slander be put away from you, along with all malice." Colossians 3:8 says a very similar thing: "But now you must put them all away: anger, wrath, malice, slander, and obscene talk from your mouth." First Peter 2:1, very similar: "So put away all malice and all deceit and hypocrisy and envy and all slander."

So what do we do? Here's what you do. You put away that stuff, and slow-pump the brakes on your anger. How? Here's Paul to the Galatians (3:27): "For as many of you as were baptized into Christ have put on Christ." The NIV says, "clothed yourselves with Christ." This means when God the Father looks at us, He doesn't see all the sin and guilt, He sees His sinless Son wrapped like a blanket around us. So if you've wrapped yourself in the sinless Son of God, who gave Himself for your sins, what on earth do you have to be angry about? You have been bought with a price. And that price is the body of Jesus.

So, put away wrath, and put on the Grace of God. This is why Paul says in Ephesians 4:32, "Be kind to one another, tenderhearted, forgiving one another." How in the world am I going to do that, God? Here's how: As God in Christ forgave you.

In the last chapter, we looked at Matthew 18, where Jesus shares a parable about forgiveness. Remember the one where there is a servant who is forgiven of a debt that he could not have paid in twenty lifetimes, then he walks out, sees a servant who owes him like a week's wage, and he goes UFC on him? The Bible says he's trying to choke him out. And everybody else is thinking, *"What's wrong with you? How in the world could you be forgiven so much and then not forgive this guy who owes you so little?"* This is what James is saying.

Do you know why we are to be quick to hear, slow to speak, and slow to anger? Because this is how God treats us. That's why. And it says, so with that in mind, therefore, put away all filthiness and rampant wickedness and with meekness receive the implanted Word that is able to save your soul. Anger is a really big deal when we think about it in the Bible. Because of anger, Cain killed Abel. Because of anger, Moses was banned from the Promised Land. Because of anger, Pharaoh lost his army, Saul lost his throne, and Balaam beat his donkey. *(That sounds way cooler in the King James. Look it up.)*

Nebuchadnezzar lost his mind. Peter cut off a dude's ear. Because of anger, Judas betrayed Jesus for thirty pieces of silver. Because of anger, the Jewish leaders had Jesus arrested and flogged. Because of anger, Lucifer tried to overthrow the Throne Room of God. We're talking about a really, really, really big deal.

So the way that we deal with this matters. The Try Harder method isn't going to work. Trust me, I have tried in my flesh over and over and over to be a kinder, gentler version of me. That's not what we're going for. We need to be in a place where you say, "You know what? No, no. I don't need to be a kinder, gentler version of me. I need to be the me that is crucified with Christ. It's no longer I who live, but Christ who lives in me."

How's this work? Paul would say, *I thought the law died to the law.* What's this mean? It means Jesus stood in my place and took my death. He died in my place. Because of this, I can put on meekness, receive the Word, and hand over the reins of my life. Because, Lord, I ain't got this on my own. I need you. I need you to help me submit not only my thoughts but my emotions to Your lordship, and I need Your help. And the reason that I need to be quick to listen and slow to anger and slow to speak is because that's exactly how You treated us.

Did you know that God is quick to listen to you? You know why we make such a big deal about prayer? It's because God is so quick to hear your prayer. He wants to listen to it right now. And God is so slow to anger. The only solution for your unrighteous anger is the Gospel. It's the only solution to the problem of your anger, because you know who you have angered? God Almighty. I mean, if you think you're offended because somebody broke a promise to you, how offended is the almighty perfect righteous God? Because every single sin that we have ever committed is a slap in the face of the almighty righteous King of the universe. If anyone has a right to be offended, it's God. But He's not. He chose to pour out His Grace upon us by pouring out His justice upon His Son at the cross.

What if God were quick to anger? There'd be a lot fewer of you reading this book right now. Actually, there'd be no book, because I wouldn't be here to write it. None of us would be here. We would all have been smoked. But instead, because of His mercy, He overlooks sin, and because of His justice, He pays for it. With His Son.

I want to make sure you understand this. Seeing the problem that is our sin, and our complete and total inability to do anything about it, Jesus Christ stands up from His throne next to His Father in heaven where He has been sitting for those last two thousand years, wraps Himself in flesh, and shows up here where He lives a perfect life that none of us could live, satisfying the righteous requirement of the law on our behalf. Then He goes to the cross—in our place—and He allows

Himself to be made our sin so that we who believe could be made His righteousness.

And while He's hanging there, draped with the sin of all humanity for all time, He doesn't look down at us with offense. He looks down at us and says, "Father, forgive them, for they know not what they do" (Luke 23:34). Then He pours out every ounce of His blood, because without blood there is no remission of sin. The Bible says the wages of sin is death, so He dies, is buried, then on the third day, because He was sinless, the grave couldn't hold Him. He puts death to death and He comes out of the grave and then ascends to the right hand of God the Father, where He's been for the last two thousand years. He's been sitting at the right hand of God, and you know what He said He was going to be doing while He's waiting to come back to get us? He's going to talk to the Father on behalf of you and me.

So be quick to listen, because God is quick to listen to you, and be slow to anger. Why? Beause that's exactly how God treats you and me. Let this sink in: This is love. Not that we love Him, not that we're trying to earn it, not that we're trying to perform, but this is love. Not that we love, but God loved us and sent His Son as the propitiation for our sin. So let me return to my question that started all this—what does God think about when He thinks about you? If you are in Christ, no matter your past, He says, "My beloved son. My beloved daughter."

Now may we, by the power of the Holy Spirit, treat other people, regardless of the offense, the way He has treated us.

So here's how I want to close this chapter. I want you to take a long, hard look at your life and ask yourself, "Who have I offended with my anger? With my reaction? With my words? Who has a legitimate right to be offended by me?" Then don't shy away from the answer. If you're anything like me, their faces are playing like a slideshow across your mind's eye right now. Funny how that works. Now I want you to take each of those people, and I want you to go to them, each one, and confess where you were or are wrong. Tell them, "Hey, I did this thing to you, and I was wrong to do that." Then I want you to go one step further. I want you to humble yourself and ask for their forgiveness. Why? Because Jesus forgave us when you didn't and I don't deserve it. I want you to use words like, "Hey, I am really sorry." And I would be specific. This isn't like it's just a blanket, "Uh, you know, we all sin, so…" No. You need to speak specifically. "I am really sorry. I was careless with my words. Regardless of my emotions I am responsible for my responses." Then ask them, "Will you please forgive me? I need Grace and I need help."

The good news is, if you have Christ, you have received His Grace, and He's sent you a Helper.

We need to be doers of the Word and confess our sins to one another and pray for one another that we might be healed. Dads, some of you might need to go to your kids and ask their forgiveness. Husbands, some of you might need to take your wife by the hand. "Hey, babe, I need to confess to you, I am so sorry. Will you forgive me?" And all of us need to get on our knees with the Father and confess, "Lord, I've sinned against You. Again. I'm so sorry. Please forgive me. Especially when it comes to my anger. Honestly, my anger is rooted in my fear because the truth is I don't really believe You're in control. I feel that You need my help running the universe. I'm sorry. That seems horrible to even say. But I confess. I'm a fearful sinner, and I need Your help. Please. Here, take my anger. I don't want it. I want faith. I want You. And I want real belief. My only hope is found in Your Grace."

Pray with Me

Our good and gracious Heavenly Father, God, we love You more than anything because You first loved us. Lord, I pray that by the help of the Spirit of God in us and under the authority of the Word of God, that we would put away filth and wickedness. God, that we would be meek, we would turn over the reins of our life to You. God, that we would be so slow to speak. God, we would be so quick to listen. And that, God, You would help us pump the brakes on our anger. God, that we would ask the question, what am I defending, what am I protecting? And if it is not You, Your name, Your people, then God, immediately we would come to You and say, Lord, we need Your help. Would You help us treat others the way You have treated us?

And then, God, for those of us who fall regularly, who struggle consistently, God, we thank You that when we fall, we fall upon the same Grace that brought us to You to begin with. So God, would You help us? Because we need it so much. And, God, I thank You that therefore now there is no condemnation for those who are in Christ Jesus, and may that lack of condemnation and may that warm invitation of conviction of the Spirit of God lead us to that abundant life in the way we handle our anger. We pray it in Jesus's name. Amen.

Chapter 9

GRACE AGAIN AND AGAIN
AND AGAIN

When you have been run over by the Grace Train, your heart beats for the things God's heart beats for. And you look different. Physically. You look like you've been run over by a train.

I want to ask you a fundamental question: Do you believe? Like, really. I know we're nine chapters in and you've made it this far, but it's worth asking: Do you believe? Because "belief in," "trust in," "faith in" Jesus is His prayer for us. In John chapter 21, we see the radical transformation and 180 that occurs in the life of someone who believes. What we see in John 21 is how belief in Jesus as the Lord, the Son of God, gives life and changes everything, about everything, for everyone.

Why does this matter in a book on Grace? Because in order to receive it, we must believe that He is who He says He is, He did what Scripture said He did, and He is still doing what He said in Scripture He said He would do. It's a really big deal. You'll never truly appreciate the enormity or magnitude or unbelievableness of the Grace offered us if you have a limited view of the One who offers it or what it cost Him to do so.

So, here we go: John 21, verse 1. "After this—" Hold it. The "this" in that statement is kind of important. It's Jesus's resurrection from the dead. The "He is risen" part. The "after He defeated death, hell, and the grave, Jesus revealed Himself to the disciples in the upper room, and breathed on them and said, 'Receive the Holy Spirit'" part. The "He let Thomas stick his fingers in the holes and showed Himself to about five hundred people" part. John says it this way in the end of chapter 20: "Now Jesus did many other signs in the presence of the disciples, which are not written in this book; but these are written so that you may believe that Jesus is the Christ, the Son of God, and that by believing you may have life in his name."

That's the "this." "After this Jesus revealed himself again to the disciples by the Sea of Tiberias [that's the Sea of Galilee], and he revealed himself in this way." John is about to tell us when and how Jesus revealed Himself again.

Verse 2. "Simon Peter, Thomas (called the Twin) [that's Doubting Thomas], Nathanael of Cana in Galilee, the sons of Zebedee [that's James and John], and two others of his disciples were together."

Jesus has already been dead, crucified, buried, and resurrected, but He has not yet given them the Great Commission, so the disciples are sort of standing around scratching their heads. They don't know exactly what they're supposed to do with the rest of their lives. Actually, they have no idea. And these men are all very different. Some of them are blue-collar. Some are fishermen. Some of them are royalty, like Nathanael. Some had different political views, such as Simon the Zealot. He talked about politics all the time and wore a "Make Jerusalem Great Again" hat all the time. There was Matthew, the tax collector, collecting taxes for Rome. Simon the Zealot and Matthew could very well have hated each other. They had nothing in common save Jesus, and yet they're still spending time together. Which means God the Father answered Jesus's prayer in John 17, that they—the disciples—might know the same love with which the Father loves (loved) Jesus.

While the original disciples of Jesus were different in interests, politics, and socioeconomics, Jesus brought them together to change the world. Which they did. And notice they're still hanging out together. That said, they're searching for a reason to still be hanging out and, in reality, they've lost their leader.

You know who's really at a loss? Peter. He denied Jesus and doesn't feel worthy to be a disciple because he did the very thing he said he woudn't. He's pretty much a mess. Verse 3: "Simon Peter said to them, 'I am going fishing.' They said to him, 'We will go with you.'"

Here's why this is a big deal. First of all, where is he fishing? The Sea of Galilee. Where's the last time they encountered Jesus? In the holy city of Jerusalem, in the upper room, where they were locked away, hiding. It's a couple days' walk. Peter is peacing out. He's trying to get away from anything that even closely resembles the place where he denied his best friend. And he's leaving what he was called to and returning to what he left. Don't miss this.

We, as people, have a tendency to return to our old lifestyle when we are confused and when things aren't going the way we thought they would or hoped. Which is exactly what Peter does. When he met Jesus, he was a professional fisherman on the Sea of Galilee. And now, feeling disqualified, disgraced, and shamed, he says, "I'm not sure how I'm going to make a living. Not sure what I'm going to do with my life. So I think I'll go do that thing that I'm most comfortable with. The thing that I used to do."

Christians, let me warn you about something. There are some of you reading this right now, and something happened in your world that threw you off, and your first instinct was to return to the person that you used to be. What we're going to see here is that Jesus does not wait patiently in Jerusalem for Peter to get his act together and return to the holy city. Jesus continuously pursues His rebellious children and goes after them. Peter is returning to his old lifestyle, but as goes the leader, so goes the whole crew.

"They went out and got into the boat, but that night they caught nothing" (John 21:3), which is a bummer. Because he's a professional fisherman. "Just as day was breaking, Jesus stood on the shore; yet the disciples did not know that it was Jesus. Jesus said to them, 'Children…'" (21:4–5). Now, this is a clue, a textual clue, that Jesus is about to jack with them.

They had words for fellas or men or brothers, but that's not what He calls them. He calls them "children." Honestly, it's a little bit insulting. They're grown men. And I think He's doing this on purpose. Hey, kids, do you have any fish?

Now, Jesus knows all things. Does He know how many fish they caught? The answer? Yes. Jesus already knows. And He's just rubbing it in. Did you catch any fish? And they answered, "No."

And He said to them—I love this part—"Cast the net on the right side of the boat, and you will find some" (21:6). Again, they're professional fishermen and they're about one hundred yards offshore, and this stranger yells, "Have you tried the right side of the boat?"

I would imagine they look at one another and think, "Who is this fool? I don't think this guy understands. Under the boat, there are not sides of the boat. It's all the same water."

Despite their tired objections, they do it.

Remember the wedding in Cana? They run out of wine, and Mary tells Jesus, *"Son, they've run out of wine."* Then she looks at the servants and gives the greatest advice you can receive on the planet. She says, "Do whatever he tells you" (John 2:5). That's it.

Which, by the way, is a pretty good definition of discipleship. What is discipleship? Do whatever He tells you to do.

Do these servants have any idea that on the other side of obedience hangs a miracle that we will be talking about two thousand years later? No. But they fill jugs with water, like He commands, and bring them to the master of ceremonies. You have to think that one of them stopped to think, "Well, gee, this is awkward. This could go really poorly for me." Listen, if you do whatever Jesus says, there are going to be times when He asks you to do something that is very, very uncomfortable, that you do not understand, and which, on the surface, makes little to no sense.

I would go so far as to say that if you haven't stepped out in faith to do something uncomfortable, then you're not doing everything He's told you to do. Back at the boat, He's talking to professional fishermen. And in their minds, they've already figured out why their way is better than the guy on the shore's way. Incidentally if you're just keeping count, their way has led to zero fish so far. But, whether it was dumb luck or by faith, they do what He tells them to do and cast the net on the other side.

Stop. Let me ask you this: What is He telling you to do?

Maybe He's telling you to do something that, in your mind, you've already figured out won't work. Why you shouldn't waste your time picking up the phone to call that person and attempt to reconcile the relationship. To finally cancel the debt that somebody else owes you and really forgive them. To share your faith with the person whom you've invited to church a hundred times and you think, "Well, I've called, but still nothing, so this will never work." I imagine the disciples feel the same way, plus they're tired, grumpy, and hungry.

But there's this stranger, calling them "children," telling them to try the other side of the boat, which is a ridiculous suggestion. And so they do. "Now they were not able to haul it in, because of the quantity of fish. That disciple whom Jesus loved therefore said to Peter, 'It is the Lord!'" (21:6–7).

Now, stop right there. One of the best ways to study the Bible is always use the Bible as commentary unto itself. What Jesus is setting up here is actually a convergence of three events in Peter's life. And they all converge right here in this moment.

Go back to Luke, chapter 5. Peter has been fishing all night, and he's caught nothing. Jesus says, *"Try the deep water."* He catches a haul of fish. He realizes that Jesus is who He says He is and says, *"Get away from me because I am an unclean man"* (Luke 5:8). Now, what we're about to see is that Peter doesn't respond that way here. In the next few moments, Peter is going to throw on his cloak and dive into the sea—toward Jesus. Notice two very important things here. One, Peter gets it. He finally understands the Gospel. According to the Bible, the last time Jesus looked Peter in the eyes was right after Peter had denied Him three times. Not his best moment. Especially when he had promised to never deny Him, never forsake Him, and that he'd lay down his life for Him.

Now, Jesus shows up, tells them to cast on the other side, and the net fills to overflowing. John says, "It is the Lord," and Peter dives off the side of the boat. He can't get to Jesus fast enough. This is the turning point in Peter's life. Everything is about to change in this moment. His running-away days are over. He is running *to* not *from*. Jesus has found him. Come to him. And that has compelled him to jump, swim, and come to Jesus.

So, stop a minute. When you sin, do you run and hide from God? Most of us do. Or do you run to Him? When we expose or confess our sin to Jesus, we remove the power of shame. It loses its grip on us. A lot of us were brought up in religion or denominations that taught us, "You're bad, He's good, try harder, see you next week." That's exhausting. Plus, we can never try hard enough. When Adam and Eve sinned in the garden, their first response was to sew fig leaves together to cover their shame. This is no different than the religion of today. The good news of the Gospel is this: Jesus invites us to come to Him when we sin. Every time we sin. No matter how often. He can handle it.

Also, in the first century, it was undignified for a grown man to be in a hurry. But Peter, at this point, doesn't care. He doesn't care what it looks like or what others think. All he knows is that Jesus is on the beach, and nothing is going to stop him from getting to Him. Also, notice something else. He doesn't tell Jesus to tell him to come to Him. To walk on water. Why? Because he's draped in shame and doesn't feel worthy to be spoken to like an apostle.

Remember in Luke, chapter 15, when the father is looking for his lost son and the son comes over the horizon and he sees him? The Bible says that the father runs to the son. Which was undignified. Humiliating. It meant that you did not have your affairs in order. Dignified men waited until others came to them. But when Peter sees Jesus, he throws on his cloak and dives into the water. "The other disciples came in the boat, dragging the net full of fish, for they were not far from the land, but about a hundred yards off" (21:8). Again, another detail, because this is history.

Also, let me point out a leadership lesson. If you're leading anything, including a ministry, notice this: Leadership is not something you do to people, it's something you do with people. Sometimes we can have a great idea and a great vision, and then we just take off running in the direction of our vision without bringing others along with us, leaving them behind to mop up the mess. And it's often because we convince ourselves: "I'm going to go be with Jesus." In truth, we've just left everyone we've been called to lead to do all the hard work. That's not leadership. But this is exactly what Peter does. He takes off into the water, and all the disciples are left to haul in the fish. For the record, maybe we could cut him some slack because his heart is pretty much broken due to his own choices, and he will soon get his act together, as we'll see in Acts 2. But he's not there yet.

And things are going to get worse before they get better. Peter's in for a surprise. When they get to land, they see a charcoal fire. In truth, they may have smelled it first. That's usually the way it works with charcoal. Only two times in the New Testament is a charcoal fire mentioned. And both include Peter. And here's why this is rare. The first is when Peter is warming himself right before he denies Jesus. The Bible says he's warming himself by a charcoal fire. Then when he lands on the beach, Jesus is cooking with a charcoal fire. Is this by chance? No way. Jesus is taking Peter back to the moment. He's resetting the scene. "When they got out on land, they saw a charcoal fire in place, with fish laid out on it, and bread. Jesus said to them, 'Bring some of the fish that you have just caught.' So Simon Peter went aboard and hauled the net ashore, full of large fish, 153 of them" (21:9–11).

There are a lot of theories about the 153. Why does the Bible record that specific number? First, because there were 153 fish. It's just a fact. The Bible is a record of true events, and John recorded the true number of fish. Secondly, in the first century, they believed there were 153 species of fish in the Sea of Galilee, you know, everything from a muddy catfish to a holy mackerel and everything in between, suggesting the disciples would soon be fishers of every kind of man. Maybe. The third theory has to do with numbers and letters. In the Hebrew alphabet, every letter is also assigned a number, which allowed the Hebrews to use their alphabet for both words and as a numbering system. This meant each Hebrew word also held within its letters a numerical total. Or the sum of all the letters added up to a numerical value. The Hebrew word "Ani Elohim" written in numerical format is: 1 + 50 + 10 = Ani. And 1 + 30 + 6 + 5 + 10 + 40 = Elohim. Or, 61 and 92. Which, added together, equals 153. Translated, "Ani Elohim" means "I am God." Some scholars think that when Jesus caused the disciples to catch 153 fish, He was reminding them that He was God Himself.

Regardless of the reason, they caught 153 fish—so many the net was stretched but not torn. And Jesus said to them, "Come and have breakfast" (21:12). You've all heard of the Last Supper, but have you heard of the last breakfast? This is it. "Jesus came and took the bread and gave it to them, and so with the fish. This was now the third time that Jesus was revealed to the disciples after he was raised from the dead" (21:13–14). John wants us to know that Jesus's resurrection was an actual physical, bodily resurrection. Spirits don't eat fish. Ghosts don't eat fish. Nowhere do we see that Jesus is trying to bite into the fish and it's falling on the ground.

And apparently defeating death, hell, and the grave and then being resurrected makes you hungry. And when they had finished breakfast, Jesus said to Simon Peter, "Simon, son of John, do you love me more than these?" And Peter says to Him, "Yes, Lord; you know that I love you."

And He said, "Feed my lambs" (21:15). I think Peter is astounded. *"Okay, you got my attention."*

And so He says to him the second time, "Simon, son of John, do you love me?"

And he says, "Yes, Lord; you know that I love you."

And He says to him, "Tend my sheep."

Peter says, *"Alright."*

And Jesus says to him a third time, "Simon, son of John, do you love me?" (21:16–17).

Now Peter understands what's going on. "Peter was grieved because he said to him the third time, 'Do you love me?'" And Peter's like, *"Oh, I see what we're doing here. Yeah. Kinda sneaky. Um, we're by a charcoal fire. And the last time I stood by a charcoal fire I denied You three different times. And that came on the heels of us breaking bread together when I promised I'd never leave You, never forsake You. And by the time the rooster had crowed three times, I'd done exactly what I said I wouldn't. When we got to Caiaphas's house, somebody recognized me and asked, 'Aren't you one of His?' And I shook my head and said, 'No way.' And then a second time while I was warming my hands by a charcoal fire, this servant girl said, 'I recognize your accent, you're a Galilean. Don't you follow Him?' And even though she didn't have enough clout for her confession to stand up in court, I said, 'No.' And then a third time I was asked and I cursed and said, 'No.' So I see what You're doing with the whole charcoal fire thing. And now You're asking me if I love You?"* And Peter said, "Lord, you know everything; you know that I love you." And Jesus said to him, "Feed my sheep."

Here's what I need you to see—the Grace of Jesus Christ poured out at the cross is infinitely greater than all of our sin. I've said this, but again, we're sheep, and sometimes we need reminding. You should write this down. Post it on your bathroom wall. There is more Grace in Jesus than sin in you. I have people come to me all the time and say, "Can God forgive me, even me? You don't know what I've done." To which I want to lovingly say to you, *Who do you think you are?* I'm not saying sin is not a big deal. Sin is such a big deal that the perfect Son of God, Jesus the Christ, had to give His life on the cross to be the ransom to pay for our sin. It's a way bigger deal than we think. It's not just a mistake. Not just a hiccup. It's not a stumble, it is sin. And every sin is a slap in the face of the almighty sovereign King of the universe, and every sin deserves to be punished by death. And it was. By the death of Jesus Christ on the cross.

And yet, simultaneously, no matter how grand your sin, it pales in comparison to the blood of Jesus Christ poured out for the forgiveness of that sin. So who do you think you are to think that your sin is beyond the saving Grace of God? And hear me, this is not license to sin. It's freedom from it. When you know that you've been forgiven by the Gospel of Jesus Christ, it does not inspire you to keep sinning. It frees you from the bonds of that kind of sin in your life. This is what Jesus offers to Peter. And this is what Jesus offers to you.

"Do you love me?" And Peter says, "Lord, you know everything; you know that I love you." And Jesus said to him, "Feed my sheep. Truly, truly, I say to you, when you were young, you used to dress yourself and walk wherever you wanted, but when you are old, you will stretch out your hands, and another will dress you and carry you where you do not want to go." And then in parentheses, John, who writes this as an older man, and who knows what happened to Peter, says, "This he said to show by what kind of death he was to glorify God" (21:17–19).

Now notice what Jesus does not say. Jesus does not say, "If you'll follow Me, I'll make everything better in your life." That's not what He says. Now, that message gets peddled on Christian TV all the time. It's known as the prosperity gospel. And it is a lie from the pit of hell. The primary argument against the prosperity gospel is what we know as the Scriptures. All of the disciples of Jesus, the apostles, died as martyrs (except, per tradition, for John). When Jesus says, "Follow Me," He's not ultimately leading us to cash and prizes. Because the reality is, if you follow Jesus in order to get something from Him, like cash and prizes, or to improve your marriage, or to get the promotion or in order to get your kids back, then ultimately what you're getting is your little "g" god, and Jesus is a means to your end, which is the worship of yourself. And Jesus will not be a means to your idolatry, He will not play that game. He is saying to Peter, *"Listen, man, you follow Me not because I promised to make your life better, but because I am better than life."*

Jesus is saying that it would be better for you, Peter, to live a shorter life, die a gruesome, brutal death, and yet do that as a follower of Me than it would be for you to gain all that this world has to offer and yet forfeit your soul. We know from church history that Peter was crucified. On the way to his execution, his executioner told him all he had to do was deny Jesus and they wouldn't kill him. They offered him a way out. "Just do the thing you already did and we'll let you go."

But he couldn't do it. Further, it is recorded that he said, "I am not worthy to die in the manner in which my Lord died." So they said, "That's fine." And so they crucified him upside down. Jesus knew that this would be his manner of death, so He says to him, *It would be better for you to die upside down on a cross with Me than it would be to live a long life without Me.*

One of the tough but great privileges of being a pastor is sometimes we get to walk with men and women in the final moments of their lives. And you know what they never talk about? They never talk about their worldly success. When I am with people in the final moments of their lives, they talk about two relationships: They talk about their relationship with the Lord and they talk about their relationships with the people who are most important to them, which, by the way, is the greatest commandment. That's what Jesus said, it's all about love God and love people.

About eight years ago, I got to meet this guy named Bob. Bob's a dude, man. He had accomplished everything you can hope to accomplish in this world. Super successful. Beautiful family. He had it all. Built companies. Sold companies. Hunted and fished all over the place. He was the picture of worldly success. His problem was that he grew up in a religious system that basically told him, "God is good, you're bad, try harder, see you next week." So he did. He tried, and he tried, and he tried, and, on the surface, he seemed like a good man. But deep down he had this gnawing sense that said, "I don't think I'm right with God."

I met him at one of our men's hunting encounters and got to know him and started walking with him. When we'd talk about the Gospel, he had the hardest time getting his mind around the Gospel.

Ultimately, he just couldn't understand Grace. Because everything in his life that he had received he had earned. He'd worked really hard and been rewarded for that hard work. Which translated into his walk with Jesus. He thought he'd be rewarded with a relationship with God if he just worked harder. This produced a real disconnect for the longest time. Then he was diagnosed with cancer.

At first, the treatments were going awesome, and then it took a turn for the worse. And somehow in that diagnosis and through that walk, he came to the place where he surrendered his life to the lordship of Jesus Christ. A few days before he passed away, his daughter asked me to come visit him in the hospital. And so I went to the hospital and I sat across from this man, and he looked terrible. He'd probably lost fifty pounds. Frail. Freezing cold. He had on pajama pants and a little blanket and a little hat for his bald head. His face was sunken in. And his breath was labored, and he looked at me, and he said something to the effect of, "I would rather have cancer and Jesus than a long life without Him." That statement floored me. And I do this for a living.

And a couple of days later, he went to be with the Lord.

This is what Jesus is saying to Peter. It would be better for you to be a disciple of Mine and be with Me forever and die the death you are going to die, than to have all this world has to offer and forfeit your soul. And then He says two of the most beautiful words in all of the Scriptures: "Follow me" (21:19).

Notice that He's saying it to the guy who keeps screwing up over and over and over and over. I think Peter looks around and thinks, "Oh, I get it. We're on the Sea of Galilee. We're here at the shore. I fished all night, I caught nothing. And then You told me to throw my nets on the other side and I haul in the fish. Which reminds me of another time in my life about three and a half years ago, on the same shore, after a similar night when we first met and You said to me, 'Follow Me.'"

In Mark 1:16 and 17, the Bible says this: "Passing alongside the Sea of Galilee, he saw Simon and Andrew the brother of Simon casting a net into the sea, for they were fishermen. And Jesus said to them, 'Follow me, and I will make you become fishers of men.'"

You see, there's a deep theological term in play here that we learned from first graders. It's called the do-over.

Do you remember the do-over? I remember it well. In my hometown of Dillon, South Carolina, we had a kickball yard. Our backyard had a fence that made a perfect home run fence. So we put in bases, and all the kids from the neighborhood would come to our yard, but we had one problem. Right field was a little jacked up because our neighbors had what we called the thicket. It was nothing but thorns and thistles. Straight out of Genesis chapter 3.

It was just a bummer if you kicked it in there, so we just decided that if you booted off the right side of your foot and it went over and into the thicket, you would just yell, "Do-over!" And then everybody would return to their place in the game as if that thing hadn't happened.

Now that I'm older, I'd love a couple of do-overs. Can I get a witness? Imagine if you were audited by the IRS, or pulled over by the police, and you said, "I'mma take a do-over." And given the rules of the do-over, all they can say is, "Carry on." That would be glorious, would it not?

I think a part of what Jesus is doing is bringing Peter back to that very first time that he ever surrendered and began to follow in the footsteps of Jesus the Christ. Now maybe you've heard that God is the God of second chances. And it looks like here that Peter's getting a second chance. And I know what you mean by that. And what you mean is fine. But here's the reality: We don't need a do-over. We don't need a second chance. Why? Because you'd just screw up again. The problem is not that you didn't have enough chances. The problem is you.

When my daughter was in the sixth grade, if I had given her an AP calculus exam and said, "Here you go, darling, give that a run," how do you think she would do? Not good. Two reasons: She's a Martin. And she's in the sixth grade.

And what sense would it make if, when she failed it miserably, I said, "Listen, in my mercy and my grace, I'm going to give you a second chance. Here's a do-over." Guess what would happen? She would just fail again. In our life here on planet Earth, we don't need a second chance. Or a third. Fourth. Or five hundredth. We won't ever get it right. What we need is a substitute.

We need somebody to take the test on our behalf and give us their grade. So we get credit for their work. Their effort.

When you hear me talk about Peter, you might think, "That's good for Peter, but he was the first pope. Peter was a big deal. Peter walked and talked with Jesus. But I don't know if God would give that to me. I don't know if He would offer that Grace to me given how badly I've screwed up."

You need to read your Bible. Do you understand what a jacked-up disciple Peter is? Somebody wrote me a few months ago and asked why I hate Peter. You're hearing it wrong. I don't hate him. I love him so much because he's just like me.

I praise God for him because if he can be a follower of Jesus, so can I. Because he screwed up everything. I mean, his highs were high, but he was his own worst enemy. Remember in Matthew 14 when all the disciples were in a boat, crossing the Sea of Galilee, in the middle of the night, the fourth watch, the disciples look out across the water and see what they think is a ghost? They cry out, *"It's a ghost!"*

To which Jesus says, *"Boys, calm down. It's Me."*

Then Peter, because he's a follower of Jesus, says, by faith, *"If it's really You, ask me to come on out on the water."*

And Jesus says, *"Come on, big boy."*

And then Peter steps out of the boat. Think about it. The Bible does not say how many steps he took. But it does say he walked. Then like almost everything else he does, he screws up the miracle. He takes his eyes off Jesus, he's filled with fear, he focuses on his condition, and he begins to sink and cries out, "Lord, save me." And Jesus says, "O you of little faith."

Peter was also part of the small group that got invited up on the mountain of transfiguration. I think Jesus was probably going up there alone, so He said to the disciples, *"Boys, you stay here,"* but then looked back at the troublemakers and thought better of it, so He said, *"Peter, James, John, get in the truck, we're going up. I can't trust you to be alone."* So, they get up on top of the mountain of transfiguration, and Jesus reveals His glory. The Bible says that His face shone like lightning. Shone like the sun. And Moses and Elijah show up on the scene. This is the personification of Romans chapter 3, that the law and the prophets would testify to the Messiah. The Bible is alive and in person there on the mountain of transfiguration. And guess what? Peter thinks, "You know what? There's Jesus, there's Moses, there's Elijah, I should probably say words now." And so he steps in and opens his big mouth and says, "It is good that we are here." Oh, you think?

To which the Father basically says, *"This is my Son, listen to Him."* Peter screws up the mountain of transfiguration.

The Last Supper. Jesus, knowing that all authority in heaven and earth had been given unto Him, shows His disciples the full extent of His love, so He gets up from the table and dresses Himself as a servant only to scrub the dirty feet of His disciples. Think about it. The Son of God washing their feet. But not Peter. He recoils. He says, *"You're not going to wash my feet."* And Jesus says, *"If I don't wash your feet, you have no part with Me."* And so Peter says, *"Well, then wash my whole body."* And Jesus just shakes His head. Peter almost screws up the very last supper.

How about the Garden of Gethsemane? Jesus says, *"Boys, come with Me, and just please pray."* Three times, He comes back to check on them, but they're asleep. *"Come on, wake up. Can you not just stay awake for an hour and pray?"* And then the guards show up. And what does Peter do? Not only is he not a good pray-er, he's not a good swordsman. He whips out his sword, and he chops off a dude's ear. Nobody goes for the ear. He was trying to kill the guy, and he can't even do that right, so Jesus picks up the ear and looks at Peter. And in my way of thinking, He says something like: "Are you even being serious right now?" Then He puts the ear back on the dude's head. The Son of God is being arrested, which is a really big deal, and Peter screwed that up.

Here's my favorite. Jesus takes the boys to Caesarea Philippi, which was like Sin City back in the day. He takes them up on this high mountain, shows them this Las Vegas of the first century, and asks the disciples, *"Who do people say that I am?"* The other disciples repeat what others are saying: a good moral teacher, etc. Then Jesus asks them, "But who do you say that I am?" And, of course, Peter, who was then known as Simon, speaks up, "You are the Christ, the Son of the living God." To which Jesus replies: *"Winner, winner, chicken dinner."* Then He tells Peter, *"Bro. That did not come from you. That was revealed to you by my Father in heaven."* So, right then and there, in front of everybody, Jesus changes his name. *"Your new name will be Petra, Rocky. And upon this rock, I will build My church."* What is the rock? The public profession of what just came out of Peter's mouth. *"Peter, I will build My church on that proclamation and the gates of hell will not prevail against it."*

It's pretty much the high-water mark of Peter's life. But watch what happens. In the same chapter, the Bible says that Jesus then lays out the Gospel. *"Alright, boys, the way we're going to build this church is this: I'm going to be arrested, handed over, tried, crucified, dead, buried, and on the third day, be resurrected. Ready, break."* Then the Bible says an amazing thing. It says that Peter rebukes Jesus. Think about this. He said, *"Jesus Christ, get over here."* Peter pulls Him aside. *"What are you talking about? Stop talking crazy. That's not happening. Not on my watch."* And then Jesus looks at Peter and says, "Get behind me, Satan!" You know how much counseling and therapy you're going to need when the almighty Son of God calls you the devil? In one page of my Bible, Peter goes from the pope to the devil. He is the consummate screw-up.

And yet on that beach, around a charcoal fire, Jesus pours out Grace upon Grace. *"Peter, your sin could never outweigh My calling on your life.*

Never disqualify you. Because when I died on the cross, Peter, it counted for you, too."

And here's what I love about the way the Gospel of John ends: Peter still has a long way to go. Think about this sweet moment. Peter hears these words, "Follow me." And how does he respond? Does he say, "For real, Lord? I thought I'd messed it up. Three times I denied You, but You bring me back to the very seashore where I first met You and once again call me to follow You just like You did when we first started"? No, he does not say this. Rather than oozing gratitude, he oozes insecurity. After hearing, "Follow me," Peter turned and saw the disciple whom Jesus loved following them, the one who also had leaned back against Him during the supper. That'd be John. And Peter says, "Lord, what about this man?" (John 21:21).

Do you see what's going on here? After Jesus gives Peter this beautiful picture of Grace, in which He re-establishes his identity not as one who denied Him, but as a follower worthy of the Gospel, Peter plays the comparison game: *"Yeah, but what about that guy?"* He immediately screws up again and compares himself to John. Jesus's response is this: "If it is my will that he remain until I come, what is that to you? You follow me!" (21:22).

Don't miss this. Peter gets the do-over and yet he screws up the very conversation about the do-over. And how does Jesus respond? Peter gets another do-over right there. That's the Grace of God. He says, "You follow me!" And, "so the saying spread abroad among the brothers that this disciple was not to die; yet Jesus did not say to him that he was not to die, but, 'If it is my will that he remain until I come, what is that to you?'" (21:23).

Verse 24: "This is the disciple who is bearing witness about these things." John is saying, *I am a firsthand eyewitness of these things.* "Who has written these things, and we know that his testimony is true." Here's the point.

When Jesus says to Peter, "Follow me," He isn't offering a second chance at life, He's offering a new life. Which He also offers to us. He's offering His life in exchange for ours.

So how did Peter answer Jesus? What was his response? Did he accept the offer? If you continue to follow the life of Peter, you find that fifty days after Passover, the Jews celebrate another feast, called the Feast of Weeks, or Pentecost, which was a celebration of the early weeks of the coming harvest. You can read about this in Acts 2. Jerusalem was full of people from all over, and God chooses that moment to make good on His Joel 2:32 promise that He would pour out His Spirit on all flesh. And the disciples were there to see and experience it.

Peter, who's always going to talk first, who's going to talk most, sees a crowd and thinks once again, "Ooh, I should probably say stuff." And yet this time, he steps up and gives maybe the second best sermon in the history of sermons. The very thing that always got him in trouble, his mouth, was the very thing that God used and redeemed. Peter preached the very first Christian sermon. Think back to that moment when he was warming himself by the charcoal fire. He intended to play it safe and secure, really concerned about what everybody else thought about him. Now contrast that with the Day of Pentecost, when he stands up and he proclaims, *"God gave us the author of life, Jesus, and you crucified Him. Repent."* It's maybe the least seeker-sensitive sermon in all of church history, but it cut men and women to the heart, and that day three thousand people surrendered their life to the lordship of Christ and got baptized.

A few days later, the boys are going up to the temple, and there's a guy begging for money (Acts 3). And this beggar is no dummy. He knows the way people's minds work: *Maybe, if I do a good work walking into the temple, then my prayer will get answered.* And so he asked the disciples, *"Hey, can you give me some money?"* And Peter looks right at him, and says, *"Silver and gold have I none, but what I have I give unto you. In the name of Jesus, arise and walk."* Peter reaches out his hands and grabs the man by faith and picks him up. And then he gets arrested for it. To which Peter responds, *"Great. I'll start my prison ministry from the inside."*

After his arrest, they drag him in front of the Sanhedrin—the very people who, with the help of the Roman authorities, crucified Jesus. The very same people who, with one word, can also have Peter crucified.

And they say, *"Hey, listen, man, you can heal people, that's fine. Everybody loves a good healing, but you got to quit with this Jesus stuff."*

To which Peter laughs. *"Hey, boo, you do you."* That's a loose translation.

Really, he says, *"You choose whatever you think you need to do. But as for us, we can't stop speaking of what we have seen and heard"* (Acts 4:20).

What happened to him? What changed Peter from denier to proclaimer? From hiding to standing on the rooftops? I can tell you what happened to him. He had breakfast with the resurrected Jesus. Think about it. Peter saw Jesus doornail dead. Saw Him breathe His last. Saw His body hang and drip blood on the dirt below. Then Peter saw Him buried and sealed inside a tomb. End of story. Who comes back from that? Who walks out of the grave having defeated hell and death?

Peter can now answer this because he had breakfast with Him on a beach and that same Jesus, *the* Son of God, revealed His resurrected and glorified self to Peter. But Jesus didn't stop there. He reached across Peter's shame and regret, wrapped an arm around His buddy, and welcomed him back. Jesus restored Peter. Just as he was before. Two words display the greatest do-over in the history of do-overs. "Follow me."

But Peter's not alone in this. Jesus offers that same restoration to every one of us. And not just once, but every time we fail or deny or betray Him. This is really difficult for us as people to wrap our heads around because we are conditioned, for lots of reasons, to think if we do X then we get Y. And this includes both reward and punishment. If we do good, we think we should get good. If we do bad, we know we deserve bad.

But when it comes to eternity and our salvation, Jesus doesn't work like that. At all. In spite of the sin we bring to the cross, He offers us Grace.

Let me say it even stronger: We killed Jesus. You and me. That may offend you, but it's no less true. Peter says this: "He himself bore our sins in his body on the tree, that we might die to sin and live to righteousness" (1 Peter 2:24). Why? Why would He do this? Because He loves us. Period. We can't earn it. All we can do is receive it. Which is why it's called Grace. It's unmerited favor. It's being given what we don't deserve. And if this knowledge doesn't humble you, maybe it should. Here's the writer of Hebrews: "Let us then with confidence draw near to the throne of grace, that we may receive mercy and find grace to help in time of need" (Hebrews 4:16). From the throne, Jesus rules and reigns and judges, but for some inexplicable reason, when we approach, He offers us Grace and mercy.

He cleanses us. He washes us from our sins in His own blood (Revelation 1:5).

On your and my best day, we deserve the death Jesus died. When we were dead in our sin, He stood in our place. I'm trying to encourage you to draw near. Bring all your shame, and regret, and bad decisions and drop them at His feet. He's not surprised by whatever you bring, and He can handle it. The cross proved that then and continues to prove it today. So come for the do-over. Whether it's your first, or your ten-thousandth, He loves you just the same. Let Jesus wrap an arm around you and restore you, and listen to His whisper.

Pray with Me

Our good and gracious Heavenly Father, we thank You that You are good. Everything You do toward us is good. And there has never been nor will there ever be one millisecond in all of eternity that You will be anything but good. It is just who You are.

And, Lord, we thank You that You are so gracious, that when we run away from You, when we return to our old lifestyle, when we deny

You by our words or by our actions, You chase us down and You pursue us and You don't chastise us, You grace us with the good news of the Gospel of Jesus Christ. And God, I thank You and I praise You that there is no one, no man or woman, no student that is too far gone from You. That we can run as hard as we can away from You. But if we would turn around, You are right there face-to-face with us, to redeem us, to rescue us, to save us. Lord, would You consistently remind us that because of Your Grace, when we sin we don't have to run from You but we are invited to run to You. Your Grace is so much greater than our shortcomings. Lord, I thank You that You have made it a habit to use ordinary, uneducated, far-less-than-perfect screwups like Peter and us to turn the world upside down. I pray this in the good, strong name of Jesus. Amen.

EPILOGUE

The scandal of Grace is that mercy triumphs over judgment.

After His resurrection, when Jesus meets the disciples on the beach with a charcoal fire, He is re-creating the same scene where Peter denied that he even knew who Jesus was. This is a do-over. He hands Peter a plate of fish and then asks him three times, do you love Me, do you love Me, do you love Me? And Peter's like, "Ahh, I see what You're doing here. I denied You three times. But apparently, I can't out-deny Your Grace. Because Your Grace poured out at the cross exceeds whatever sin I can bring to the equation here."

Some of you need to hear that.

We're a couple hundred pages in, and it still hasn't sunk in, so let me be blunt: You cannot out-deny, out-sin, out-betray, or out-offend the Grace of Jesus, which He lavishly poured out on us at the cross. And yes, if you are on death row, this includes you. Because here's the truth—we are all on death row. Dead in our sin. Awaiting an impending execution.

Then Jesus.

His Grace exceeds any and all of your sin. It's not even a competition. Some of you say, "Yeah, but you don't know what I've done." You're right. I don't. But He does. And He still pours out Grace upon Grace. Maybe the real question is whether you will get over yourself and receive it.

While I was writing this book, my son, JP, was finishing his junior year in high school. One morning he was driving to school, with his sister,

Reagan, my thirteen-year-old, in the seat next to him. They came out of our neighborhood, took a right, drove about two or three lights, and then got in the left-hand turn lane, where they were in the pole position. First in line. Nobody in front of them. His light was red. He was just chilling. I'm pretty sure they were not listening to worship music and sharing prayer requests. You know what I mean? He's seventeen, she's thirteen, just regular, normal kids on the way to school.

Out of nowhere, a truck ran the red light and T-boned this little sedan. Boom! Right in front of them. The sedan flipped over, then slid thirty or forty yards into the corner gas station. On instinct, JP put his car in park, said, "Reagan, stay right here," popped out, ran across the traffic and to the car that flipped over. The car was mangled. Four women inside were screaming at the top of their lungs. There was blood everywhere. The people in front were able to crawl out, but the people in back were hanging upside down from their seat belts. He tried to open the door, but it was mangled and wouldn't really open. Another grown man ran over, and the two of them managed to strong-arm the door open. One lady had a big gash in her head, and her leg was broken. Just mangled. Turned up like a candy cane. JP got her unbuckled, she hit the ground, and he put his arms under her armpits and dragged her out. She looked up at him, blood still pouring everywhere, and she said, "Thank you, thank you, thank you." And she was still screaming because of the pain.

So, I asked JP, "Who else was helping you? What was everybody else doing?"

And then his tone began to change. He said, "Daddy, what is wrong with people?"

I said, "What do you mean, dude?"

And he said, "I'm a seventeen-year-old kid. I'm a junior in high school. There was one other person helping. And when I get this lady out, there was a whole bunch of adults standing around in a circle and everybody just had their phone out and everybody was just videoing it for YouTube." And he began to get a bit agitated. I mean, he's got some of me in him, right?

"Dad, what is wrong with people? Man, they're grown people and I'm a kid, I'm a junior in high school, and it's me and one other man doing the thing and everybody else is just videoing." And he said, "Those people, they're a bunch of..." and you could tell that he was trying to choose what word he's going to share with his preacher father, and he began, "Those people are..."

I jumped in. "Just say it, dude."

And he said it, and yeah, there was an adjective followed by a noun of sorts. "Those people were a bunch of..." And it was the perfect description for that moment.

To which I said, "You're dang right they were, buddy. You're dang right. And while they were paralyzed in fear, bro, you weren't. Good job playing the man. Good job playing the man. Because you were. You are. And they weren't."

Later that night, I asked Reagan, "What happened?"

Now to be honest, my thirteen-year-old daughter is not in the habit of giving superlatives to her big brother. You know what I'm talking about? You got teenagers? I said, "Baby, what happened today?" And she put down her phone. She looked deep into my eyes and said, "Daddy, JP was a hero."

That's right. Hero. And he was. And is.

Church should be the kind of place that when the car flips over, we run to the blood, we turn to the screaming, we run to the lost, we run to the hurting, we run to the people. Where everybody else may be making videos about them, but not us, man. We run to the mayhem. Not from it. JP later told me, "Daddy, all I could think was that if I was in that car, I sure would want someone to come help me."

I am not suggesting you and I are heroes. Jesus is the hero of our story. When we got T-boned, blood everywhere, leg mangled, He ran toward the wreckage of our lives and dragged us from the scene. Triaged

Epilogue

our wounds. Stopped the bleeding. Comforted our soul. Got us to the hospital. Jesus Christ, the Son of God, at great expense to Himself, came on a rescue mission for you and me and dragged us from death to life and calls us son. From beggar to heir in a nanosecond.

That's us. Run over by the Grace Train.

And when we are run over by the Grace Train, our heart beats for the things God's heart beats for. You can't earn it and you don't deserve it, but that matters not at all to Jesus. He pours it out anyway. All of us are no different than the thief on the cross next to Jesus.

Last time, here's the truth: There is more Grace in Jesus than sin in you and me. If you believe otherwise, then you mock His cross and you're saying, "It didn't work. Not good enough." When, according to Jesus, His death on the cross was perfect and perfectly fulfilled the law and perfectly forgave all of our sin for all time and perfectly rescued us and perfectly brought us back into relationship with Him, and now our Father perfectly makes us sons and daughters, heirs of God. That's the result of His Grace.

Jesus rescued all of us who believe from the hotel on fire. The singular thing that sets the Gospel of Jesus Christ apart from every other religion is Grace. Only Grace. And not cheap Grace. But the kind of Grace that required the death of the Son of God.

Will you receive it?

Several years ago, I received a prayer card. In our church, we place those things in the seat backs. When folks fill them out, we download them, scan them at all of our campuses, upload them to some cloud somewhere, then send them out to our care team, and every pastor. And we pray over every one every single week.

I usually look at the prayer cards on Thursday nights because when I walk up to preach, it helps me know what's happening around me and in the seats in front of me. So a few years ago, I was reading through one, and I can't even remember exactly what it said, but it was something like, "I know Joby will never see this, but I'm in a very dark place."

And I felt like the Spirit of God said, "Call her."

Now, listen, I'm not a hyper-charismatic person. I'm more of a charismatic with a seat belt. I ask the more Pentecostal-leaning folks in our church that if they're going to bring their tambourine or flag, please just do it back there because it kind of throws me off. You understand what I mean?

But I've pre-decided that if I feel like God is nudging me to do something that lines up with His Word, I'm just going to say yes. Because when I stand before Him and He says, "You know I told you to call that girl. Why didn't you call her?" I don't want my answer to be, "I was scared." Or, "I was too busy." Or, name your excuse. I'm not having that conversation. I'd rather stand before Him and have Him say, "Dude, I didn't tell you to call that girl." Then I'll just shrug and say, "Oh, that's my bad. I thought You said that."

She wrote her number on the card, so I dialed it. And she answered. Which, honestly, is a major faith move. See a number you don't recognize and answer. If I did that, I'd be answering my phone fifty times a day because some nice person in Bangladesh is concerned about my automobile warranty expiring.

When I was growing up, we had a phone with a cord attached to the house. And when it rang, we had no idea who was calling because there was no nice little screen showing the number. It was anybody's guess. Today, we all have these fruit phones, and one thing they do really well is tell you who's calling so when it rings, you can glance and decide. Yep or nope. But evidently, even though she didn't know my number, she said, "Yep," because she answered. "Hello?"

Just being honest, I was surprised she answered, but I said, "Hey, this is Pastor Joby."

To which she said, "No, it's not."

It took three minutes to convince her.

"Really. It's me. I promise."

"No, it can't be."

"What do you think? We got voice actors at the church?"

So she just jumps in. "Who told you?"

"Told me what?"

"Who told you?"

"I just read your prayer card and felt like God told me to call you. So, I'm calling."

Pause. Silence. Then she said, "I just took the cap off the bottle. The pills are in my hand. I'm about to end my life."

That's about the time the Spirit of God in me really rose up. "Nope. No, you're not. That's not what we're doing. You're coming to church. Right now. Right this second. And if you're not here in five minutes, I'm coming to you."

Five minutes later, she showed up, which was just a few minutes before our Thursday-night service, which starts at 7:22 p.m. I didn't know what to say. Didn't have the words. And neither did she. So we just sat with her. Talked. Prayed. Helped her get counseling. I got her with some girls from our church to come around her, walk with her. And then every week, I told her, "Just come see me at the end of every 7:22 service. I want to lay eyes on you." Now, note: I am not her messiah. I'm not her savior. I'm not her Holy Spirit. But something in me just felt like she needed to be needed, to be known, to be valued, and she needed to know that somebody was looking forward to seeing her.

Fast-forward a few years. I'm standing in the ocean during one of our beach baptisms. And she walks out into the water. I almost didn't recognize her. Her entire countenance had changed for the better. She was one of the 644 people that day who walked out into the ocean to declare Jesus Christ as their Lord and Savior. Before I dunked her, she told me she's engaged. And she's now a first responder. And God uses the darkness that she walked through as the platform from which she's able to minister to people. I still see her every Thursday night sitting in about the fourth row with her soon-to-be husband. She was run over by the Grace Train.

I tell you this story because I'm a few pages from closing this book, and I can't help but wonder if there's someone out there with the top off, holding a handful of pills, just waiting for someone to call. Someone to see you and recognize your pain. If that's you, I'd say this—this is your phone call. "Hey, it's me—Pastor Joby. Please don't. Please flush them. That will not stop the hurt but I know One who can. Come see us. Right now. No kidding. We've got lots of people who would love to pour into you, pray for you, and walk with you out of this place and into the place of freedom to which Jesus wants to bring you."

Let me end with this: There is a sound in the distance. Getting closer. It's the sound of the Grace Train. And He has come for you. Yes, you. And when you say "Grace" you should try and sound like Braveheart and trill your "r." "Grrrrrrace." The glory of God manifests itself in the Grace of God, which points to the glory of God, which once again manifests itself in the Grace of God...you get the point. Grace is found on almost every page.

We know from the psalmist that Grace is poured out on the lips of Jesus (Psalm 45:2). John tells us that the law came through Moses, which condemns us, but Grace and truth come through Jesus Christ—who saves us (John 1:14). From His fullness, we receive Grace upon Grace (John 1:16–17). That's like Grace squared. How do we get it? Both Peter—the disciple—and James—the brother of Jesus—tell us that God resists the proud, but gives Grace to the humble (1 Peter 5:5; James 4:6). How do they know this? Two ways: personal experience. They walked with Jesus. And the Bible says so. They're quoting Solomon—the wisest man to ever live (Proverbs 3:34).

Our salvation is dependent upon "believing in" Jesus, but He knows we can't just decide to all-of-a-sudden believe. Something has to happen on the inside. Specifically, He has to do something in us. So, how do we get there? Do we muster it up ourselves? Can we? No. This indescribable thing called "the Grace of God" leads to belief (Acts 18:27). One of my favorite Scriptures is this one: "And because of him you are in Christ

Jesus" (1 Corinthians 1:30). Pretty short, but it says a whole lot. Notice: What did we do in that transaction? Nothing. Not one thing. He initiated and completed it. Now look at this one: "He greatly helped those who through grace had believed." How did they believe? Grace. Period.

Here's the kicker. It's Paul writing to the church in Ephesus: "Even when we were dead in our trespasses, [He] made us alive together with Christ—by grace you have been saved—and raised us up with him and seated us with him in the heavenly places in Christ Jesus, so that in the coming ages he might show the immeasurable riches of his grace in kindness toward us in Christ Jesus. For by grace you have been saved through faith. And this is not your own doing; it is the gift of God, not a result of works, so that no one may boast" (Ephesians 2:5–9). Our salvation, our guaranteed eternity with Jesus, is a blood-bought gift. We are saved by Grace through faith. When we were dead, He made us alive. He saved us. Raised us. Seated us with Him. Why? To show His immeasurable Grace.

If you are "in Christ Jesus," then when God looks at you, He sees you as totally and completely, 100 percent righteous. How? Paul, in his pastoral letter to Titus, writes that we are justified by Grace (Titus 3:7). "Justified" is a big word that means that when God looks at us, He sees us just as if we'd never sinned. Or, in other words, righteous. How? How does He take wretched, blackhearted sinners and cause them to be seen as blameless in the eyes of God? Only Jesus. His death on the cross, His shed blood, His once-and-for-all payment that satisfied the wrath of God, means we are no longer held under the law, but under His Grace (Romans 6:14). To say otherwise is to pervert the Grace of God and deny that Jesus is the Son of God and the only way to God (Jude 1:4).

Let me give you one more. Look at the last line of the entire Bible. The very last line of John's Revelation: "The grace of the Lord Jesus be with all. Amen" (Revelation 22:21). Why would John end this way? Why not "and the miracles" or "the power" be with us all? Why the Grace? Because John understands that all of that is contained in that one word. John knows that it is by Grace alone, through faith alone, in Christ alone.

This is why I call it THE GRACE TRAIN. It's the most powerful thing in the universe and also the most beautiful. And when you grab hold, you do not feel bigger. You just grab a seat and enjoy the ride.

If you are reading this, if you are within the sound of my voice right this second, then He is calling your name. The train has arrived. And truth be told, you don't even have to climb aboard. Just receive the pardon and let it run you over. So let me ask you—will you take the ride to glory? Will you surrender your will to His? Will you bow to the King of Kings?

I'm praying like crazy that you do.

Pray with Me

Our good and gracious Heavenly Father, may we be utterly and completely different because of Your Grace. When we are tempted to try and earn Your Grace, will You remind us that it is a gift to be received, not a wage to be earned? Lord, when we get lazy and are tempted to blame our lack of activity in pressing forward the Kingdom of God on Your Grace, would you convict us to boldly push forward? Would You remind us that Grace is not anti-effort? Grace is anti-earning. God, when lies of the enemy get so loud in our minds and we are tempted to believe that we are too far gone, that we have sinned too much, that we are outside of Your reach, would You please remind us that no one can outrun the reach of Your Grace poured out on the cross? Lord, may Your Grace change us completely, that we would be molded and shaped and formed into the likeness of Your Son, Jesus Chirst. Full of Grace and full of truth. Lord, I pray that we would be so changed by the Gospel that whenever we come in contact with friends or family members or coworkers, that they would know that we have been run over by the Grace Train. Amen.

ABOUT THE AUTHORS

Joby Martin is the founder and lead pastor of The Church of Eleven22 in Jacksonville, Florida. Since launching the church in 2012, he has led a movement for all people to discover and deepen a relationship with Jesus Christ. In addition to providing The Church of Eleven22 with vision and leadership, Pastor Joby is an author, national and international preacher, and teacher. He has been married to his wife, Gretchen, for more than twenty years and they have a son, JP, and a daughter, Reagan.

Charles Martin is a *New York Times* bestselling author of over twenty-five books, translated into more than thirty-five languages.